Social Change, Social
Welfare and
Social Science

To Alice, Gabriel, Joseph and Susan,
for forbearance and diversion.

Social Change, Social Welfare and Social Science

PETER TAYLOR-GOOBY
University of Kent at Canterbury

HARVESTER
WHEATSHEAF

New York   London   Toronto   Sydney   Tokyo   Singapore

First published 1991 by
Harvester Wheatsheaf,
66 Wood Lane End, Hemel Hempstead,
Hertfordshire, HP2 4RG
A division of
Simon & Schuster International Group

Printed and bound in Great Britain by
Billing and Sons Ltd, Worcester

British Library Cataloguing in Publication Data

Taylor-Gooby, Peter
  Social change, social welfare and social science.
  I. Title
  361

  ISBN 0–7450–0869–0
  ISBN 0–7450–0870–4 pbk

---

2   3   4   5   95   94   93   92

CONTENTS

TABLES

FOREWORD

'Of making many books there is no end, and much study is a weariness of the flesh.' The preacher should have been in the social welfare business. Books on the predicament of the welfare state are now coming out faster than the scholar can decently read them. The justification for adding another to the pile is twofold. First, there is the feeling of new departures in the air. So much current literature is concerned to document the failure of the grand tradition of the welfare state and to sketch out the alternatives of the mixed economy, the social market, quasi-privatisation, pluralism, civil society and 'bottom-up' socialism, that something from a different perspective might hope to slip in without making much difference. Second, the positive case for the welfare state is sufficiently powerful to sustain restatement when the institutions of welfare are under attack from so many directions.

The first six chapters of this book are concerned to confront interpretations of evidence and new developments in social theory which nourish the claim that the time of state welfare is past. The remainder considers how arguments about human need and moral hazard may be used to establish a secure moral foundation for a citizenship right to welfare. All things being equal, basic needs entail an obligation on the community. The problem is that services organised on this principle may lead the ingenious to dodge their responsibilities – the problem of moral hazard. The real difficulty is not the erosion of motivation to engage in paid work, but the perverse incentives which encourage men to evade a duty to share in the unwaged labour of social care. This problem justifies the display of the defining feature of the state – monopoly on the legitimate use of violence – in the arena of welfare, in order to ensure equal enjoyment of welfare rights for both women and men. It is important to be clear that establishing mechanisms which will enable citizens to meet their needs as equals is as much about resisting the power of the strongest groups as it is about devising an apparatus of beneficence for the excluded.

Thanks and acknowledgements are due to the Nuffield Foundation, who generously financed a term's study-leave to enable me to write this book, and to Roger Jowell, Sharon Witherspoon and Lindsay Brook of Social and Community Planning Research, who produced the data used in Chapter Five. Responsibility for interpretation rests with the author. This book would not have been written without the help and support of many people – my family, numerous students at the University of Kent, Vic George, Ian Gough, Claus Offe, Ray Pahl, Peter Townsend and Alan Walker and other colleagues, Clare Grist at Harvester Wheatsheaf and, not least, the British Government of the past decade, whose contribution is, unfortunately, obvious.

Peter Taylor-Gooby,
University of Kent,
January, 1991.

CHAPTER 1

WELFARE UNDER ALTERED CIRCUMSTANCES

There is in public affairs no state so bad . . . that it is not preferable to change and disturbance.

Michel de Montaigne

Introduction: not with a bang but a whimper

As the capitalist world limps from the crises of the 1970s and early 1980s into the recession of the early 1990s, the viability of the democratic welfare compromise is again called into question. The attack on state welfare was based on the assertion that the provision of high quality public services cost more than the economy could afford. The long-term balancing act between the appeasement of both capital and the mass citizenry threatened to come to an abrupt end. An official conference on 'the crisis of welfare' in 1980 concluded that: 'the first priority seems to be to make clear . . . that social policy in many countries creates obstacles to economic growth' (OECD, 1981, rapporteur's summary, p.31).

In the event, the predicament of welfare capitalism was resolved and growth restored through a policy mix of welfare cuts, industrial protection and fiscal discipline varying from country to country. At the level of academic discussion, the argument that the welfare state stood in contradiction to the capitalist economy was deflected by the demonstration that state services provide a substantial 'return flow' of benefits to the capitalist sector, and that the cost of state provision is unlikely to constitute an intolerable burden. The fiscal crisis of the welfare state was resolved both in policy and in theory.

In the 1990s, both academics and policy makers are again viewing state commitment to the continued provision of mass welfare services with disquiet. However, the present critique of welfare capitalism is not based on an assumed conflict between state welfare and growth. It asserts that the welfare state is obsolete. The social context in which the traditional pattern of state provision is embedded has altered in fundamental ways, and social policy is no longer able to meet needs effectively. The implication is that government should politely stand aside from the business of providing welfare services for the mass of its citizens. The era of the welfare state is coming to an end, not with a bang but a whimper.

This book is concerned to review arguments about welfare provision and social change and to present a positive case for the welfare state. It will attempt to show that the state as central guarantor of citizen welfare is at risk of premature interment. This chapter provides an overview of the debate. It is followed by four chapters which discuss the three main claims advanced against the welfare state. These are, first, that a review of the recent history of the welfare state indicates a failure to achieve the main goals laid down in its policies (Chapter Two); second, that objective factors – in particular projected increases in the population groups who make the greatest demands on state provision and the economic burden of maintaining welfare services – present formidable problems for capitalist economies (Chapter Three); and third, that increasing social inequality demonstrates the incompetence of state welfare and will undermine the viability of collective welfare at a subjective level, because better-off people are less willing to finance benefits for the poor (Chapters Four and Five).

Chapters Six, Seven and Eight review some recent developments in moral and social theory that are relevant to the debate. New developments in theories of social stratification have led sociologists to conclude that people's aspirations and interests are organised in a more intricate pattern than previous theory suggested. The structure of social locations is seen as too complex to be managed by a welfare state approach based on redistribution between social classes and income groups. New approaches to need and to rights seek to undermine the idea that guaranteed access to welfare services is a crucial component in citizenship. It is at the level of moral theory that the strongest arguments in favour of the welfare state can be found.

The discussion in this book is focused on the policy debate in the UK. The argument therefore pays particular attention to the specific features of the national setting. This is characterised by a determined commitment to welfare spending constraint and privatisation and by very high levels of unemployment and a rapidly widening gap in living standards between better off and poorer people. Since much of the evidence used in the debate refers to issues emerging in several countries, cross-national data will be used where appropriate. First, we review the main strands in recent discussion about the proper role of government in the provision of citizen welfare.

The former crisis of the welfare state

Post-war discussion of social policy in Britain has been dominated by the assumption that government must be the chief architect of welfare provision. Practical debate focused on the question of how best it might achieve that goal. The economic crisis of the mid-1970s brought the 'long boom' of secure growth to an abrupt halt. Real social spending in the welfare capitalist countries, which had risen at a rate of over 6 per cent a year between 1960 and 1975, declined to about 4 per cent between 1975 and 1980 and to 2.5 per cent between 1980 and 1985. Unemployment took off in the 1970s, rising from under 3 per cent in 1970 to peak at nearly 12 per cent in 1985; negative growth in the mid-1970s was not recouped until 1977 (OECD, 1988, Table 2; 1989, Tables R1 and R18). In Britain the impact of the crisis was more severe and the policy response sharper. Inflation peaked at 26 per cent in 1975, negative growth in the mid-1970s was repeated in the early 1980s and at the beginning of the 1990s unemployment rates remain at nearly twice the average for the seven major capitalist countries. By the mid-1980s the rate of increase of social spending was less than 2 per cent a year – lower than in any major western economy except Germany.

Within the overall framework of a slackening in welfare effort, different countries responded to the economic pressures in different ways. The social traditions that have moulded government involvement in welfare vary from country to country. Esping-Anderson identifies three basic patterns derived from the interaction of political developments with the structure of social class formation (1990, pp.26–33). In the 'social-democratic' regimes, typified by the Scandinavian countries, the alliance of left-wing workers' parties with small farmers dependent on state subsidy to form a rural-urban alliance generated pressure for state commitment to a full-employment welfare state providing a wide range of universalist services. In corporatist regimes, typified by Germany, Austria and France, conservative forces in central government developed a system of occupationally-segregated social insurance welfare to ensure both middle and working-class loyalty and the integration of the trade union movement into the state. In liberal welfare states, characterised by the United States and the Anglo-Saxon nations, a basic class alliance was never achieved, with the result that highly selective state welfare is directed at the poor and a dual system of private and occupational services caters for the needs of the middle class. The UK represents a special case, wherein some elements of social democratic universalism are combined with the Anglo-Saxon tradition of selectivity and class-divided provision. The pattern of services is particularly sensitive to the political orientation of the government in power.

The crisis of the welfare state emerged most powerfully as an ideological issue in the liberal regimes, despite the fact that these spent least on state welfare. Mishra uses cross-national data to show that in these countries, where the notion of welfare as a major component in legitimation crisis was taken up by governments influenced by the political ideas of the New Right (most noticeably the USA and the UK, but also New Zealand), the most substantial cuts in provision resulted (1990, pp.116–19). In those Anglo-Saxon countries where governments of the centre or centre-left took power, such as Canada and Australia, cut-backs in welfare provision were less striking, but still greater than in social democratic Sweden or corporatist Austria.

The particular circumstances in which the British welfare state developed ensured a neat division between the services for the needy and those for the mass and the middle class, while the politics of the radical Conservative government of the 1980s generated especially stringent demands for constraint in welfare spending. As a result the cuts were visited accurately on the poorest groups. In short, the crisis of the British welfare state imploded. The most needy groups within the state system experience severe welfare losses, while the structure of state welfare remains intact. As a result, government remained firmly at the centre of the social welfare system, despite its pursuit of exceptionally severe cuts in response to the economic crisis. State welfare provision for the most needy groups simply followed the national tradition of social division and meagre commons at the lower end. The traditional structure of state welfare survived.

The second challenge

Over the past decade, a second challenge to the welfare state has emerged. It is at once subtler and more broadly based. If earlier critiques derived their force from an economic crisis that made the case for a radical retrenchment in welfare spending persuasive, the new critiques draw strength from the renewal of economic growth and the real rise in living standards in most advanced countries. By 1983, economic growth in western countries had returned to a level of over 3 per cent a year. The annual rate of increase in private consumption expenditure (which had fallen to 2.5 per cent between 1973 and 1982) regained the average level of over 4 per cent of the 1960s.

The new approaches are better adapted to more prosperous times. They do not claim that state welfare is threatened by a crisis that offers to tear the system apart under the pressure of inherent contradictions between private profits and the public good, nor that a collapse in economic growth signals the end of the welfare state. Instead, they pursue a more moderate line of reasoning, claiming that there is a continuing demand for restructuring in the pattern of provision to meet changing conditions. The state will dwindle in importance as a provider of welfare, and other agencies bear the brunt of provision.

This perspective emerges throughout the social policy literature of the late 1980s. For example, Judge (1987) and Klein (1984) assert that the pattern of provision is in point of fact shifting away from a state dominated system towards a mixed economy of state, private, voluntary and family care, whether government likes it or not. Johnson entitles his recent book: *The Welfare State in Transition* and argues that 'the current predominance of the state in welfare provision is unsatisfactory. While the state should exercise a regulative role and remain the chief source of finance, its role as a welfare provider should be considerably diminished, and a correspondingly greater role should be accorded to the voluntary, informal and commercial sectors' (1987, p.2). Friedmann and his colleagues (1987) examine the trend to a decline in the centrality of government in welfare provision in a comparative study of a number of societies. The argument seeks to examine 'a period of transition during which the welfare state is experiencing not so much a fundamental change in scope as an evolution from one stage of development to another' (1987, p.xi). It concludes:

> The mixed economy of welfare in which the state is an enabler, and private participation is possible through greater individual contribution of fees and the contractual provision of services, seems to be the direction in which many welfare states are moving. In response to pressures for decentralisation, demands for greater social participation and questions raised about citizen–state relationships, the mixed economy of welfare offers a flexible framework for reshaping modern welfare states according to national objectives (p.289).

From a different standpoint writers on the left acknowledge the desirability of a move away from the dominance of government. A study by the Sheffield Group, setting out a 'new policy agenda for the 1990s' commends a dual strategy for reform. On the one hand, the state must guarantee stronger democratic rights. However, these must be complemented by 'bottom-up democratic control within civil society, to ensure at local and community level that services are geared to the varied real needs of people' (1989, p.269). An alternative approach is contained in market socialism, which advocates a shift towards consumer sovereignty as an antidote to paternalism, with the role of government restricted to the equalisation of initial incomes to ensure a fair start in the race (Le Grand and Estrin, 1989).

Two further developments strengthen concern at the power of government bureaucracies and their responsiveness to needs articulated by weaker groups. In the UK, central government has added to the armoury of state power in legislation against trade unions and local government and moved against the traditional bastions of a free society – the education system, the press and television, even the church. At the same time, the collapse of East and Central European communism in the late 1980s has generated new opportunities for social development over a considerable area of the world's surface. This has led to demands to strengthen the influence of citizen agencies outside central government. A number of writers are striving to draw together the various strands in discussion of civil society understood as a 'non-state sphere comprising a plurality of public spheres – production units like voluntary organisations and community-based services – which are legally guaranteed and self-organising' (Keane, 1988, p.14).

In all these developments, the central tradition of social policy displays a growing unease at the primacy of the state in welfare. To the right of this tradition lie the concerns with the mixed economy of welfare; to the left the development of market socialism, the reconstitution of local democracy and the rebasing of civil society. Social policy writing is seeking alternatives to the post-war system of state dominance.

The economic crisis of the 1970s produced the political response outlined above, in which the division between welfare for the middle mass and the poor enabled a new right-wing government in Britain to carry out the sharpest welfare cuts for over half a century, without losing much in popularity and without abandoning the basic structure of state welfare provision.

The focus on the state remained a central feature of the analysis of welfare policy. Debate between left and right centred on the question of what, if anything, government could be expected to do about economic disaster. Now the perspective has shifted. Academic discussion questions the continued relevance of state welfare to life under altered circumstances. It seems hard that the grand tradition of welfare statism should survive the major post-war crisis of capitalism, which threatened its destruction, to suffer the fate of simply being put on the side lines as capitalism recovers.

The new perspectives on welfare

The different approaches share a growing concern with the continued viability of state welfare. They draw on a common core of empirical evidence, and the interpretation and theoretical presumptions share many elements. The most authoritative statement of the key features of the new perspective is contained in an Organization for Economic Cooperation and Development report which discusses the impact of social change on state welfare spending and patterns of provision by the non-state sector. This document argues that despite the resumption of consistent growth through most of the capitalist world after the oil crisis of the 1970s 'the agenda for social protection has changed in some important respects' (1988, p.17).

The report identifies basic issues in three main areas: the process of 'policy learning' has led politicians and commentators to become more sensitive to the past shortcomings of welfare strategies, and more cautious about developing too great a reliance on the state in the future. Second, changes in the social context of welfare – 'the policy environment' – call into question the capacity of governments to maintain the present level of provision. Increases in the size of the population groups which make the heaviest demands on state provision have important implications for the future cost of state welfare. At the same time, the experience of recession has cast doubt on the capacity of governments to finance expanding welfare programmes. Third, rising real incomes enable people to afford a wider choice of welfare, which may imply greater reliance on the non-state sector. The widening of income inequalities may pose a threat to the social solidarity on which it is often assumed that support for collective welfare is predicated.

The argument does not draw explicitly on theoretical developments in social science. Academic disenchantment with the welfare state has been reinforced by current themes in sociological theory and in social philosophy. The neo-Weberian view that status combines with economic class as a major determinant of the political power of social groups is attracting renewed attention in sociology. This argument is used to nourish the claim that the traditional bases of support for state welfare are now being undermined by changes in the status order. Normative discussion of needs, citizenship and welfare rights, which draws on long-standing traditions in social policy writing, throws doubt on the capacity of the state to serve people's welfare interests satisfactorily. We will consider these five aspects of the critique of welfare statism separately.

The failure of the state

Two aspects to the short-comings of state welfare have been identified by critics. The first contends that the welfare state has failed to achieve objectives which are widely regarded as appropriate. The yardstick against which the overall performance of the state has been measured in recent debates is the advance of social equality (George and Wilding, 1976, Chapter 6; Ringen, 1987, p.167; Le Grand, 1982, Chapter 6).

The second aspect of failure is that the welfare state not only fails to achieve the ends it sets itself, but is also subversive of desirable social goals. Thus well-intentioned government becomes repressive. Hayek provides the classic statement of the methodological individualist claim that government which intervenes to achieve particular goals is starting along a road which leads ultimately to serfdom. This approach asserts that failure is inevitable, since it is in principle impossible for any planning agency to gather together the information scattered in a large number of individual minds about aspirations and capabilities. In the attempt to construct a plan, however, the system must become vulnerable to attempts to supplant general knowledge with particular knowledge, especially the claims that are in the interests of particular groups, expressed through the majority voting system. The interventionist state sets up a system to serve the general good and presents such groups with a perfect apparatus to impose their own will on the body politic (Hayek, 1960).

Left-wing versions of the argument that the state is an apparatus for oppression can also be constructed. These assert that ruling classes tend to gain control of the state apparatus (as some Marxists argue), or that powerful groups become entrenched vested interests to which government must accommodate (Crossland, 1964). An alternative strand in left-wing analysis charts out the role that ideology plays in capitalist society. The centrality of the system of free exchange of private property in market capitalism leads to the establishing of property interests as legitimate. It thus becomes difficult for the state to adopt policies which conflict powerfully with them (Holloway and Picciotto, 1978). In addition, many feminists identify repressive and coercive elements in state policy, which facilitate the restriction of women to the role of unwaged family carer, and which damage opportunities for women to enter formal employment on an equal level with men (Cass, 1990; Pascall, 1986, p.28). The oppression of black people through social policy is seen as more direct, since practices which deny opportunities in a way comparable to those affecting women are allied to overtly repressive policing and restrictive housing policies (Williams, 1989).

A further aspect of state failure concerns the unintended consequences of state policy as it affects other social institutions which meet needs. Thus a number of writers argue that government policies create an unsatisfactory climate of dependency, so that people are reluctant to shift from reliance on state welfare to the use of work and family as structures to meet needs. In recent debates and practical policy initiatives in Britain and the USA, this argument has been used by the right to defend welfare cuts on the grounds that these increase incentives for people to become independent (for example, Murray, 1990; Minford, 1987, 1988). These approaches claim that income derived from waged work or from the gifts of other family members constitutes independence, whereas income derived from citizenship benefits involves dependence. Other writers avoid this distinction and stress the difficulties that the stringency, stigma and heavy policing of state welfare put in the way of those wishing to find work (Dean, 1990; Bradshaw and Deacon, 1984) and the way in which restrictions on family support have tended to damage rather than nourish family cohesion (Finch, 1989).

The failure to achieve equality and the extent to which government policy involves the oppression of particular groups or fosters a self-stultifying dependency have been prominent features in the discussion of state welfare for a considerable period. The striking feature of present debate is the widespread acceptance of the thesis that the traditional form of the welfare state is unsuccessful, even among those groups which defended it most strongly in the past.

Social forces as external agencies: certainty and supposition

Social change is a continuous process. New patterns of social life have attracted particular attention during the 1980s and are seen as likely to exert a major influence on the future development of policy. In much discussion, these issues are understood as objective social forces. They are conceived of as developing autonomously and bearing externally on social policy. Government has no choice but to adapt to them. The notion of the 'objectivity' of social change is implicit in the OECD report's distinction between policy – which the state can control – and the policy environment – which it cannot. The forces which threaten current patterns of provision are formidable. However, their characterisation as ineluctable must rest on assumptions about the inevitability of change in some areas of social life while current patterns are maintained in others.

The argument that objective social change constitutes an external threat that makes the continuation of present patterns of state welfare unfeasible has been developed along three main dimensions. These concern economic pressures on state provision, changes in the population structure and new patterns of family life which influence both the level of social need and the availability of care. Some discussions include the trend to greater inequality in incomes which may influence popular support for mass services. However, the relation between inequality and support for state policy is uncertain and involves consideration of subjective factors. It will therefore be discussed in a separate chapter.

The first line of argument claims that government spending constitutes a burden which damages economic performance and which it will be difficult to sustain. Thus state provision must be cut back and a greater proportion of the burden of care laid on the private sector. This argument can only be assessed in the context of debate about the extent to which social spending imposes a real pressure on growth, and of projections about the future development of spending.

The second argument concerns changes in the age structure of the population and reinforces the first. Analysis of population statistics coupled with evidence that elderly people use more social services than younger age-groups indicates that a serious problem will face the welfare state in future years (OECD, 1988; Halsey, 1988, p.103). Coupled with the contention that welfare in any case imposes a burden on economic growth, this evidence constitutes a powerful reason for concern about the future sustenance of current forms of provision.

The third argument concerns changes in family life. Much social care, especially for children, the elderly and sick and disabled people is carried out through the family – largely unrecognised in and weakly supported by official policy (Finch and Groves, 1983). Continuing changes in patterns of family life suggest that it may be increasingly difficult to sustain this pattern of care activity (Finch, 1989). In particular, there is a long-term trend to an increase in the proportion of families headed by single parents, which is particularly marked in Britain and the USA. Projection of current trends suggests that by the end of the century, half of all children in Britain will live in single parent households (Kiernan and Wicks, 1990, p.43). There is also a continuing trend to a reduction in household size, so that the proportion of young and especially very old people in the population in single person households continues to rise. In themselves, these trends imply nothing about extra burdens on state policy. However, within the present system of access to housing, work and child-care provision, lone parents constitute a vulnerable group. A high proportion depend on relatively meagre social security benefits. Elderly people are more likely to need health and social care. In the absence of a partner, the onus of provision is likely to fall on the state.

Two developments are seen as reducing the available pool of carers. First, there has been a long-term tendency for families to be completed at an earlier age and to be smaller, so that elderly people are less likely to have younger children in the household and to have fewer children and particularly daughters who may provide care. At the same time, women, who do the lion's share of care-work, are more likely to be involved in paid employment and less likely to have the time to look after elderly relatives. One British authority estimates that a typical couple married in 1920 and retiring in the 1960s would have some forty-two female relatives, fourteen of them not in paid employment when they entered their eightieth year. A comparable couple married in 1950 and reaching their eighties at the end of the first decade of the twenty-first century will have only eleven female relatives, of whom three will not be in paid employment (Eversley, 1982). Social policy based on the assumption that women in the family are available to provide care will be forced to change.

The argument that the economic burden of state welfare spending sets limits to the growth of social policy which have already been reached is difficult to substantiate. Examples of both successful and unsuccessful economies with relatively high and relatively low levels of state welfare spending can be found. Even in Britain, where the long-term weakness of the economy makes the argument initially more plausible than elsewhere, it is difficult to demonstrate that low growth is the result of social policy. More sophisticated arguments stress the detail of the organisation of social interventions, rather than their sheer size as important in determining their social impact. This implies that it is inappropriate to seek practical limits to social welfare in the proportion of Gross Domestic Product (GDP) devoted to it. The claim that pressures from demographic and family change constitute a substantial challenge to the present pattern of state provision rests on two ideas. First, change in these areas is seen as presenting novel problems. Second, it is often assumed that current patterns of provision and the context of social institutions in which they are embedded will remain unchanged, so that the shifts to which attention is drawn must be accommodated within this context.

Substantial demographic changes have taken place in most advanced countries throughout the post-war period. To give one example, the proportion of the population in the highly dependent group aged 75 or over increased by two-thirds to 5.4 per cent between 1960 and 1986 in the OECD as a whole, with much sharper increases for Germany, Japan and the Netherlands, where it more than doubled (OECD, 1988, p.11). In no advanced western country is the rate of increase in this group over the next quarter-century expected to be anything like as great. However, many discussions of policy throw great weight on the financial implications of future patterns of aged dependency. Anticipation of demographic pressures has led to widespread reform of state pensions to reduce the cost.

The context of social care has been discussed above. More care is needed and fewer middle-aged women are likely to be available to provide it. This raises the issue of whether middle-aged men or younger people will take on the task. The argument about the increase in numbers of single-parent families assumes that access to paid employment and child care will remain as inadequate as it now is. Discussion of the economic impact of population change assumes current patterns of social need among the different age groups.

All these issues involve supposition about the way in which social life will develop in the future. The idea that one category of potential problems for the welfare state can be demarcated as objective, as based beyond the uncertainties that afflict other areas of life in society, appears unfounded. Arguments about inequality and social values are explicitly presented as dealing with subjective issues. The central assumption is that support for state welfare will be eroded by social change.

The subjective dimension: social polarisation and support for collectivism

Over much of the post-war period, the dominant trend in advanced countries has been to greater social inequality. Since the mid-1970s this pattern has been reversed, most noticeably in Britain and the USA (Esping-Anderson, 1990; O'Higgins and Jenkins, 1989; Room, Lawson and Laczko, 1989, p.165). There are a large number of competing explanations of this phenomenon, drawing attention to changes in employment patterns and the structure of the labour market, which constitutes the major source of income for most people; the changes in family and household patterns discussed in the preceding section; and changes in state policies on job creation and social security. Choice of explanation has important implications for the view taken on whether it is change in the policy environment (employment patterns and household structure) or in state policy itself that is responsible for the shift. The most influential work in the late 1970s and early 1980s favours the former account, but more recent studies paint a different picture (Flora, 1985, p.13; Buck, 1989).

Processes of inequality are also seen as affecting other social groups, in particular women and black people. Analyses of employment patterns indicate that progress towards equality has been limited, especially for working-class women. Detailed analyses of local labour markets in Britain show that 'despite the passage of equal opportunities legislation . . . , women have made few inroads into the more exclusively male areas of employment . . . significant success in getting "mainly men's" jobs has so far been limited to professional women, who have been able to take advantage of greater equality of access to higher education' (ESRC, 1990, p.5). Black people are still mainly confined to low-paid work, and find it hard to gain employment commensurate with educational qualifications.

The widening of inequalities is often seen as an objective process. Its implications for welfare policy operate largely through subjective factors. This is because social division and state policies designed to mitigate it have attracted attention through their presumed effect on people's values and behaviour as individuals.

There are two main approaches. The first focuses mainly on the values and behaviour of the poor, considered as an 'underclass', while the second concerns itself with the impact of change throughout society. The central idea of the underclass thesis is that poor people constitute a group who are different in their social values, behaviour or both from the rest of society. It is sometimes paralleled in accounts of the rich as an overclass. Discussion of the idea as an example of the counter-productive effect of state welfare policy earlier focused on the extent to which it supplies a convincing account of the behaviour of welfare benefit recipients, that supports the claim that they act in ways that damage general social interests. Here we are concerned with values. There are left and right wing versions of the thesis that poor people are demoralised by their circumstances. The former stresses benefit stigma, the insecurity of employment for unskilled people in many areas and the low wages paid and the difficulty of shifting from benefit to work (see for example, Dean, 1990). The latter argue conversely that state benefits erode the incentive to seek paid work because they are over-generous. The question that arises is whether poor able-bodied people share the work-ethic values of the mass of the population.

An alternative approach focuses on the implications of inequality for values and behaviour among all groups in society and often leads to debate about social cohesion and social polarisation. Better-off people find that their interests, opportunities and needs are increasingly distant from those of poorer and less secure groups – 'comfortable Britain' is detached from 'miserable Britain'. This has three effects.

Secure groups are less inclined to sympathise with increasingly remote needy groups. Second, they are less willing to pay tax to support welfare payments which they see as going to these groups. Thirdly, they are more likely to demand greater control over their own welfare provision and greater flexibility in patterns of services to meet their needs, and this leads them to use private services (Heidenheimer, Heclo, and Adams, 1990; Harris and Seldon, 1987, p.5; Saunders, 1990, Chapter 1). In a polarised society, the idea that many poor people constitute an undeserving underclass, corrupted by state aid, is likely to find a ready audience among the advantaged, since it confirms their own merit, and gives a moral gloss to the material gulf between the established and the marginal. The upshot is that the social solidarity which buttressed the welfare state declines until the point is reached at which there is a structural gap between the basic services targeted on the poor and the variety of private provision available to more wealthy consumers. Discussion of polarisation and underclass issues requires the analysis of detailed evidence on values and attitudes, which is in short supply, as well as data on people's behaviour. We now move on to consider developments in social theory which call into question the assumption that the state can function satisfactorily as an agent of the common interest in a stratified society.

The new sociology of welfare: status, stratification and privatisation

The mainstream in the sociology of welfare over much of the post-war period flowed comfortably alongside the development of the welfare state. The centrality of government as the appropriate agency to regulate and supply need went largely unchallenged. The principal themes of debate concerned the identification of disadvantaged groups and the best state policies to meet their needs.

Earlier discussion noted the double rebuff experienced by this perspective in the mid-1970s. The practical politics of welfare states in recession proved no longer willing to support the further extension of services. New theoretical standpoints informed by Marxism, market liberalism and feminism challenged the underlying conception of government as a guarantor of services in the common interest. By the 1990s, events had outdistanced the contention that the welfare state faced a terminal crisis. A major new theme in the sociology of welfare, however, replaces the premonition of disaster with a persistent disquiet at previous assumptions about the role of the state in welfare.

It is particularly striking that such a perspective should emerge in the UK at this period, for three reasons. British social policy had never been dominated by the egalitarian social democratic tradition that prevailed in the Scandinavian countries, so that the extent of welfare state intervention remains lower than in some other countries. Secondly, the response in Britain's divided welfare system to the economic pressures of the previous two decades had been to cut back provision and safeguards for the poorer groups while retaining the framework of mass welfare, so that the previous structure remained more or less intact. Thirdly, the evidence to be examined in more detail in Chapter Four indicates that the incidence of need for welfare provision, measured in the basic terms of income poverty, unemployment levels or reductions in services, had become especially acute by the mid-1980s in comparison with many other countries. The paradox lies between the unease at state interventionism and the high level of need for welfare services.

Two developments in sociology reinforced concern at welfare statism. The first and principal source of nourishment for this view was a shift of emphasis in basic sociological accounts of stratification. The Weberian model, which emphasises that individual social location is a function of position in three separate hierarchies – the market order, the status order and the order of political influence – was powerfully restated by a number of

writers. Since this approach stresses the mutual independence of
the threefold roots of social stratification it is capable of reinter-
pretation from a variety of viewpoints. The approaches that
received particular attention stressed the extent to which the
combination of the three orders to produce welfare state citizenship was essentially plastic, to be determined by the interaction of
stratification factors in the political system. This throws a strong
emphasis on the role of empirical study to investigate the operation of these factors in particular contexts.

The work that developed on this basis led to two conclusions,
both damaging to the traditional model of the welfare state. First,
there was a substantial emphasis on the complexity of the foundations of individual identity, and a strong suggestion in much work
that people were moving away from social class position as the
basis of their self-identification to a more individual approach,
where privatised consumption patterns, kinship networks, home,
hearth and family become more significant. This was seen as a
result of the impact of economic crisis, and the failure of class
based political and trade union organisations to advance the
interests of the mass of the population. The importance of the
occupational order was denied at the level of political consciousness. Working-class demands, articulated principally through
Labour party politics, had traditionally been seen as the principal
engine behind the post-war expansion of the welfare state in
Britain. Now one support for state interventionism was cut away.

The second aspect to the new approaches concerns the operation of the state itself. If the market order – social class and income
group – are no longer of such moment, policies designed to
redistribute between them become of less importance. The traditional strategy of the welfare state is thus declared obsolete.

The dual significance of neo-Weberian approaches for the
sociology of welfare are worked out in a number of studies –
Turner's work on citizenship and status groups, the renewal of
interest in the role of kinship obligation in meeting need, stratification studies of the emerging ideology of privatism and the political
sociology that substitutes consumption sector for social class as the
principal cleavage in political consciousness. The question of how
far the evidence supports the view that reliance on the state as the
main producer of welfare is no longer appropriate is hotly contested. Chapter Six reviews evidence indicating that the changes

outlined above can be accommodated within the model that emphasises the market-order as a central element in class divisions and argues that the state should retain a central role in welfare.

A second and minor strand to the sociological critique of state interventionism is contained in attempts to reassert the significance of civil society in people's lives. This has attracted particular attention on the left. The broad notion of civil society includes the market order, and also kinship, family and community systems. It commands attention because it takes seriously feminist work which strives to draw attention to the political significance of the private sphere of home and family; because it resonates with contemporary disillusion with the practice of state welfare; because many on the left feel disenchanted with the failure of traditional institutions to allow space for the entry of the new social movements – the women's movement, the green movement, the peace movement – into mainstream politics; and because a feature of the 1980s was the attack by the right on central civil society institutions – the education system, the union movement, local government, the media, voluntary organisations and even the established church. The defence of civil society gains force because it is a reaction against centralised state power as much as a positive value in its own right. Similar themes are incorporated into New Left defence of radical, participative democracy (Sheffield Group, 1989; Beresford and Croft, 1986). There are also strong analogies with right-wing arguments that stress the importance of individual choice. The critique of civil society has not played such a major part in the generation of sociological unease over state interventionism as the broader approach to stratification.

These new developments in recent sociology constitute a major departure in social science perspectives on the welfare state. Through much of the post-war period, sociology was the discipline most closely identified with state interventionism and with the charting out of the inequalities and deprivations which justified the adoption of the government policies designed to mitigate them. Recent developments in empirical work call into question the success, relevance and potential of the state perspective. At the same time the new perspectives emerging from the direction of social theory nourish a sense of unease at the whole welfare state project. The new perspectives have not so far been satisfactorily grounded in empirical data. Nonetheless, the sense of disquiet remains.

The new moral debate: individualism, collectivism, and citizenship rights

The issues debated in controversy over the future of the welfare state have normative as well as empirical aspects. Often these are confused in discussion, so that empirically based arguments about the existence or conversely the vulnerability of a particular state of affairs are used to imply that support should be extended or withdrawn. In relation to the 'failure of the state', evidence of the ineffectiveness of policy on redistribution is used as evidence of 'the bankruptcy of the welfare state ideal' (Gray, 1989, pp.48–62); change in population structure is presented as explanation of why it is necessary to curtail pension commitments (DHSS, 1985); new forms of family life become compelling reasons for a shift in the balance of state and informal sector in social care (DH, 1989b); the fact of social inequality becomes a justification for the accept- ance of a widening gap in living standards as part of the policy environment (Joseph and Sumption, 1979, p.30).

Much recent work in moral and social philosophy has been concerned with the question of whether a stable foundation for welfare citizenship can be defended, and whether a theory can be constructed which will generate an uncontested list of the welfare rights which the state has a duty to guarantee. Governments may of course use a variety of means to protect citizenship rights, and may depart from present structures in doing so. However, the establishment of a moral basis for welfare provides a starting point in the argument about how government should respond to changes in the social context of its policies and in the way in which it meets need.

The point of departure for one important approach to this issue is the Kantian notion of 'respect for persons'. In the work of Plant and others this is developed into a theory of human needs, which suggests that survival and autonomy are basic, because they are essential to the pursuit of any moral life. There is thus an obligation on the state to provide the means to these ends for all citizens. The question of how governments are to interpret and guarantee these needs becomes a matter for political debate.

This argument provides a useful tool for developing a normative criterion for the involvement of the state in welfare. However, it suffers from two problems in the context of our argument.

First, it is ill-developed to take into account the social context of individual need, since it is based entirely on conceptual analysis of the idea of moral choice. This is especially significant in relation to arguments based on social choice. Second, the notion of welfare citizenship that it provides says little in concrete terms about the extent to which government should seek to meet specified needs. It suggests that for the practical expression of the commitment to meet human needs, we must rely on the outcome of political debate which cannot be prejudged in social theory.

Recent work seeks to adapt this approach to a social context by introducing elements into the account of basic needs that are rooted in Marxist social analysis. The capacity of an individual in an advanced society to satisfy needs for survival and autonomy is dependent on the existence of social systems of production, reproduction, communication and authority, since without these there could be no society and no individual life. From this perspective, these are also basic needs.

All social formations must meet these needs in order to endure, and in fact do so in radically different ways. The problem now is to find a way of justifying a particular approach to the meeting of need, when the approaches that are embodied in existing societies involve at an individual level different levels of provision in relation to autonomy and survival. The argument now refers to a Hegelian concept of social progress. It identifies the core need to which autonomy is directed as emancipation through access to knowledge. Some approaches to meeting need are better able to provide these than others. In this way the problem of cultural relativism is avoided, and the use of the level of need satisfaction that can be attained in more technically advanced societies justified as a yardstick for social policy.

Discussion of citizenship rights indicates that there is no good reason in the traditional arguments why welfare rights should not constitute an element in the package guaranteed by the government, alongside the political and legal rights acknowledged by all theorists of the modern state. A powerful argument for the maintenance of a substantial level of state provision is the claim that the enjoyment of citizenship rights should be shared out on an equal basis, so that one person's social or welfare claims do not infringe another's. This does not in itself provide a compelling reason for reliance on direct state provision in itself. However, there is good empirical evidence that, within the existing welfare system, the government is better able to protect equal access by disadvantaged groups than is the non-state sector.

The most powerful argument against the translation of equal needs into a system of equal rights to welfare is the possibility of moral hazard – that access to state-guaranteed welfare as of right will diminish work incentives. The evidence discussed earlier in relation to the problem of the underclass indicates that this is unlikely to be a serious problem at the low levels of welfare provision currently available. However, it is necessary to construct needs-based welfare rights in such a way that the obligation to make an appropriate contribution to the common good is not undermined.

This point has strong implications for the citizenship rights of women. Pateman (1989) and others point out that welfare states ignore the contribution made by the unpaid care-work carried out for the most part by women. There seems to be no good reason why the moral hazard argument should not be extended to include participation in such unwaged but socially necessary work for all, including men and young people, as a component in citizenship.

The theory of need implies a range of equal citizenship welfare rights. State provision will guarantee these most effectively. However, such a system must be predicated on contribution through participation in socially necessary paid and unpaid work by both men and women. The core justification for the welfare state is ultimately that, while appropriately supervised market systems may well be (at a pinch) able to meet needs with more or less success, state power is essential to the harsher side of welfare – the enforcement of equal citizenship for weaker groups against the structure of perverse incentives implied by provision according to need in a market society.

Conclusion

This chapter has discussed the emergence of a new critique of state welfare which has supplanted the dominant analysis of the 1970s and 1980s, and has outlined some of the disparate empirical and theoretical strands of which it is composed. These are combined with different emphases by different writers.

Review of the available evidence indicates that the welfare state is not yet obsolete, nor that it lacks the licence of popular endorsement. There is a strong moral case for the expansion of state intervention, to guarantee citizenship rights. The remainder of the book considers arguments and evidence in greater detail.

CHAPTER 2

THE FAILURE OF THE WELFARE STATE

Beware of energetic governments. They are always oppressive
. . . . If we can prevent government from wresting the labors of
the people under the pretence of caring for them, we shall be
happy.

Thomas Jefferson

Always keep a hold of nurse,
for fear of finding something worse.

Hilaire Belloc

The imperfections of social policy

By the early 1980s, many commentators argued that the traditional
pattern of the welfare state had outlived its usefulness: 'fresh
guiding principles are required . . . in particular a reappraisal of
the role of the state in social welfare' (Hadley and Hatch, 1981,
p.2). The principal strategy pursued by the state to meet welfare
needs was the provision of universal services as a guarantee of
common citizenship. This was the objective set out in Beveridge's
notion of a 'national minimum', in the slogan of 'secondary
schooling for all' and in Bevan's goal for the National Health
Service (NHS) of a 'uniform standard of service' (see Glennerster,

1990, pp.12–15 for a discussion). The declarations of politicians may be misleading. Government policy does not carry its intentions branded on its forehead. Most commentators agree that if the idea of common provision is interpreted to mean simply that most people should have access to a basic level of service, the welfare state has been reasonably successful. The most recent statement is by Le Grand, who concludes from an exhaustive review of recent evidence: 'there has been a steady improvement, at least in the average levels of key welfare indicators'; 'the welfare state acted with increasing effectiveness as a safety net over a period of economic crisis and restructuring' (1990, pp.348, 350). However, a different approach gauges the success of policy by a more demanding criterion:

> social institutions – property rights and the organisation of industry, and the system of public health and education – should be planned, as far as possible to emphasise and strengthen, not the class differences which divide, but the common humanity which unites them (Tawney, 1935, pp.48–9).

The object of policy was increasingly seen as the reduction of the social distance between those in the safety net and more fortunate groups, especially by Labour party politicians and by Fabian academics. When assessed by this standard, the performance of the welfare state becomes more controversial.

A second, stronger version of the thesis that the state has failed suggests that government welfare policy is counter-productive: the extension of citizenship rights damages the capacity of society to attain other desirable ends. Discussion centres on the reinforcement or legitimation of the power of particular groups, on the development of particular ideologies, and on the relation between government and other institutions which sometimes meet peoples' needs, such as the family and the market.

Much welfare debate has involved conflicts between individualist right-wing, collectivist left-wing and feminist viewpoints. These differences have been intensified in recent controversy about the future of welfare. Debates about selectivism and universality, the role of the family and the scope of government tend to follow the fault-lines of these ideological divisions. The claim that the welfare state has failed to meet expectations cuts across them, and is advanced by left, right and feminist analysis.

The goal of equality

A major axis of controversy between the central mid-twentieth-century social policy tradition of Fabian reformism and other approaches has been the question of whether government policy can achieve egalitarian ends. 'You cannot make the poor richer by making the rich poorer', Joseph and Sumption (1979, p.22) argue. This forms part of a larger, established debate about the extent to which equality can be achieved in modern societies which are at once democratic and divided on lines of class and gender (Hindess, 1987, pp.33–42). It is hardly surprising that, while there are relatively few statements of the desirability of equality as a policy objective, the failure of government policy to achieve a substantial advance in equality has been discussed at length in a number of social policy texts. Much of the discussion has been in terms of the so-called 'social division of welfare' (Titmuss, 1955; Abel-Smith, 1958). Inequality is understood in terms of access to or exclusion from different services. Unequal outcomes are assumed to follow the use of the most highly prized sectors.

The social division of welfare is seen to operate primarily along the axes of social class. Major examples of the division concern private and occupational welfare services which are heavily state subsidised. The value of tax reliefs and allowances for owner-occupied housing was officially estimated at £10.9 billion in 1990, those for occupational pensions at £11.9 billion and those for personal pensions at £1,000 million (Treasury, 1991, p.102). In addition, the cost of the rebates and incentives designed to encourage people to switch from state earnings-related to private pensions is estimated at £9.3 billion between 1988 and 1993 (National Audit Office, 1990). Official statistics are not published for private schooling and medical care. The state subsidy to the private school system through direct bursaries, charitable status, and tax relief on savings schemes for fees is estimated at about £300 million in 1986–7 (Papadakis and Taylor-Gooby, 1987, p.93). The subsidy to private and occupational medical insurance through the premium off-set against corporation tax introduced in 1981 is estimated to exceed £100 million on the one and a half million occupational policies by 1989. Since 1981, further concessions on subscriptions by low earners and retired people have been introduced (Higgins, 1988, p.92).

These subsidies are concentrated on middle- rather than working-class people, and (especially in the case of pensions) on men rather than women, as Table 2.1 shows. Recent information on the class distribution of private schooling is not available. An exhaustive study of the schooling of men born between 1913 and 1952 divided into cohorts by year of birth showed that private schooling was almost exclusively an upper class preserve. The most recent official data refers to 1976 and shows that private school pupils for that year included over 70 per cent with a professional or managerial class father, against 7 per cent from the Junior non-manual group, and a third of 1 per cent from a manual working-class background (OPCS, 1978, Table 7.1). By the late 1980s there was little difference in the proportions of male and female pupils in private schools, although boys were rather more likely to be included in post-16 private education (19 per cent, against 15 per cent of girls – CSO, 1991, p.52).

Home-ownership subsidies are likely to be concentrated on men, who form the majority of home purchasers, but precise

Table 2.1 Private welfare and social class

	Covered by private medical insurance (1987)		Covered by employers' pension schemes (1988)		Mortgagees (1988)
	Men	Women	Men	Women	
Professional	27	27	79	33	75
Employers and managers	24	22	70	55	74
Intermediate and junior non-manual	10	8	74	58	63
Skilled Manual	4	3	53	25	58
Semi-skilled Manual	2	2	51	27	39
Unskilled Manual	2	1	45	17	24
Overall	10	8	62	51	40

Source: OPCS (1989) *General Household Survey, 1987*, Table 4.11; and 11.23.

statistics are not available. Access to pension and mortgage subsidies is more widespread among working-class people. The benefits available are considerably lower than those enjoyed by middle-class people. The average annual value of tax relief on mortgage interest is £1,360 a year to people with an income over £40,000, but only £420 to the less well off on incomes under £5,000 (CSO, 1991, p.144). Information on the social distribution of pension reliefs is not conveniently available. A review of the literature concludes: 'the objection common to all tax reliefs applies . . . those with the highest incomes making the greatest provision for retirement get the most help from the state, and those with the lowest incomes get the least' (Wilkinson, 1986, p.35).

This perspective shows how the pattern of state subsidy to private provision is moulded by the inequalities of class and gender. Further social divisions exist within the heartland of universal state services. Evidence of this problem contradicts the equation of common citizenship with equal welfare rights, which is the traditional rationale for state welfare.

An influential book distinguishes five inter-related dimensions of equality, to do with variations in the amount of public expenditure, the use of services, the private costs imposed on users and the final outcomes between different groups, and the overall redistributive effect. The conclusion has had considerable impact in shaking the confidence of proponents of the welfare state: 'almost all public expenditure on the social services in Britain benefits the better off to a greater extent than the poor. This . . . is also true for services whose aims are at least in part egalitarian, such as the National Health Service, higher education, public transport and the aggregate complex of housing policies' (Le Grand, 1982, p.4). Explanation is complex: poorer groups are deterred from using some of the most costly services, or face greater private costs; tax-subsidies benefit those with high incomes; access to some costly provision (for example, higher education) is determined by class-related criteria. Le Grand attributes the failure of the 'strategy of equality' to the fact that an 'ideology of inequality' is so deeply entrenched in British public life that egalitarianism will always face an uphill battle, and will always lose.

The factors that make British public policy such a potent engine of inequality are reproduced in a number of other systems.

Haveman shows that the War on Poverty and Great Society programmes in the United States do 'not appear to have imposed large net losses on the non-poor, on whose political support such efforts rely' (Haveman, 1987, p.87). Goodin and Le Grand analyse the tendency for the 'non-poor to invade programmes originally targeted on the poor' in discussion of means-tested welfare in Australia (1987, p.124). A detailed cross-national analysis of trends in welfare states 'concludes that some social programmes in the United States serve people who are above the established level of financial need for such intervention' and 'that such Canadian programmes as family allowances and old age security, have benefitted equally all classes of Canadian society' (Friedmann, Gilbert and Sherer, 1987, p.295). Comparable evidence of inequality in social expenditure and in social benefits between the poor and the rich also appears in Israel (Friedmann, Gilbert and Sherer, 1987, p.195).

This discussion operates along the dimensions of social class and income group inequality. A further set of arguments applies to the redistributive impact of state policy between men and women. There is no study of the overall impact of state welfare on inequalities between men and women comparable to the body of work on the social division of welfare. Since gender inequalities involve analysis of informal relationships as well as formal ones and interact with income inequalities, the problems of producing an equivalent account are severe.

Social division and gender

The most basic test of equal citizenship is the extent to which different groups escape poverty. Analysis of the impact of social security on poverty among women demonstrates the inadequacy of a system that in most areas of policy gives women the same formal citizenship rights as men. Women constitute the majority of those in poverty and have done so over the life of the welfare state. Lewis and Piachaud show that women make up some three-fifths of supplementary benefit recipients in the 1980s, a rate almost exactly identical to the proportion of poor law recipients at the turn of the century who were women (1987, p.47). In the eighties, the principal causes of poverty among women were old age, sickness and disability (which accounts for some 60 per cent of the women who were at or below the supplementary benefit poverty level), unemployment (20 per cent) and lone parenthood (10 per cent).

Benefit rules for women are, with some exceptions, no different from those that apply to men. However, women are more likely to earn low incomes, to have interrupted employment records and to work part-time for part of their working lives, so that their national insurance benefit entitlement is less secure than that of men and produces earnings-related benefits of lower value. Women are also less likely to be covered by occupational pension and sick pay schemes. Hakim estimates that, in 1987–8, four-fifths of the 2.2 million low-paid and marginal workers who fell completely outside the National Insurance system were women (1989, p.480). It has been frequently pointed out that the structure of benefits for single parent families provides a disincentive for many lone parents to work, since they lose benefit when their earnings exceed a low threshold (Bradshaw, 1985, pp.207–8).

Changes in the 1980s have exacerbated these problems. The 1986 Social Security Act cuts back rights to inherit spouses' pension entitlements by 50 per cent. Although the rules apply equally to all, they will penalise women far more than men, since women are more likely to survive their spouse, and less likely to have a high entitlement in their own right. The formula for the calculation of the benefit is also weakened. Sick pay responsibilities have been transferred to employers, who are less likely to run occupational schemes for women workers. The value of the only benefit designed to help mothers, child benefit, has been eroded by an uprating freeze from 1987 to 1991.

The consequence of the failure of social security to take into account the circumstances of women is that women are more vulnerable to poverty than men. Thus nearly two-thirds of single women pensioners live at or below the poverty level, compared with about half of single men pensioners. The statistics are 61 per cent for women lone parents as against 43 per cent and 33 per cent for single non-pensioners as against 30 per cent (Glendinning and Millar, 1987, p.14).

The failure of government policy to adapt to the obvious needs of women for a specific pattern of support, so that the risk of poverty might be equal between the sexes, is compounded by three other factors. First, state policy generally stops at the front door. The redistributive impact of welfare provision within the household is simply not a theme for government intervention. As a result, benefit allocation and official analyses operate on a household basis and assume that the distribution of living standards within households is egalitarian, or at any rate, non-problematic. 'What evidence there is on the distribution of resources within households shows clearly that it is perfectly possible for women to experience substantial poverty and deprivation in families whose family income brings them above the poverty line' (Glendinning and Millar, 1987, p.10).

Pahl's careful analysis of the distribution of income within married couples shows that women in couples are likely to have less command over income than men. Over four-fifths of women in couples had a personal income of less than £57 a week compared with about one in twenty of the men (J. Pahl, 1989). However, women's incomes were more likely to be spent on family consumption, and less likely to be spent on personal consumption than men's: 'put simply, if a pound entered the household economy through the mother's hands more of it would be spent on food for the family than would be the case if the pound had been brought into the household by the father' (J. Pahl, 1990, p.130; see also Edwards, 1981). As a result, men in couples were more likely to have money available for leisure pursuits than their partners. Glendinning and Millar conclude from a review of the evidence that: 'the disproportionate degree to which women suffer the consequences of poverty in terms of reduced consumption is obscured by the assumption that all household members share the same standard of living' (Glendinning and Millar, 1987, p.10).

Second, state policy has been reluctant to intervene in the central arena of capitalist class relations – the labour market. Since women command lower pay (on average about 68 per cent of men's gross weekly earnings for those in full time work in 1988 – CSO, 1991, p.86), the lack of state help means that women's resources, their access to occupationally related welfare and their capacity to exert social influence through trade union politics remains less than that of men. Equal Opportunities and Sex Discrimination legislation passed in the 1970s has made little progress against the widespread segmentation of employment.

This is especially true for working-class women who find it most difficult to gain qualifications in order to jump over the barriers between low- and high-status jobs. The most substantial recent study is based on a sample of over 4,000 men and women interviewed for the *Social Change and Economic Life* survey in 1986. This shows 'a clear relation between sex, gender segregation and promotions which works to the disadvantage of women and to the advantage of men . . . . For the vast majority of women, class compounds gender, accentuating the depressive effects of their domestic constraints' (Scott, 1991, pp.21–2).

Cross-national analysis also supports this view. Esping-Anderson concludes that the 'vast literature on occupational segregation . . . , by and large, . . . finds support for the job-segregation argument' (1989, p.208). The review of recent evidence on developments in the US, Germany and Sweden shows how the politico-economic structure of the societies and in particular the role of the state sector and the degree of industrialisation exert a considerable influence on the pattern of segregation. 'Swedish women have done exceedingly well, but at the price of an unusually strong sectoral-occupational segregation' – essentially 'a heavily male private sector and a female-dominated public sector' (1989, p.215). By contrast in Germany with its relatively small state and large industrial sectors, women are concentrated in 'junk-jobs'. In the US, women are doing rather better, and 'Hispanics are increasingly filling the unpleasant jobs being vacated by women and Blacks' (p.216). In general women do not have equal access to the most desirable sections of the job market, although the Swedish example indicates that the expansion of the welfare state may improve their position to some extent.

Third, assumptions about the role of women in social care influence the pattern of state provision. As Evandrou points out (1987, p.21), the issue has two dimensions: discrimination against women as recipients, and against women as carers. Studies of the operation of the home-help service indicate that among elderly people living alone men are more likely to obtain help at lower levels of dependency (Hunt, 1970; Wenger, 1985). There is also a substantial body of evidence that women carers receive inferior levels of support compared to men carers. Hunt's work showed that home help organisers were more likely to provide help if the main carer was an employed son rather than an employed daughter. An Equal Opportunities Commission study a decade later concluded that male carers were much more likely to receive help at an earlier stage in the onset of dependency (Charlesworth, Wilkin and Durie, 1984). Support for carers is also related to age and marital status. Re-analysis of the General Household Survey shows that 'carers who are married women under 65 obtain the least domestic and personal health care support . . . among disabled elderly people living alone, men receive somewhat more domestic and personal health services than women' (Arber, Gilbert and Evandrou, 1988, p.153). In a detailed review of the literature, on which this paragraph draws, Evandrou concludes that: 'women caring for disabled elderly husbands were less likely to receive . . . support than married men caring for disabled elderly wives' (1987, p.32; see also Bebbington and Davies, 1983).

The failure of social security and social care services to achieve a greater measure of equality in outcomes for women and men despite formally equal rights demonstrates the weakness of a universal welfare citizenship that fails to compensate differences in social status that affect the extent to which groups can use those rights. The outcome is a social division of welfare along the fault-lines of gender, which cuts across class and income divisions. However, it is not clear that the evidence supports a wholesale critique of state welfare as an instrument of egalitarianism.

Inequality and progress

The most striking finding in *The Strategy of Equality* derived from analysis of the use of the NHS – the flagship of the welfare state: 'the top socio-economic group receives 40 per cent more NHS expenditure per person reporting illness than the bottom one' (Le Grand, 1982, p.46). It is this assertion that presses home most powerfully the failure of welfare policy by Tawney's criterion – the fact that government does not appear to be on the side of the egalitarians, by a wide-ranging list of definitions of equality as a social policy objective. The claim has prompted a number of studies. More detailed analysis of primary care (Collins and Klein, 1980, 1984; Maynard, 1985, p.155) indicate that there is little class inequality in the use of this aspect of the service. Examination of more recent General Household Survey data on hospital and primary care utilisation indicates that poor people receive rather more in the way of NHS resources than do the better-off, but concludes (perhaps with a sense of irony) that this does not necessarily mean that the strategy of equality is missing its target in the other direction by being too generous to the poor. 'The pro-poor distribution found . . . may be consistent with allocation according to need' (O'Donnell and Propper, 1989, p.1). Further work on data for the 1980s indicates that 'there has been some movement towards greater equality of treatment relative to need over the period' (Le Grand, Winter and Woolley, 1990, p.125).

A similar conclusion is supported by analysis of the social class distribution of the principal objective of medical care – good health. There is strong evidence of substantial and unjustifiable inequalities between social groups in their standards of health. These inequalities have persisted over time, despite the intervention of the NHS. A necessary condition of health is survival. Over the twentieth century average mortality rates have fallen by about two-thirds between 1901 and 1985, with the improvement being rather more marked for women than it is for men (Halsey, 1988, pp.400–1). Much of the improvement is due to the dramatic reduction in mortality from infectious diseases in the first half of the century and a decline in infant mortality – the final stages of what is sometimes termed the 'demographic transition' from a high birth-rate/high mortality society to low birth and high survival rates. Differences in mortality by social class have persisted, as the Black report and the updating of it by Whitehead emphasise (Townsend, Davidson and Whitehead, 1988).

More recent work enables the picture presented in reports based on differential mortality ratios to be fleshed out. Fox and Goldblatt (1982) followed up a 1 per cent sample from the 1971 census over ten years. Their analysis showed that a wide range of indicators of standard of living, including not being a home owner, not having access to a car, having a lower educational level and being in a lower social class are all related to higher mortality. Similar findings are reported by Wilkinson in an analysis of the relation between mortality and the living standards of different social groups (1989, p.307). Davey-Smith and his colleagues review studies of Civil Servants and army personnel in the 1970s and 1980s which all show a sharp class gradient (1990, p.374). A tentative appraisal of cross-national data supports the view that social class is closely linked to differential mortality. Studies in Norway, Denmark, Switzerland, France, Japan and Australia all show 'relations similar to those in Britain, with raised mortality among manual groups being seen for most causes of death' (Davey-Smith *et al.*, 1990, p.374). In addition 'the difference between France, England and Wales and Sweden was considered to reflect the different degrees of inequality in income between those countries, and the current ranking of mortality differentials does follow that of inequalities in income.'

However, statistics showing a persistent social class gradient in mortality do not in themselves show that it is the welfare state that is causing inequality. There are problems in using social class as the main dimension of health inequality. Good data are only available for men aged 15–65, and deaths in this group only constitute a small fraction of all deaths (some 40 per cent of male deaths in 1921 falling to 26 per cent by 1983 – Illsley and Le Grand, 1987, Table 2). In addition, the structure of class inequality itself has changed. The manual groups have grown smaller, and the gradations of inequality between them and the rest of the population grown wider. Using a rather different measure of health – age at time of death – Illsley and Le Grand are able to show that there has been a trend to greater equality in the population as a whole by this measure. This is due mainly to the decline in incidence of respiratory diseases, which tend to affect poorer people. This pattern contains within it the persistent inequality of mortality rates by class among people of working age. In one sense, the health of the population has grown more equal over the period of the welfare state. Nonetheless, the poorest groups suffer a substantially greater burden of morbidity and of early death than do those who are better off.

Health outcomes are unequally distributed, although there is some progress in the direction of equality. The most recent evidence indicates that access to and resources received from the NHS are not unequally distributed by social class. There are grounds for concluding that, despite the inegalitarian impact of state subsidies to the private sector in health care (and elsewhere), and of access to state education services, state universal services are not entirely unsuccessful as an avenue to equal citizenship.

Comparable evidence in relation to gender inequalities is

difficult to find. The creation of universal services in the welfare settlement at the end of the Second War helped women, because it gave them more secure access to provision in areas like health and education. Men had enjoyed greater access to the former through National Health Insurance 'panel' services and friendly society provision. Thane writes of the creation of the NHS that: 'in particular, working-class wives received access to medical care as never before. Female health benefited decisively from the new service' (1982, p.236). A similar point may be made about the development of secondary schooling for all. By 1938 roughly half of all the children attended some form of secondary schooling. This was heavily weighted towards the middle-class and towards boys (Thane, 1982, pp.229–30). The Butler Act in 1944 increased access for women, and especially working-class women, to a greater extent than for men. In this sense, the growth of the welfare state resulted in real advances for women.

Equality and the panoply of welfare interventions

In addition, a series of approaches broadens the scope of analysis to include other aspects of state activity which bear on welfare. The most important areas which are not fully covered in analysis of direct state services are taxation and cash transfers. In Britain, as in many other countries, direct taxes tend to be mildly progressive and indirect taxes regressive so that the net impact of taxation cancels itself out (Sawyer, 1976). Over the period of welfare state expansion this problem has become more acute. The cross-national study mentioned above concludes: 'rates of taxation, which have been one of the main means of financing social expenditure, have risen dramatically in the past few years. But the tax system has been found to be regressive . . . The establishment of various taxation-based expenditures has made many tax systems extremely complex with the brunt of the tax burden falling on the less prosperous sections of society' (Friedmann *et al.*, 1987, p.292). This effect is compounded by the cuts in marginal tax rates for higher earners, which have fallen in all of the principal fourteen Organisation for Economic Co-operation and Development (OECD) member countries, by an average of 18 per cent, between 1975 and 1990 (Heidenheimer, Heclo, and Adams, 1990, p.211).

On the other hand, cash benefits tend to give rather more to poorer people. The reasons for this depend on the nature of the system – means-tested benefits are, by definition, directed at the poor, although their success in reaching all the target group is variable. Other benefits (and in advanced countries the largest programmes concern retired people) are directed at those whose labour market income is interrupted or terminated, and who are therefore less well-off than they would otherwise be.

A re-analysis of Family Expenditure Survey data is published annually by the Central Statistical Office for the period from 1961 to 1986. This series estimates the redistributive impact of state intervention on market incomes, taking into account the impact of direct and indirect taxes and the receipt of state benefits and services. The analysis produces a ranking of households by market income, by disposable income (after payment of direct taxation and receipt of social benefits) and by final income, including the additional effect of the main forms of indirect taxation and the use of services in kind. The evidence shows that the trend to greater equality in market incomes between the top and bottom fifths of the income distribution came to an abrupt halt in the mid 1970s, and by the early 1980s had gone into reverse. Inequalities in final incomes after the effect of government tax and welfare provision reflected the trend to greater inequality. However, inequalities at the end of the process were substantially less marked than those that appeared in the market. In 1975 the bottom fifth of households received some 0.8 per cent of market incomes, and 7.4 per cent of final incomes, whereas the top fifth got 44.4 per cent in the first place and 37.9 per cent after the impact of state policy. By 1986 the corresponding figures were 0.3 and 5.9 per cent for the bottom group and 50.7 and 41.7 per cent for the top group. The net impact of the welfare state is not to eradicate inequalities. Redistribution has lost ground as market pressures exacerbate the inequalities which are the starting point for the operation of government policy. However, the impact of the state is still to shift the overall distribution in the direction of greater equality.

The official series has been criticised on a number of grounds: it ranks the population by households, which may give a misleading picture of the extent of inequality, since the poorest households tend to contain fewer people and thus represent a smaller proportion of the total. In addition, income distribution within households is likely to be unequal. The method assumes an equal benefit for each user of a state service, and thus ignores the point that those who have access to some parts of the service – for example, post-16 schooling in an A-level class rather than in a vocational course – receive more resources per head. A considerable proportion of state spending (about two-fifths in the 1980s) is not allocated to any income group. A more detailed analysis avoids some of these problems and reaches the same general conclusions: that the net effect of state intervention is to increase 'the share of resources going to lower income groups . . . . In Britain in the 1970s and early 1980s, although state spending has not brought about greater overall equality . . . it has combated and significantly modified the impact of pressure towards inequality' (O'Higgins, 1985, p.303; see also Barr and Coulter, 1990, pp.323–7 for a similar analysis).

Cross-national data show a broadly similar picture. A recent review of the field remarks that 'numerous studies . . . have been conducted in a large number of countries over the last ten or fifteen years' and concludes from an examination of the evidence: 'the entire system of transfers and taxes is redistributive in favour of the poor in the sense that there is less inequality in the distribution of disposable and final income than in the distribution of market and gross income' (Ringen, 1987, p.174). Similar findings are reported in examination of data from Canada, Israel, Norway, Sweden, the UK, the USA and West Germany for 1979–80 by the Luxembourg Income Study (Smeeding, O'Higgins and Rainwater, 1990, pp.51–54). A study of Poland in the early 1980s reports that 'benefits from social expenditure can partially conceal the increasing inequalities due to these factors [increasing wage inequality] but cannot totally even out the effect of inequalities in original income' (Okrasa, 1987, p.2). This work does not contradict the evidence that better-off groups do well out of some aspects of directly-provided state services, but places it in a context where the successes of the welfare state are also highlighted. Cautious and comprehensive analysis suggests that the welfare state may deserve one-and-a-half cheers as a motor of equality.

Equality: alternatives to state welfare

The third set of issues are conceptual. Claims that a given policy has a particular impact involve a counter-factual: that the outcome would be absent if the policy were not pursued. In the case of welfare, the counter-factual is unsubstantiated. There are no examples of advanced societies where welfare policy is entirely absent, and the answer to the question of what would happen if the welfare state disappeared tomorrow is contested. For the argument about the impact of welfare state citizenship on the position of the least-favoured groups, the real question is what would happen to them if they did not have access to the welfare state services they currently share with others.

The counter-factual assumed in critiques of the strategy of equality is typically the abolition of welfare state services and the use of people's market incomes to buy the welfare they need. Table 2.1 shows how unequal access to private welfare purchased out of market incomes is at present. The abolition of the welfare system would presumably make it more difficult for those groups who currently depend on state benefits to purchase housing, health care or education, so that inequalities in the use of these services would grow larger. To prevent this, those who wish to see state provision abolished often propose radical systems of income redistribution in order to give low-income people better access to services through the market (Le Grand, 1982, p.140; Harris and Seldon, 1987, p.65). If you want to make poor people more equal to those who are better off, it is not entirely unreasonable to give them money.

A similar argument may be advanced in relation to women. Rather than including women in equal formal rights to men, which they cannot fully enjoy because they are constrained by the burdens of unpaid domestic care-work and unequal status in the labour market, it might be appropriate to insist that these burdens are shared more equally. To achieve this, it would be necessary for government to intervene more directly in the family and the factory – spheres in which it has been reluctant to play an active role (Pateman, 1989; Finch and Groves, 1980, pp.503–5).

The problem with such approaches is that they are utopian. Class and gender inequalities within welfare echo in a somewhat muted form the structure of inequalities that exists in the society in which the welfare state is situated. It is optimistic to expect that long-standing class and gender privileges will be abandoned. Universal citizenship does not produce equality in an unequal society. It can have the effect of reducing inequalities to some extent, as the CSO studies show in relation to social class, because it includes both privileged and less privileged groups and allows sufficient headroom for the advantage of the one for them to tolerate a system that gives some degree of access to services to those who are less advantaged. The strategy of equality is only *partially* successful. This is the chief defence and the chief virtue of universal citizenship welfare.

The answer to the question of whether the state succeeds in redistribution depends to a considerable extent on how redistributive you expected it to be in the first place. The central weakness of the case against the state as a failed engine of egalitarianism, as Hindess points out, is that it assumes too much: 'far from showing that the strategy of equality has been tried and failed, the record shows that it [equality] has played at most a limited role in the development of the British social services' (Hindess, 1987, p.99). Nonetheless the record shows that social policy, despite its failings has moved in an egalitarian direction.

A stronger version of the 'failure of the state' argument claims that welfare interventions are not only unable to meet their objectives but that they are also counter-productive because they subvert other desirable social goals.

Welfare as subversion – the underclass

Social policy involves the government in interaction with other institutions that meet social need – in particular, the family, the community and the market. In all these areas it has been suggested that state welfare undermines basic social values. The welfare state is cast in the role of saboteur. Such arguments are pursued from left, right and feminist viewpoints. The main differences lie in the analysis of the problem and the solutions proposed. The right tends to see the shortcomings of the welfare state as arising from the misplaced munificence of government whereas feminists and the left draw attention to meagreness and constraint in welfare policy.

The notion that state welfare is counter-productive because it generates an 'underclass' has been a long-standing feature of discussion of government interventions to help the poor. Dean traces the notion back to the Victorian characterisation of the disreputable poor as the 'dangerous classes', the 'residuum', the 'lumpen proletariat' (1990, pp.2–3; see Stedman-Jones, 1971, p.11). The resurgence of the idea in post-war British policy is associated with Sir Keith (now Lord) Joseph's sponsorship of a large scale research initiative to identify a 'cycle of deprivation' in the 1970s (see McNicol, 1987, pp.293–4). More recently, the governments of the 1980s developed the idea as an explanation of the persistence of poverty in a prosperous society, linked to an equation of the use of market or family support with healthy independence, and the use of state welfare with unhappy dependency. In this they were heavily influenced by the work of American commentators, such as Gilder (1981), Glazer (1988), Mead (1986) and Murray (1984; 1990). The determination to restrict the availibility of benefits and enhance the pressure to work is seen by Barr and Coulter as marking a new departure in social security policy in which the goal of the reduction of inequality is displaced by an over-riding concern with economic efficiency (1990, p.275).

The central point of the underclass thesis is that some groups among the poor are isolated by both their values and their behaviour. This social exclusion is damaging both to the poor themselves and to the wider society. Moreover, it is nourished by unwise social policies. Left and right wing approaches differ both in diagnosis and in solution. The right typically bases analysis on individualist premises, which locate the genesis of behaviour in economic self-interest. Thus high relief rates are a disincentive to work; support for single parents encourages family break-up. More recent accounts have also incorporated cultural factors as a reinforcement to the process. For example, run-down neighbourhoods may be seen as infecting their inhabitants with the values of demoralisation. Left-wing approaches typically use a social-structural account which emphasises the role of developments in the labour market, in family structure and in policy in actively excluding the poor from access to the life-styles of the wider society (Julius Wilson, 1987; Walker, 1990; Townsend, Corrigan and Kowarzik, 1987, p.82; Field, 1989). Some accounts also stress the operation of cultural factors (Dahrendorf, 1987).

Charles Murray is probably the most significant American writer on the underclass. His work has had considerable influence on British policy-makers through feature articles in leading newspapers (Murray, 1989) and meetings with the Prime Minister. He divides low-income people into two categories – the 'honest' and 'dishonest', the 'respectable' and the 'undeserving, debased, depraved, disreputable or feckless poor' (1990, p.2). His work is thus a conscious contributor to the long tradition of 'moralising the poor' (Novak, 1988, p.200). The argument identifies three key characteristics of the underclass – high illegitimacy rates, work-shyness and criminality – as perverse products of welfare. The earlier work tends to focus primarily on work incentives and the latter on illegitimacy as the key indicators. This marks a shift from a model that operates purely in terms of economic incentives to the inclusion of cultural factors in explanation.

The method of argument combines an economic psychology derived from public choice theory with sociological arguments about status. The former sees monetary incentive as the link between behaviour and values. The latter, which occurs more forcefully in later work, is concerned with the moral impact of state maintenance on the disreputable poor. The main problem is that welfare benefits for single parents and for unemployed people act as a subsidy that encourages such behaviour; at the same time, they act as a system of social sanctions that legitimate it. Murray argues for the 'scrapping' of the whole social welfare system and the establishment of a structure in which 'effort is often rewarded with success – often, not always' (1984, p.226). Philanthropy should be encouraged, but should be concerned to distinguish between the deserving and the undeserving poor. Green comments succinctly on the policy conclusions: 'perhaps it is time for social policy analysts to adopt a new rallying cry: Bring back stigma; all is forgiven?' (1990, p.x).

The empirical data on which Murray's thesis is based has been heavily criticised – he is selective in his choice of time-period in order to demonstrate the link between the expansion of relief rolls and the generosity of benefits in the US: the extension of the data into the 1980s would indicate a continued expansion in the numbers claiming although benefits levels have been cut back, suggesting a closer link with recession than with the perverse effects of subsidy (Manning, 1989). He also chooses an area unusual in the high level of benefits (Pennsylvania) for his example: other areas would not show a financial incentive for the behaviour he sees as irresponsible. Comparisons between areas with different relief rates do not reveal the differences in behaviour that would be expected if behaviour were simply a response to cash incentives (Marmor, Mashaw and Harvey, 1989, p.112). Murray's use of British illegitimacy figures fails to engage seriously with the evidence that 'inferences about changes in the number of lone mothers based on the increase in births outside marriage would be misleading' because many cohabit; and that 'the most important cause of one-parent families remains marital dissolution' (Ermisch, 1990, p.14). There is no evidence that poor people have different evaluations of work or family than the rest of the population and no attempt to identify corresponding immoral behaviour among the 'over-class' of the rich, who may well have greater opportunities (Taylor-Gooby, 1991a).

The left and the underclass

Arguments from the left and feminists tend to disagree with right-wing commentators about the size of the underclass, seeing the 'excluded poor' as a much smaller group. They also see the mechanism of exclusion as socio-structural rather than the result of rational economic choice compounded by cultural factors.

These approaches place considerable emphasis on the role of government policy, especially benefit cuts and the failure to tackle unemployment, in generating a deprived underclass, although socio-economic change also plays a part. Julius Wilson has developed an influential analysis of social exclusion operating in a dynamic framework of socio-economic change in his discussion of the black underclass in US cities: 'the inner city is experiencing a crisis because the dramatic growth in joblessness and economic exclusion associated with the ongoing spatial and industrial re-structuring of American capitalism has triggered a process of hyper-ghettoization' (Wacquaint and Wilson, 1989, p.8). These accounts have in common their critique of the extent to which mechanisms of social exclusion are reinforced by government policies. The state has failed the poor, not because it is too generous, but because it is too mean.

In the British context, Field follows a strong tradition in social policy writing to use Murray's language of 'underclass' to identify a group among the poor conceptualised in a radically different way. Murray stresses the argument that the disreputable poor exclude themselves from the common pattern of social life by their different values and behaviour, their refusal to 'make the effort' to be like everyone else. Field, in common with Townsend and Julius Wilson claims that the poor underclass are excluded from the mainstream of social life by changes in the organisation of society. To focus attention on the lifestyle of the poor is to put the cart before the horse:

> the personal pathologies of many of the underclass, and the culture induced by poverty, need to be seen as part, but only part, of a score of social and economic maladies against which action needs to be taken. Above all it is vital to get away from the notion that the part of the underclass of working age is in some way responsible for their own exclusion from the mainstream of society. Such an exclusion undoubtedly exists . . . but members of the group are equally characterised by a wish to regain membership – through a job – as soon as possible' (Field, 1989, p.8).

The social rejection of poor people has been the principal theme in Townsend's work on inequality, summed up in the title to a collection of essays, which describes the poor as *The Social Minority* (1973). Here he draws on a long-standing tradition which stresses the way in which policy can embody shared values, community or welfare citizenship (Titmuss, 1970; Marshall, 1950). Empirical discussion of poverty is concerned to chart in detail the extent to which poor people are unable to participate in the normal activities of everyday life – below a certain income level, access to a whole range of consumption activities, from entertainments to clothes to diet becomes markedly worse (Townsend, 1979, Chapters 6 and 7). This analysis complements the claim that many poor people are excluded also from production activities – from the world of work.

The structural account may be reinforced by a cultural argument. Dahrendorf writes of a 'syndrome of deprivation which often leads to a "ghetto" existence' which results from the difficulty which unskilled young people find in entering the labour market at a time of high unemployment. However, a process analogous to the deviancy amplification identified by deviancy theorists then bolsters the formation of the underclass: 'they are not clinging on precariously to a 'normal' world of jobs and life-chances, but settling into a life cycle . . . sufficiently different from the rest to make them feel they have no stake in the official society' (1987, p.4). Once structural changes marginalise some groups of poorer people, they behave in a way that strengthens the process of exclusion.

The view that the processes whereby other people shut out the poor are far more important than the process whereby the poor exclude themselves leads to the conclusion that the logic of the underclass argument is itself an attack on the poor:

> the underclass, like all our previous attempts to individualise the causes of poverty, diverts our attention from blaming the mechanisms through which resources are distributed, including the role of government, to blaming, in William Ryan's famous phrase 'the victims' (Walker, 1990, p.58).

A clear distinction may be drawn between writers on the right who see the solution to the problem of the underclass as the restriction and stringent targeting of welfare benefits so that work and family ethics are not subverted, and those on the left who argue that the social forces that generate an underclass can only be diminished by a more generous social policy designed to make work more readily available, and support those excluded from the world of work at a level that enables them to participate in the common life-style of the population. Feminist writers have extended these themes in discussion of the state and family life.

Subversion and the family

The preservation of the family has become a key theme in social policy discussion in recent years: 'it all really starts in the family, because not only is the family the most important means through which we show our care for each other, it's the place where each generation learns its responsibility to the rest of society' (Mrs Thatcher, 1981). Or as another Prime Minister put it: 'the family is the most important unit of our community . . . Our aim is straightforward: it is to strengthen the stability and quality of family life in Britain' (Callaghan, 1977, quoted in Coote, Harman and Hewitt, 1990, p.12). Friedmann and his colleagues' cross-national study finds a similar pattern in recent debate in Italy and Japan (1987, pp.196-7 and 246).

The arguments about dependency culture and the underclass developed by the right often see state policy as subversive of the norm of the two parent family as the social unit defining legitimate relations of dependency. A number of recent policy measures have been designed to strengthen the responsibility of the family for the care of old and young, and the obligations of spouses. Independent social security rights for young people have been curtailed. The 1986 Social Security Act cut back the level of last resort income support benefits for those under 26. The 1988 Act denies benefit altogether to most 16 and 17 year olds, on the grounds that they should be supported through training scheme allowances or by parents.

Similarly, official policy wishes to locate social care in the community, rather than in state institutions. 'Care in the community has increasingly become, as per the intentions of the 1981 White Paper, care by the community, meaning care by women. Ideally the private sphere of the family is to be left free from public interference, thereby ensuring its autonomy' (Lewis, 1989, p.136). The central assumption of responsibility in couples is implicit in the structure of family means-tests, so that entitlement to income support rests on a partner's income as well as the claimant's. Social Fund loans are recoverable from a spouse's benefit. Poll tax obligations also fall on spouses.

These policy directions are designed to strengthen family responsibility. They have been criticised for two reasons. First they are seen as concealed cuts in provision, throwing the burdens of care-work and poverty on to women through the mechanisms discussed earlier. Secondly, they may weaken rather than strengthen the family.

In a detailed review of the literature on family and kinship obligation, Finch shows that government policies designed to strengthen the family by enhancing incentives for family support through the withdrawal of alternatives have often been counter-productive, because people have refused to co-operate with severe tests of family responsibility:

Several times during the last centuries . . . governments have tightened the screws, to try to ensure that people relied on their families rather than on the state for financial assistance: the New Poor Law of 1834; the tightening of Poor Law regulation in the late 19th century; the creation of household means-tests in the 1930s . . . On each occasion when government was attempting to impose a version of family responsibilities which people regarded as unreasonable, many responded by developing avoidance strategies: moving to another household, losing touch with their relatives, cheating the system. If anything it has been the state's assuming some degree of responsibility for individuals – such as the granting of old age pensions – which has freed people to develop closer and more supportive relations with their kin (Finch, 1989, p.243).

The discussion of the impact of policy in the 1930s is supported by an interesting re-analysis of the raw data from the New Survey of London, conducted in the early 1930s. This concludes that: 'the role of the family was small' (Gordon, 1988, p.1), and remarks on a 'virtual absence of charity and kin as income sources' (p.42).

There is some evidence that current policies to enforce family responsibility are similarly self-stultifying. The curtailing of social security rights for 16 to 18 year olds has been associated with a sharp increase in the number of homeless young people living marginalised lives in big cities – from about 30,000 in London alone, in the mid-1980s to over 100,000 by 1989 (see Chapter Four). The reduction of support for family care is likely to lead to a lowering of standards, although it is difficult to find good evidence on this point. What is clear is that the system of informal care without adequate backup imposes severe psychological and financial stresses on carers. Ungerson (1987, Chapter 1) reviews evidence of the former. Evandrou points out that carers with a dependant in the same household (mainly women) run roughly one and a half times the risk of living in poverty as do other adults (Evandrou, 1990, Table 13). An authoritative review criticises the new policies to implement community care contained in the White Paper *Caring for People* (DH, 1989b) because they fail to include 'explicit resources that will be available for carers', and comments that 'the government's new social security legislation does not suggest that this is likely' (Glennerster, Falkingham and Evandrou, 1990, p.15). The implication is that the lack of state support for community care will increase the vulnerability of both dependants and carers to poverty.

Many writers interpret the evidence that married people are more likely to be unemployed when they have unemployed partners as indicating that social security rules designed to enforce reciprocal responsibility in fact damage work incentives, because a partner's income is likely to affect the unemployed partner's benefit rights. In 1987, about three-fifths of women whose husbands were in work were also in employment, as opposed to less than an eighth of those whose husbands were unemployed (OPCS, 1989, Table 9.19). The system of responsibility for Social Fund loans has increased the numbers below basic Income Support level because the loan is being deducted from benefit (Craig and Glendinning, 1990). The system of spouse's responsibility for the individual community charge 'may lead to a reluctance to accept responsibility for the care of an elderly or disabled person . . . it may add to the difficulties of those whose marriages are in the process of ending' (J. Pahl, 1990, p.136).

These arguments suggest that, like any other prop, the family is more likely to be damaged rather than strengthened by adding to the burdens imposed on it. In addition, the evidence that the differential power of men and women is reflected in differences in living standards within the home as well as outside indicates that increased family burdens will be borne disproportionately by women. This reinforces the case for intervention to enhance equal citizenship discussed earlier.

Subversion and state power

A strong theme in political theory, especially among market liberals, is that state intervention is counterproductive: 'we have since learnt that the very omnipotence conferred on democratic representative assemblies exposes them to irresistible pressure to use their power for the benefit of special interests, a pressure a majority with unlimited powers cannot resist if it is to remain a majority' (Hayek, 1979, vol.3, p.128). Friedman refers in a similar vein to the 'tyranny of momentary majorities' (1962, Chapter 1). On the left, the debate has focused more on the extent to which the welfare state produces legitimating ideologies for an unequal and exploitative society.

Norman Barry gives an admirably succinct summary of Hayek's argument as a 'process theory' – the understanding of society is to be carried out in terms of the understanding of the processes of exchange and interaction in which the individuals who make up society participate, rather than the 'end-state' to which their actions tend (1988, pp.19–20). In process theory, social justice cannot be understood in terms of collective outcomes, but only in terms of individual action under general rules of just conduct. 'Since outcomes are the products of the unintended consequences of human action, moral concepts of approbation and disapprobation are entirely inappropriate. We can no more blame the outcomes of a process, such as the market, for its injustice than the British people can blame the weather for its inequitable distribution of sunshine between these islands and Spain' (pp.60–1).

The evaluation of policy in terms of its success in attaining a particular end-state, such as equality, social justice or growth, has justified the extension of state intervention. Such a process contradicts itself, for two kinds of reason: first, it is inefficient. Human energy is directed to the pursuit of self or group interest through political activity (aimed at redistribution), rather than through productive activity (aimed at the increase in the total amount of resources available). Olson's ingenious analysis of *The Decline and Fall of Nations* uses such arguments to show how conditions of political stability tend to lead to economic stagnation because they create ideal circumstances for such a diversion of effort. Ultimately, pressure groups behave 'like wrestlers struggling over the contents of a china shop' (1982, p.44).

The second counter-productive aspect of interventionism concerns the kinds of decision that welfare state governments are likely to pursue. The right argue that since deciding the best way to allocate resources in a real economy is exceedingly difficult (in Hayek's model, logically impossible) state planners are vulnerable to the persuasions of special interests articulated through the democratic political system. The result is that interest groups tend to curtail the freedom of the mass to serve their own ends, and the welfare state becomes the road to serfdom (Hayek, 1944).

It is not clear that either of these arguments is convincing.

Cross-national studies find no clear relationship between level of welfare spending and economic growth rates (as the evidence given in the next chapter shows). The point that intervention contradicts autonomy depends on the assumption that freedom is to be equated with non-interference, rather than enhanced access to resources.

Comparable arguments on the left claim that the welfare state finds it difficult to attain its objectives, because it operates in an environment hostile to welfare. State policy must make the productive capacity of the capitalist economic system a prime objective because it depends on this system for resources. This limitation undermines the pursuit of egalitarian policies. The classic statement of this approach is contained in Miliband (1971). Social policy is a prisoner to the 'logic of the situation' in which government operates (Walker, 1984). Secondly, welfare systems are based on private property and the reallocation of rights to it through redistributive policies. The problem here is that such an approach reinforces and develops the ideology of possessive individualism inherent in many of the interactions of social life in market society. The outcome is that the welfare state faces an uphill battle in any serious attempt to put welfare high on the political agenda, because the necessary redistribution of resources and opportunities contradicts a dominant strand in popular values.

The difficulty with the arguments of both left and right that see the welfare state as subversive of human welfare is that they expect too much. The evidence reviewed earlier in the chapter indicates that state policy can make some headway against class and gender inequalities, though there are clear limits that prevent it moving very far in the direction of equality. State intervention can be particularly successful in breaking down inequalities in earnings and conditions of work as in Sweden where there has been a strong political commitment. It has been less successful in eroding segmentation in the labour-market. Similarly, it is hard to see meagre government welfare benefits as the primary mechanism in the production of an underclass when the operation of labour markets excludes a sizeable group in the population from normal life-styles, by denying them access to employment.

The conflict between state intervention and family values over-states the influence of government against popular values about obligation. It also masks the extent to which inequalities within the family may themselves subvert other welfare objectives such as equal citizenship.

A priori arguments from the right that see the state as necessarily subversive of efficiency and human freedom in the market ignore the evidence of real but partial practical successes in interventionist policy. They rest ultimately on a particular and limiting construction of the notion of freedom as the absence of interference rather than the provision of opportunity. Conversely, the claim that government is constrained by its insertion in a capitalist economy exaggerates the extent to which welfare policy challenges the system of private property. The evidence of studies of the impact of tax and welfare indicates that modest shifts in the direction of greater equality may be made without subverting the structure of social class.

Conclusion

The evidence presented in this chapter indicates that the provision of universal state services can have mildly egalitarian effects. Intervention does not necessarily exclude poorer groups from participation in the social life and values of the community at large through a misplaced generosity that undermines their capacity to sustain a core value of independence. If anything, the reverse is true. Finally, the exercise of state interventionist power does not appear to contradict individual freedom.

Critics of the welfare state often tend to have high hopes for the influence of policy. The failure of the state as an instrument of equal citizenship is more striking if you imagine that the achievement rather than the advance of equality is a feasible objective. Similarly, the view that state intervention is subversive implies that government policies are sufficiently powerful to frustrate the values of the market and family systems. Given the relatively low level of benefits, this may seem an exaggeration.

We move on to consider a more brutal form of the argument against the welfare state. This is not that it has failed and should therefore be rejected, but simply that changes in the external environment of policy render state welfare obsolete, whatever your preferences in the matter.

CHAPTER 3

ECONOMIC PRESSURES AND POPULATION CHANGE

The age of chivalry is gone. That of sophisters, economists and calculators has succeeded, and the glory of Europe is extinguished forever.

E. Burke

Introduction: the challenge from the policy environment

The record of state welfare in the recent past may be judged as moderately successful, provided the standard set is not too optimistic. Critics claim that new developments will undermine the capacity of social policy to meet its targets. These arguments assert that factors outside the domain of government constitute objective social forces which jeopardize the stability of the welfare state settlement, willy nilly. The two most important problems concern the relationship between state welfare and economic growth and the impact of changes in population structure and family make-up on future possibilities for welfare. Public spending on a mature welfare state is presented as a burden that capitalist economies can no longer sustain. This difficulty is compounded by a secular trend to growth in the groups seen as dependent threatens to outstrip the capacity of government to meet their needs. Such arguments have been used with particular force in official discussions of the future of social policy in Britain.

Growth and welfare

'Public expenditure is at the heart of Britain's economic difficulties' (Treasury, 1979, p.1). The oft-quoted opening sentence of the public spending white paper issued by the incoming Conservative government in 1979 lays the blame for Britain's weak economic performance squarely at the door of government policy. Since social spending constitutes the lion's share of government expenditure (about two-thirds in the 1980s), this approach has stringent implications for the future of the welfare state. Britain has suffered from unsatisfactory economic growth rates relative to its major competitors for a considerable period, variously dated to the sixties (Bacon and Eltis, 1978, p.3), the Second World War (Ball, Gray and McDowell, 1989, p.29), the late nineteenth century (Gamble, 1985, p.xiv) and the Roman conquest (quoted in Gough 1990, p.3). Long-run problems are highlighted by the weak performance of the British economy in the recession following the two oil shocks of the 1970s. The economy contracted more rapidly and unemployment rose to a higher level in the early 1980s than in any other major OECD country. The gains in productivity and enhanced growth rate of 1987 and 1988 have not been sustained in the recession of the early 1990s. The UK economy suffers either from a specific individual problem or is excessively vulnerable to a common malaise. If welfare policy stints the goose that lays the golden egg, there is an especially strong case for retrenchment in this country.

The question of whether state welfare spending is part of the explanation for poor economic performance, as official policy implies, may be approached from three directions. First, a number of cross-national studies seek to identify a direct statistical link between spending and growth by attempting to correlate the two. All things being equal, the notion that public spending is a burden implies that countries which spend more on welfare will suffer economic penalties compared to those who spend less. A second more indirect approach considers particular aspects of welfare policy which might affect economic success and considers whether the welfare system crowds out more profitable sections of the economy, or undermines incentives. A third approach attempts to integrate sociological and political insights with economic theory to study the processes that produce and sustain welfare states in advanced economies. The results indicate that the link between welfare and economic growth is far more complex than the theory that one is a burden on the other implies. Welfare spending is not simply a luxury to be abandoned when times grow hard.

Welfare spending and economic growth: direct links

An authoritative series of analyses based on OECD data carried out by Cameron in the mid-1980s (1984, 1985) point to two interesting conclusions. First, those nations in which the debate about state welfare and growth has been waged most intensely over the last two decades do not in fact have particularly high rates of state spending. Governments in Britain and the United States have been most active in restructuring welfare spending in order to improve economic performance. These countries spent 18.7 and 16.9 per cent of GDP respectively on the main social programmes

Table 3.1 Economic growth and social spending 1960–1991

	Average annual GDP growth rate			Social spending as % GDP		Average annual social spending growth rate	
	1960–74	1975–85	1985–91	1960	1985	1960–74	1975–85
US	3.4	2.6	3.0	10.9	16.9	6.5	2.5
Japan	8.6	4.3	4.4	8.0	14.8	8.5	5.7
Germany	3.8	2.0	3.2	20.5	24.1	4.8	1.4
France	5.0	2.1	3.0	13.4	28.4	7.3	4.4
UK	2.6	1.5	2.8	13.9	18.7	3.9	1.9
Italy	4.6	2.2	3.2	16.8	27.7	5.5	3.4
Canada	5.1	3.3	3.4	12.1	21.0	7.6	3.0
Average	4.7	2.6	3.4	13.7	21.7	6.3	3.2

Sources: OECD (1990) Table 24, (1988) Tables 2 and 3 and (1985) Table 2.

in 1985, less than any other major OECD power with the exception of Japan, and substantially lower than the average of nearly 22 per cent (see Table 3.1). Since both countries have also experienced sluggish economic growth rates over the post-war period, it is plausible to attribute concern at the burden of relatively low levels of welfare spending to the search for a scapegoat. An analysis by Gough points out that 'Britain has been protected by its oil from some of the new competitive pressures of the 1980s . . . . In part the British welfare state has been eroded despite the pressures of international competition' (1990, p.46).

Cameron's second point derives from correlational analysis. Using data for the twenty largest OECD countries, he is able to show that the link between growth in state intervention (whether measured as total government spending, government's share of consumption, the receipts of government or specific social welfare programme spending) between 1964–5 and 1980–1 is only weakly related to gross capital formation. However, there is a modest and negative link between the size of expenditures and capital formation. The conclusions he draws from this are equivocal: 'we cannot escape the possibility that the public economy of advanced capitalism has intruded in some yet to be determined way upon the accumulation – investment – growth – job-creation process' (1985, p.21). However, it does seem difficult to pin the blame for low growth on social welfare as such when high spending nations have as high economic growth rates in the 1980s as low spenders.

A similar conclusion emerges from the analysis by Thurow and others for an international conference in 1980. His data focus on the relation between growth and government policies designed to mitigate inequality for the twelve largest OECD countries over the period of expansion from 1960 to 1977. He concludes: 'there is no rank order correlation between performance, the degree of inequality, or the extent of redistributional effort' (OECD, 1981, p.137).

Casual examination of more recent evidence on economic growth rates and increases in social spending reinforces the impression that it is difficult to identify a direct link (Table 3.1). The data on economic growth rates cover the period from 1960 to 1991, divided up to show the impact of the recession following the oil shock of 1974 and recent developments. Unfortunately, nationally comparable data on social spending are not available to cover the late 1980s. However, variations in the growth of social spending are not sufficient to alter the relative position of countries along this dimension.

The table shows that the relationship between growth and welfare spending does not correspond to the model implied by the argument that the latter damages the former. There are clear national variations in growth rates. These fell sharply in the late 1970s and have been restored with varying success, to deteriorate again in the recession of the early 1990s, especially in the UK and the USA. It is possible to find examples of high growth and low spending, such as Japan. However, there are also cases where despite low spending growth remains low, as in the UK, or is moderate, as in the USA. Conversely, high welfare expenditure is associated with moderate growth rates in France, Germany and Italy, and moderate welfare spending with high growth in Canada. Economic success in the recent recession appears to relate to high annual spending rates. This may indicate simply that cuts are fiercer where recession bites most urgently. In the conditions of the late 1980s, low spending countries such as the UK and the USA do not do spectacularly better than those which maintain a high rate of increase in spending, such as Italy and Canada. The economic burden model of welfare spending can tell only part of the story.

Welfare spending and economic growth: resources and incentives

The problems in demonstrating a direct relationship between welfare spending and growth have led to attempts to investigate more indirect processes whereby social welfare policy might influence economic success. The argument that over-generous state welfare creates a counter-productive dependency culture at the individual level has already been discussed in Chapter Two. At the level of more general analysis, two lines of argument have been significant in recent debate. One suggests that state provision diverts resources from the wealth-creating parts of the economy, whereas the other claims that the high rates of taxation necessary to finance extensive welfare programmes undermine the incentive to work, so that the economy becomes less productive than it might otherwise be.

The classic statement of the case that the welfare state preempts productive resources is by Bacon and Eltis. In an influential book, they attribute Britain's economic problems to the expansion of the non-marketed state sector in the 1960s and 1970s at the expense of the marketed sector. The nub of their argument is that it is 'the marketed output of goods and services taken together which must supply the total private consumption, investment and export needs of the whole nation' (1978, p.27). State expansion, especially in the welfare area, has diverted resources to non-marketed services such as health and education, and reduced the resource base which must supply industry.

This approach is misleading when applied to state welfare systems. First there is little evidence that the crucial resource cited by Bacon and Eltis – labour – was denied to industry by welfare services. In the decade of expansion from the mid-1950s to the mid-1960s, these industries called principally on new entrants to the labour force, particularly married women (Parry, 1985). It is even more difficult to suggest that state welfare is pre-empting skilled labour in the high unemployment of more recent years. Second, state welfare is not simply a burden on the productive sector but may be 'indirectly productive', providing a return flow of services and benefits which enable the marketed sector to realise greater profits, as Gough points out (1979, pp.108–27). The crucial issue is not the size but the nature and organization of the welfare system, in particular whether it expands markets for the directly productive sector, enables individuals to buy its products and equips labour to work more effectively. British industry certainly suffers from serious problems. Labour productivity in the manufacturing sector remains lower than in any of the main OECD countries, despite an improvement in the annual rate of increase of productivity from less than 1 per cent in the 1970s to 4.5 per cent by 1987 (National Institute of Economic and Social Research, 1989, p.88). Low productivity is associated with low investment, weak profitability and low incomes in a logical and vicious circle (Ball, Gray and McDowell, 1989, p.33; Coutts and Godley, 1989; Layard and Nickell, 1990). However, it is difficult to demonstrate that the presumed burden of welfare spending makes a major contribution to these problems. After all, the rate of spending is lower than in more successful economies, and there is no convincing evidence that the welfare state pre-empts resources and crowds out productive industry. A second argument about the way welfare spending might affect economic development concerns incentives.

Welfare spending and incentives: the impact of high tax rates

The suggestion that state welfare undermines individual incentives has already been considered in the discussion of arguments about dependency culture as an aspect of the failure of the state in Chapter Two. The point made there is that the expansion of welfare may also provide the resources to enable people to function more effectively in the economic system. Welfare provision can be seen as buttressing the market system as well as eroding it. These arguments may be reinforced by evidence about the impact of state welfare on incentives at a more general level. One suggestion is that the tax burden required to finance the welfare state undermines work effort because people receive less of the money they earn, and thus have a smaller incentive to work. If work is less well rewarded, there is a tendency to substitute leisure for work. However, it is equally possible to argue at a theoretical level that a reverse effect will also apply. As people pay more of their income in tax, they have an incentive to work harder, to make up the money they are losing to government.

Empirical evidence provides no clear guide to whether the 'substitution' or the 'income' effect of taxation is dominant. An authoritative cross-national review of the evidence by the OECD (Godfrey, 1975) concluded that taxation does not have a large effect on the overall amount of 'work effort'. This conclusion is reinforced in the findings of a number of British studies (Fieghan and Reddaway, 1981; Beenstock, 1979; Brown, 1980). However, new theories about the impact of tax which became current in the mid-1980s give the debate an added political point.

Arguments associated with the American economist Laffer have had considerable influence on fiscal policy in the US and the UK (Canto, Jones and Laffer, 1983). The theory claims that the disincentive effects of high rates of taxation undermine work incentives in particular and economic growth rates in general to such an extent that incomes are lower than they would otherwise be. The long-term effect is to restrict the capacity of government to finance its spending programmes through taxes such as income tax. The rational strategy for a government which wishes to maximise tax revenue is to reduce tax rates so that individuals are encouraged to work harder, growth increases, larger incomes are available for taxation and the amount of revenue gained actually rises. Higher tax rates may not only undermine growth, they actually cut state revenues. Greedy government starves itself.

This argument was given added support in the UK by the evidence that the tax paid by the highest earning 5 per cent of tax payers increased from 24 to 27 per cent of total tax revenue between 1979 and 1986, despite the fact that the highest marginal rate dropped from 83 to 60 per cent in 1979 and other changes benefited this group (Hansard, Written Answers, vol.131, col.220, 1987–8). The Chancellor of the Exchequer in his 1988 Budget speech argued:

> excessive rates of income tax destroy enterprise, encourage avoidance and drive talent . . . overseas . . . . As a result, so far from raising additional revenue over time they actually raise less. By contrast, a reduction in the top rates of income tax can . . . result in a higher, not lower, yield to the Exchequer (Hansard, House of Commons Debates, vol.129, col.1012, 1987–8).

The 1988 budget cut tax sharply, reducing state income by some £6 billion (or 3 per cent of general government revenues) over a full year. One enthusiast for the Laffer argument predicted an 8 per cent rise in state revenues once the enhanced incentives had fed through (Minford, 1988).

Detailed analysis of the increase in the share of tax paid by better off people in the 1980s suggests a different explanation, and one in tune with the evidence on trends to increasing income inequality discussed in the next chapter: 'the plain fact is that the incomes of the highest paid tax-payers have grown much more quickly than the income of the rest of tax-payers, and this is what explains most of the increased share of tax revenue contributed by the rich' (Kell, 1988, p.32). The Laffer arguments do not provide additional support for the contention that over-expansive state welfare damages incentives. A careful review of recent evidence concludes that tax cuts do not make people work harder or for longer hours than they otherwise would have: 'there is little evidence to suggest that there will be any significant increase in short-run labour supply as a result of the increase in allowances or the cut in the basic rate of tax. The evidence from both sides of the Atlantic is about as firm as any empirical evidence in economics' (Brown, 1988, p.106 – see also Dilnot and Kell, 1988). Arguments which seek to link state welfare spending to the health of the economy find little support either from attempts to correlate growth and spending statistics directly, or from evidence about the impact of policy on resources and incentives. An alternative approach explores the way in which economic, social and political factors interact in the development of welfare states in order to understand responses to economic changes.

Welfare spending and economic growth: institutional factors

Theories about the social processes that generate advanced welfare states have developed rapidly in recent years, encouraged by technical advances that make the analysis of large cross-national data-sets less cumbersome. A whole series of statistical studies of increasing sophistication have re-examined the thesis originally stated by Wilensky and his colleagues, that economic growth is the main motor behind the development of state welfare. Wilensky's original work on a sample of sixty countries showed that the main factors explaining the level of social security spending are economic product and the proportion of the population over the age of 65, with the age of the social security system itself playing a subsidiary role (1975). Taken together, these factors explain some 83 per cent of variation in spending. Since the sample included both developed and developing countries, with wide variations in national product and level of spending, such a broad-brush outcome is hardly surprising. Wilensky's subsequent work focuses on twenty-two richer countries and shows that the main additional explanatory factor among this group is the extent to which major economic interests are incorporated into the political process.

This finding has been sharply contested by sociologists and

political scientists, who claim that social and political factors have a major role to play (Castles and McKinlay, 1979; Stephens, 1979; Skocpol, 1985). These factors include the role of left-wing parties, the strength of the labour movement and the part these institutions play in societal bargaining processes. A number of writers show how methodological differences influence conclusions (Uusitalo, 1984; Paloheimo, 1984; Weir *et al.*, 1988). A recent paper by O'Connor and Brym (1988) clarifies the differences in analysis and conceptualisation that underlie the divergent conclusions of those who, like Wilensky, place strongest emphasis on economic and structural factors, and those like Castles and Stephens, who emphasise the role of the political and social system. Wilensky tends to focus on social security spending as defined in International Labour Office statistics, which leads to an emphasis on pension systems. Other writers include the whole range of state interventions in society, measured by such indicators as the level of non-military spending, and including health care, education, housing and other benefits. Some attempt to cover policy orientations in such areas as unemployment and income inequality. In discussion of political factors, those who favour economic accounts tend to focus simply on the role of left- and right-wing parties in government, whereas those who stress the significance of the political system discriminate more finely between social democratic and communist parties, and include measures of class mobilisation outside parliament and of trade union organisation and influence. Stress on pension spending as a measure of state welfare intervention directs attention to an area where there is relatively little political controversy. The more limited the notion of politics, the less likely it is to provide a strong discrimination between different social policy regimes.

The most successful quantitative analysis of the growth of welfare states in a technical sense is by Hicks and Swank (1984). These authors succeed in explaining 95 per cent of the variance in cash transfers across a sample of eighteen OECD countries for the period 1960–71, using a statistical model that includes a sophisticated account of political as well as economic factors. They conclude: 'in short, institutional and extra-institutional class-linked politics along with economic growth seem largely to determine welfare payment changes' (p.81).

The new perspectives have been strengthened by an increased

sensitivity to the importance of social changes in influencing the context of policy-making. Such changes do not take place in a vacuum. Skocpol and Amenta point out that 'social policies, once enacted and implemented, themselves transform politics' (1986, p.131). In other words, there is a feed-back from current to future policy through the pattern of interests which existing policy nourishes and the organisational opportunities it has to express itself. Analysis must remain sensitive to the fact that social policy enters into the determination of the future scope for action.

One of the most impressive pieces of analysis from this perspective is Skocpol's own account of the 'zig-zag' trajectory of American social policy, responding to the exigencies of patronage democracy in the Civil War era; of the weakness of any institutional base for the establishment of a citizenship social insurance system in the progressive period at the beginning of the twentieth century; of the popular political pressure for a solution to the misery of the Depression; and the slackening of such pressure in the post-war boom. Developments at each stage are moulded by the context of existing provision and the political institutions that allow interests to express themselves (Weir, Orloff and Skocpol, 1988, pp.24–5; Skocpol, 1989). This analysis follows the 'new institutionalist' approach to the state, incorporating a dual perspective on government, as an actor pursuing particular ends and as a responsive institution constrained by the political-economic context in which it is located. Actions by government in the present can contribute to shaping the context of future policy making (Skocpol, 1985, p.28).

Other studies point to similar conclusions. Hage, Hanneman and Gargan (1989) who use both detailed case-studies and time-series statistics in a study of Germany, Italy, France and Britain, show that both economic and political factors are important at different points in the history of policy development: 'states are both responsive and active, and their particular stance in one time-period shapes whether they are responsive or active in the next' (p.283). Esping-Anderson and Korpi (1984) and Esping-Anderson (1990) are able to show in studies of policy development in Europe and America that the process by which left-wing parties and the labour movement press for change creates a pattern of vested interests in society which will bring pressure to bear on future policy development. Both social structural factors, to do with the level of economic development, the structure of the population and the organisation of the governmental system, and political factors, to do with the extent of class conflict and the opportunities for it to express itself and influence the political system are likely to influence welfare outcomes. The more the focus of debate shifts from the level of spending to the detail of policy across a wider range of areas, the more politics comes to the fore in accounts of the development of welfare states.

Growth and welfare: the impact of recession

This brief review shows how the analysis of the relationship between growth and welfare has led to debate between those who emphasise economic development and those who stress the operation of the social and political system. This debate has produced a new level of analysis which argues that these factors interact in complex ways – which perhaps is not surprising to anyone who has examined the development of a particular social policy in an individual welfare state in any detail. The debate about growth and welfare has been given an added impetus by the crisis in social spending of the mid-1970s. The faltering of economic growth, coupled with a surge in unemployment, consumer prices and inflation, led to concern about the availability of resources for future social policy.

Studies of the way welfare states have responded to the economic crisis indicate that different combinations of economic, political and social factors produce different outcomes in different national contexts. Cross-national statistical analysis of welfare spending shows an increasing divergence in patterns of welfare intervention after 1973 (O'Connor, 1988, p.232). More recent studies reinforce the impression that different welfare regimes are following different pathways. Hicks and his colleagues extended their analysis of the interaction of political and economic factors contributing to the development of state welfare. They conclude that after 1973 there is

a bifurcation of processes generating welfare expansion . . . . In nations where labour unions are organisationally strong . . . political actions of left parties evidently still affect welfare policy fairly directly. In nations where unions are organisationally weak, aspirations for greater welfare effort are perhaps better directed towards . . . the emergence of a new era of economic expansion (1989, pp.424–5),

with the result that political pressure for redistributive policies is muted.

The divergence in response extends beyond welfare spending to embrace other aspects of policy. Mishra (1990) argues that capitalist countries may be divided into two groups – those who responded to the recession by retrenchment in state spending, and those who strove to maintain the level of provision. The United States and Britain typify the policy of cutting back, whereas Sweden and Austria were able to sustain provision under difficult circumstances because they had institutional arrangements which incorporated the labour movement into the process of economic decision making.

Through detailed analysis of policy development, Mishra demonstrates that social spending patterns in the four countries do not show a simple contrast between new right retrenchment and social democratic maintenance (in fact, by 1985 Sweden had cut back the rate of increase in social spending to an annual average of 0.1 per cent, whereas the USA at 2.7 per cent exceeded the OECD average of 2.6 per cent (OECD, 1988, Table 2). However, if the definition of social welfare is expanded to include employment levels and the impact of provision on poorer groups, analysis highlights the success of policies in Sweden and Austria in holding unemployment below 3 and 4 per cent respectively throughout the 1970s and 1980s, in contrast with the US where it exceeded 9 and the UK where it exceeded 11 per cent (OECD, 1988c, Table R 18).

The contention that divergence in policy-development results from the operation of different factors in internal political economy also emerges from Therborn's analysis of unemployment. The striking cross-national differences in levels of unemployment arising since 1975 are seen to reflect different response to economic crisis: 'the differentiation among our sixteen countries took place in the two cyclical troughs of the crisis, which suggests that it is the capacity and the resolve to resist the onslaughts of the international storm, rather than the ability to ride the waves of recovery that have been decisive' (1986, p.21). The explanation of the difference between the countries which maintained low unemployment (Austria, Japan, Norway, Sweden and Switzerland) and those which suffered large increases in the early 1980s (Belgium, Canada, Denmark, the Netherlands and the UK) is the 'existence of an institutional commitment to full employment' in the former (p.23). This commitment must include the use of counter-cyclical macro-economic policies, specific mechanisms to moderate the working of the labour market, and the decision not to use unemployment as a means to attaining other goals, such as the limitation of wage demands, or a reduction in inflation. Like the work of Mishra and 'new institutionalist' writers such as Skocpol, this analysis demonstrates that it is not simply the level of economic challenge or the political complexion of the party of government that determines the policy response to external pressures, but that the detail of the organisation of political institutions is also important.

It is difficult to account for the development of state welfare simply in terms of economic change. Political and social factors play an important part, and this role has become more significant in the different responses to the economic crisis. Sociologists such as Sabel (1982) and Lash and Urry (1987) have attempted to identify new configurations in capitalist political economy, which they contend are succeeding the regimented 'Fordist' system of mass production as the dominant influence on economic and social life (see Aglietta, 1976). The mass production system led to an organised working class, the concentration and centralisation of industrial, financial and commercial capital and the articulation of pressure for Keynesian intervention and national state welfare systems, providing uniform citizenship rights in a way that bolsters the work ethic. If new systems of production, dependent on small-scale flexible enterprises satisfying particular niches in an increasingly sophisticated and differentiated market emerge, these may foster different patterns of political struggle and of state intervention, emphasising decentralisation, differentiation between individual needs and capacity to pay and private control over services. A pattern could emerge in which the uniformity of economies on a national and international scale breaks down, to be replaced by a system in which different politico-economic arrangements are successful in different areas.

It is difficult to establish with certainty whether such changes are in fact taking place. These arguments must remain speculative at this stage. However, there do seem to be significant differences in the relation of economic growth and welfare provision in different countries. These are brought out in the different patterns of Table 3.1 and highlighted in the different responses of national governments to the crises of the 1970s and 1980s. There is no evidence of a simple· and direct relationship between economic development and social welfare policy. For this reason, it is simplistic to construe state welfare spending as a burden on growth and to argue that economic exigencies demand expenditure cuts.

We now move on to consider academic debates about the other main factor identified in theories as an objective social force likely to curb the feasibility of the continuance of state welfare – changes in population structure. Again we will consider some cross-national argument and then focus on the debate in the British context.

Population change and the cost of social welfare

The most significant – and most widely – quoted discussion of the relationship between demographic change and social spending over the next half century is the OECD's authoritative report *Ageing Populations* (1988d), which is an important influence on *The Future Of Social Protection* (1988), and on arguments about the limits to social policy elsewhere. Trends in the age structure of the population and their implications for social policy have not only attracted great interest in the cross-national policy community. They have also generated interest among sociologists (for example Turner (1989) uses the possible distributional struggles surrounding age-divisions to illustrate a modified neo-Weberian theory of stratification) and public choice theorists (for example, Browning (1975) examines the potential for coalitions between different age groups in a system of pay-as-you-go financed pensions).

The OECD report points to two phenomena that are affecting demographic structures, with an impact that varies in force and timing in different local contexts. The first is often termed the 'demographic transition' associated with the development of a mature industrial society. It is characterised by a substantial decline in mortality rates, followed by a similar decline in fertility. This contributes to the ageing of the population through an increase in the numbers of elderly people and a reduction in the proportion of younger people. In most Western countries, the decline in mortality occurred most strikingly in the first three quarters of the nineteenth century, and the decline in the birth-rate over the period up to the beginning of the Second World War. The second change is the sharp increase in the birth rate after the Second World War, which produced a boom in the school age population in the 1950s and 1960s and will feed through into the elderly population in the first quarter of the twenty-first century. Taken together, these changes imply that the proportion of elderly people in the population will tend to increase, until the changes in mortality and fertility stabilise, and their impact is absorbed into population structure over the life span.

The transitional decline in fertility came to an end in most western countries in the early 1970s. However, more recently, fertility rates have again fallen: 'fertility is now below the level required for replacement of the population . . . in all [OECD] countries except Ireland and Turkey' (OECD, 1988d, p.14). The lowest rates occur in a group of European countries, including Austria, Germany, Denmark, Italy, Luxembourg, the Nether-lands and Switzerland. The average rate of live births required for stability is estimated at about 2.1 for each woman in the popula-tion. In these countries it had fallen to about 1.5. The trend to a reduction in mortality has also continued into the post-war period, with an increase in average life expectancy at birth of about 8.5 years for women and 6 years for men between 1950 and 1980 in the OECD as a whole. The main reason for this increase is the continued fall of death rates in the early years of life in most countries.

The second phenomenon identified as contributing to future patterns of dependency – the post-war baby boom – is superim-posed on the ageing of populations as a result of the changes in birth and death rates. Fertility rose in most countries in the early 1940s. In Western Europe it slackened and then went into decline from the late 1940s onwards, whereas in the US, Canada, Australia and New Zealand it continued to rise until the mid-1960s. In Japan there has been an almost continuous decline from the 1940s. The effect of the rise in births in the 1940s will be to produce an additional cohort of elderly people in the first quarter of the next century, extending rather later in some countries.

The report analyses the likely impact of these demographic shifts on future population structures and on patterns of demand for social services in some detail. The appraisal leads to four conclusions: first there will be a considerable increase in the numbers of elderly people in the population of OECD countries over the next half century; secondly, the average age of the group of elderly people itself will tend to rise in the early years of the twenty-first century as the cohort of baby boomers feeds through into retirement and into advanced old age; thirdly there will be a shrinkage in the relative size of the young and working age populations (and in many cases of the absolute numbers in these groups); fourthly, women will considerably outnumber men in the elderly population because they live longer. The ratio of women to men among 65–69 year-olds will shift from 1 to 0.82 to 1 to 0.91 between 1980 and 2040 (OECD, 1988d, p.23).

These projections are based on estimates of mortality, fertility and migration rates. Migration plays a relatively small part in the calculation. Mortality rates are assumed to vary little over time. Future changes in birth rates are difficult to predict. Thus estimates of the young population for the last years of this century and the early years of the next must be uncertain, as must calculations of the working age population from the second quarter of the next century onwards. However, estimates of the elderly population over the next sixty or seventy years and of the working age population for the next thirty or so can be treated with some confidence (assuming the absence of cataclysms, health care miracles or mass emigration to Mars) because they are based on knowledge of changes which have already taken place. Table 3.2 gives some estimates of the proportion of the population in the various age-groups and of the implications for social spending based on the OECD statistics.

The proportion of young people in the populations will fall, from 23.4 to 17.9 per cent on average for the OECD as a whole, with particularly sharp reductions in Germany and also in Denmark and the Netherlands. Populations of working age will start to shrink in absolute terms from the second decade of the twenty-first century onwards, with the most rapid shrinkage in

Table 3.2 Population projections for the principal OECD countries

	Canada	France	Germany	Italy	Japan	UK	USA
Percentage of population aged:							
0–14							
1980	23	22	18	22	24	21	23
2000	20	19	16	17	18	21	21
2020	17	17	13	15	17	20	19
2040	18	18	15	17	17	18	19
15–64							
1980	67	64	66	64	67	64	66
2000	67	66	68	68	67	64	67
2020	64	63	65	66	62	64	65
2040	59	59	57	59	60	62	61
65–79:							
1980	10	14	16	14	9	15	11
2000	13	15	17	15	15	15	12
2020	19	20	22	19	21	16	16
2040	23	23	28	24	23	20	20
80 or over:							
1980	2	3	3	2	1	3	2
2000	3	3	4	3	3	3	3
2020	4	5	5	5	5	3	3
2040	7	7	7	6	6	5	6
Percentage increase in total dependency ratio, 1980–2040:							
	42	20	47	27	38	10	23
Percentage increase in aged dependency ratio, 1980–2040:							
	168	74	106	97	180	43	89
Percentage increase in financial burden per head of working population required to maintain social spending:							
2000	3	0	6	−1	15	−7	−4
2020	25	16	24	16	42	11	7
2040	45	32	54	39	54	11	31
Average annual rate of GDP growth necessary to finance the increases in social spending due to demographic factors over the period 1980–2040:							
	1.05	0.41	−0.05	0.11	0.56	0.16	0.84

Notes: Total dependency ratio is defined as the population under 15 and over 64 divided by the population between 15 and 64.

Aged dependency ratio is defined as the population aged 65 or over divided by the population aged 15 to 65.

The financial burden is the ratio of social spending (projected to take account of demographic change) to the population between 15 and 65.

Sources: OECD, 1988d, Tables 6, 7, 13, 14, 21 and 22 and author's calculations.

Germany, Italy, Portugal, Spain and Switzerland. Only Turkey and Australia do not experience an absolute decline. The proportion of the population over age 65 will nearly double in the OECD as a whole between 1980 and 2040 with the biggest increases in Germany, Italy, Switzerland and the Netherlands. More optimistic assumptions about mortality rates (essentially that the rate of increase in life expectancy between 1950 and 1980 is maintained for the next half-century) imply a rough doubling in the proportion of the population over 65 and a trebling of the proportion of very elderly people over 80 years of age by the second half of the next century. This however is speculation.

The report goes on to estimate the impact of demographic change on social spending. Since elderly people use the most expensive single programme – pensions – and are the heaviest users of health and social care services, the tendency toward ageing in the population will produce a substantial increase in expenditure. To the extent that there is a relative reduction in the size of younger age groups, there will be savings on family benefits, education and health care for children and younger people. The balance in social spending by age-group varies between countries according to age structure and the organisation of the social security and medical care systems – particularly the part played by government. In 1980, the twelve largest OECD economies spent 2.7 times as much per head on average on welfare for the over-65s as on the under-15s. The ratio varies between nearly 4 times as much in countries with strong programmes for the elderly (like Italy) or weak programmes for younger people (like the US) and twice as much in countries with relatively meagre pensions (like the UK) or strong support for children (like Denmark – OECD, 1988d, p.35).

On the assumption that the level of provision remains at the current rate, it is possible to calculate the cost of maintaining services in the future, as the population balance shifts. The lower rows of the table show the increases in financial burdens implied by the changes in dependency. These vary substantially from country to country. The changes can be usefully expressed in terms of the burden of finance placed on each member of the population of working age, since it is the working population who pay the taxes required to finance most state-run schemes. The conclusion to this analysis provides the nub of the argument that changes in population structure will set real limits to the expansion and the maintenance of social policy. For the twelve major countries,

> expenditure and financing capacity will remain in balance until after the turn of the century . . . . After 2010, however, social expenditure is projected to grow more rapidly than the working age population in Australia, France, Sweden and the US. A similar situation arises in Canada, Italy and the Netherlands from around 2005, from the mid-1990s in Germany and from about 1990 in Japan. In Belgium, Denmark and the UK the projected growth rates of expenditure remain below those of the working-age population until 2015 or 2020 (p.41).

The document goes on to consider the sensitivity of the calculations to assumptions about future patterns of social spending, changes in levels of employment and economic participation, mortality and fertility rates and concludes that they are reasonably robust.

The argument of the OECD report has been described at some length because it is basic to a cluster of documents which provide an international commentary on the development of social policy, and because similar arguments recur in national documents. The implications of the demographic argument for the future of state welfare are gloomy. The discussion of pension reform, for example, argues that 'the necessity for policy change is obvious' (OECD, 1988, p.37) and discusses benefit cuts, raising the retirement age, increasing revenue, and privatisation as options. Major pension reforms involving the limitation of indexation of benefits have occurred in France, Germany, the Netherlands, Sweden and the UK in the 1980s and benefits have been frozen in cash terms in New Zealand; retirement ages have been increased in Japan and are to be increased in the USA. Contributions have also been increased substantially in France, the UK and the USA. Navarro writes of the US: 'an inter-generational conflict is assumed to occur, with the working population . . . increasingly reluctant to pay social security taxes for another generation' (1988, pp.227–8). Legislation passed in 1983 will reduce the cost of providing for the post-war 'baby boomers' by raising the retirement age from 65 to 67 from the year 2000, and increasing contributions from the late 1980s onwards. In the context of the claims about the economic burden of social spending discussed earlier, it is hardly surprising that demographic claims are often used as a justification for cutting back on state welfare provision.

The UK has the lowest increase in dependency ratios of the seven major OECD countries discussed in Table 3.2 (and indeed of all the other OECD countries except Iceland, Ireland, Portugal and Turkey where very sharp falls in the proportion of young people are anticipated). The pattern of social spending and the fall in the British population of working age imply an estimate of the proportion of GDP required to maintain spending that is not so low as in some other countries, but is still not enormous. However, as in the USA, demographic change has been presented by government as a compelling reason for a radical reduction in state social security commitments.

The official review of the social security system in the mid-1980s argues: 'if the best estimate available to us leads us to question whether we will be able to afford the promises we are making, then we have a duty to re-examine the position. It would be an abdication of responsibility to hand down to our children an obligation which we believe they cannot fulfil' (DHSS, 1985, p.18). The estimate, by the government actuary, is that the number of national insurance contributors for each pensioner will fall from 2.3 in 1984–5 to 2.0 by 2015–6 and to 1.8 by 2025–6 (Government Actuary, 1984, p.2). Independent calculations by Ermisch (1990, p.1) indicate that: 'an ageing population will demand a radical overhaul of pension policies'. Since elderly people consume a high proportion of health care and social care services the demographic shift is also seen as imposing additional burdens on these services.

The changes in population structure raise serious questions for social policy. However, it is premature to draw the conclusions reached by some policy makers in the UK and the USA, that demographic change incapacitates the welfare state. There are three reasons for this. First, the calculations typified by the OECD report pay little attention to previous experience in coping with the impact of change. Second, they may be an incomplete guide to the future because they say little about relevant social changes. Third, the whole question of how ageing is related to dependency requires more detailed consideration.

Welfare spending and population change – the post-war period

The proportion of the population aged 65 or more in the seven largest OECD countries rose from 8.6 to 12.5 per cent in the thirty years between 1950 and 1980 – the heyday of welfare state growth. The projection for the next seventy years, to 2050, implies an increase to 21.6 per cent, roughly the same arithmetic rate of increase. The circumstances of the different countries vary, but only in Canada, France and Japan does the rate of increase in the later period exceed that in the earlier. The impact of change on spending is complicated by policy and by changes in the number of younger people. It is these factors which lead to the calculation of high and alarming ratios of dependency. However, if the cost is presented in another way, it becomes less striking. The OECD report calculates the average annual growth rate of GDP required to maintain social expenditure at a constant level for the various age-groups as they change in size. The results are summarised for the seven major countries in the bottom row of Table 3.2. Only in Canada and Australia does the growth required exceed 1 per cent. Demographic change in the other countries demands substantially less, with the US at the top of the range, Japan and France around the middle, and the other countries at the bottom. In Germany and Denmark the requirement is actually negative.

Looked at from this point of view, the demographic burden seems less of a problem. Growth rates of social spending considerably in excess of these figures have existed throughout the post-war period. This has enabled the countries to cope with demographic burdens while making substantial real improvements in provision. As welfare states approach maturity with programmes that now cover most groups in the population, insistence on improvement is likely to grow less marked. It seems reasonable to conclude that demographic pressures will not prove insuperable in most countries, unless there is a complete and unprecedented economic collapse.

It is striking that the concern about demographic pressures should be so great in Britain, where the likely burden in extra spending is relatively low, at less than 0.2 per cent of GDP a year. This represents less than a fifth of the average annual rate of increase in government spending, or an eighth of the increase in social spending under the Conservative government of the 1980s, which was vehemently committed to constraint. The significance of this point has tended to be obscured by the focus on the area most sensitive to demographic increase – pensions – in official debate, and the expression of costs in terms of the burden on the working population rather than as a proportion of GDP. If anything, the UK seems peculiarly well-placed to cope with demographic shifts. It is difficult to identify obvious practical limits to social policy in this country. This point is reinforced by more detailed analysis of the logic of arguments based on dependency.

Social change and dependency

The notion of dependency ratio that figures in the debate about pensions is normally based on the comparison of retired and working groups. For convenience, these are typically operational-ised as those over pension age and those of working age. This is roughly what the OECD does, assuming common cut-off ages throughout the member countries. The calculations of the Govern-ment Actuary and others in Britain, however, keep more closely to the actual configuration of local circumstances. Thus the Actuary contrasts pensioners to National Insurance contributors, and assumes that unemployment remains at a constant 6 per cent, and that the proportion of contributors in the working age population remains constant. Both these assumptions are highly contestable. The future pattern of unemployment is hard to predict. However, it is certain that the expansion of the numbers of working age over the past two decades has now come to an end, and that this group will gradually shrink in numbers from the early years of the next century onwards. At the same time, it is likely that the established trends to the expansion of higher education will continue (Ermisch, 1990, p.30). These developments will lead to a tighter labour market. The result may be immigration (as in the tight labour market of the 1950s), a steepening of the trend for women and particularly married women to enter paid employ-ment in greater numbers and possibly a reversal of the trend to early retirement, and an effective raising of the retirement age. These changes would increase the proportion of contributors, and would also cut back the numbers of retired people receiving pensions. If the problem is that there are too many elderly people and too few workers, it is difficult to see levels of unemployment that are exceptionally high by any historical standards as likely to continue.

A further issue concerns participation in the labour market. Women's participation in paid employment has increased rapidly since the 1960s, whereas that of men has undergone a slight decline (CSO, 1990, p.70). Among the younger age cohorts, participation rates have become roughly equal for men and women, if women are assumed to take some four to five years out of paid employment to carry out the child rearing duties, which current social arrangements assign predominantly to them (Joshi, 1986). As increased participation feeds through all age cohorts, a rise in the number of contributors is likely, but this will reach a ceiling which cannot be passed without substantial improvements in child care provision.

Falkingham (1989, p.227) provides a detailed analysis of the official calculations of the burden of providing for increased numbers of pensioners in the next century. Her work shows how the labour force participation of both men and women over the post-war period has been strongly influenced by conditions in the labour market. She takes into account the likelihood of a fall in the level of unemployment and of an increase in the work force through the participation of married women at all ages and through an increased tendency to work beyond minimum retirement age. Developments in these areas may well reduce the pressure on pensions from aged dependency. For example, the assumption of a fall in unemployment from ten to two per cent over the thirty year period from 1990 cuts the official projection of increased dependency more or less in half. Unemployment over the last two decades has had a much greater effect on social security spending than change in population structure (Barr and Coulter, 1990, p.290). Estimates of dependency used to support radical changes in pension policy may be misleading because they ignore likely changes in unemployment rates and in patterns of paid work especially among women.

Dependency and need

The third point concerns sociological analysis of dependency and its relation to need. In much of the literature the relationship of old age to need is simply assumed, and taken as the positive relation implied by law and policy that links retirement to a particular age and provides differential health and social care for those above and below that age. This assumption is increasingly challenged. First new sociological approaches see the phenomenon of old-age dependency as a sociological rather than a biological construct. Second new evidence is emerging to challenge previous assumptions about the tightness of the link between age and the demand for extra social spending.

In industrial society, old people suffer a generally low social and economic status compared to younger people. 'This is characterised by financial dependency on the state, and by restricted access to a wide range of other resources' (A. Walker, 1987, p.41). Sociologists of welfare policy, such as Townsend (1981), Phillipson (1978) and A. Walker (1987) explain this through a 'political economy of ageing'. The analysis points to the interests of capital and of the labour movement as the main determinants of the overall pattern of policy in advanced capitalist societies. It has two principal elements. On the one hand, capital has an interest in the maintenance of a flexible group in the population to function as a reserve army of labour, since demand fluctuates over the business cycle. It is rational to use those workers whose retraining in contemporary techniques is most expensive – the oldest – as one group in the reserve pool, alongside guest workers, unemployed people and some categories of women. On the other hand, the restriction of the work force is also in the interest of existing workers, so that there are likely to be strong pressures from elements in the labour movement to construct mechanisms for compelling exit from paid employment, rather than, for example, shortening the working week and spreading wages more thinly over an extended work force. Both these interests make it possible for flexible mechanisms of exclusion from paid work to be constructed, of which retirement is one. The details of the status of retirement are fought out in the complex struggles of practical politics, and the interest of workers in providing for their own individual future sustenance and of capital in the maintenance of the labour reserve leads to pressure for the provision of pensions.

end result is that social policy creates a 'structured depen-
's Townsend terms it, in which those of particular ages are
from the labour market and become dependents on
⟶nd other benefits. The level of state provision is
⟶y the balance of forces in struggles in which capital
⟶west rate of support and labour a higher return. In
⟶e balance of political forces ranged about welfare
⟶ and the US has swung in favour of capital, with
⟶al cuts in welfare for the retired are the subject

's of retirement is seen as a creation of policy
⟶ objective social fact which furnishes a justifica-
⟶ιcy change, the arguments about demography and
⟶ency emerge in a new light. The logic of the OECD
⟶gument and of that pursued in the British government documents is of a simple equation of age and dependency. The critique
by Falkingham and others points out that additional factors must
be taken into account in the calculation. The thesis that dependency is socially constructed claims that the concern about the
burden of the maintenance of aged people contains a paradox. The
system of work constitutes aged people as a dependent group in
the first place. This insight throws open the whole debate about
age-structures. In practical terms it reinforces the point that the
status of retirement is socially negotiable. An increased demand
for workers in the next century may lead to an effective raising of
the retirement age and the extension of the working years. As
Walker points out (1987, p.46) retirement is a relatively recent
phenomenon. Between 1931 and 1971, the proportion of men aged
65 or over who were retired increased from under one-half to 78
per cent, and by 1984 the figure was around 94 per cent. Under
modern pension systems a noticeable proportion (about 10 per
cent) choose not to retire and to defer state pension entitlement,
and this group is likely to increase as pressure on jobs slackens.

The second aspect to the new critique of dependency concerns
the relationship of age and need. It is repeatedly pointed out in
discussions of public spending that elderly people cost the state
more than younger people. Much of this spending is in the form
of the pensions and income benefits discussed above, but a
considerable proportion (varying from country to country) concerns health and social care. Comparative statistics on social care
spending are not conveniently available. For health care, the cost

of services for those over 65 is on average four times the cost for younger people, with wide variations between countries. For those over 75, it is nearer six times (OECD, 1988, p.43). Unlike pension spending, which is in general greater for the younger groups among the elderly since pensions are not always adequately inflation-proofed and do not fully reflect gains in wages made by the working population, health care demands tend to be higher among the older groups.

In the case of health and social care spending the discussion of the social construction of dependency has been reinforced by a re-evaluation of the evidence about physical dependency. There are two important points. First the fact that there are more physically dependent people and more sick people among elderly groups should not be allowed to obscure the point that most people over the age of 65 are neither dependent nor ill. As Townsend (1986, p.24) points out even among those over the age of 75, less than half reported a limiting long-standing disability in the early 1980s in the General Household Survey. Although disability increases with age, over 90 per cent of those aged between 65 and 74 can cope with the normal tasks of everyday life – washing themselves, walking down the road, managing the stairs. For those aged between 75 and 85, the proportion falls to about to about 85 per cent, and for those over 85 less than 80 per cent (Henwood and Wicks, 1984, p.16). Over 95 per cent of the population live in their own homes until the age of death. On the assumption that existing standards of provision are maintained, Ermisch estimates that population ageing only implies an increase of 12 per cent in health and social care spending by the end of the first quarter of the next century (1990, p.41).

There have also been substantial improvements in mortality rates among old people. Between 1946 and 1985 mortality rates for those aged between 65 and 74 have fallen by 14 per cent for men and 30 per cent for women, among those aged between 75 and 84, by 13 per cent for men and 31 per cent for women, and even among those over 85 by 8 and 15 per cent respectively (Wells and Freer, 1988, p.xvi). Freer (1988, p.4) concludes from a review of recent survey evidence that 'the majority of older people live reasonably happy lives . . . and there is no evidence of a decline in happiness or life-satisfaction with age'.

The second point concerns the debate about old age and

morbidity. The American geriatrician, Fries, contests the prevailing view that an increase in the number of elderly people necessarily implies increased problems of social provision. He claims that: 'the number of very old people will not increase, that the average period of diminished vigour will decrease, that chronic disease will occupy a smaller proportion of the typical lifespan, and that the need for medical care in later life will decrease' (1980, p.130). A careful review of the evidence by Bury shows that the claim that mortality is being compressed into a briefer period around the age of 85 may be misleading. Many aspects of health are improving, and consequently the overall need for health care may diminish. However 'the terms "rectangularisation of mortality" and "compression of morbidity" turn out to be frustratingly elliptical: intriguing notions to conjure with, but difficult to use in focusing on current health experience and health service interventions' (Bury, 1988, p.27). There is still considerable variation in morbidity and mortality along social dimensions. Substantial welfare interventions will be required, especially for working-class groups. This is the obverse of the conclusion that dependency in old age is socially constructed. If so, the pattern of need involved is likely to reflect patterns of class and gender power in society, with working-class people and women most likely to become defined as dependent, and most strongly in need of social welfare services.

These two points imply that the link between health and social dependency, which initially appears more intractable than the link between retirement age and pension spending, may also be capable of modification. The extent to which it is possible to arrive at an estimate of future demand for social spending by the arithmetical method of dividing the population by age groups is again called into question. However, changes in patterns of family life do raise issues about the development of policy for social care.

Changing patterns of family life

Many writers have pointed out that family and voluntary provision play a major role in supplying health and social care. Estimates of the impact of social change on the provision of care must attempt to take this into account. Precise calculations of the value of such care are impossible since it does not take place in an obvious commercial context. Working from a 'conservative estimate' derived from the 1980 General Household Survey of 1.3 million carers providing an average of five hours a day care (which is rather less than the average of over seven hours found by the Women and Employment survey in the same year (Martin and Roberts, 1984)) and costing the care at the rate of pay of a home help, Henwood and Wicks estimate the price of informal provision at some £7.4 billion in 1984–5 (1985, p.370). This is about three times the amount spent by government on personal social services in that year, or half the cost of the NHS. Other estimates provide similar or higher figures – as high as £24 billion, or six times the cost of personal social services, in 1987 according to a recent Family Policy Studies Centre study (Nissel and Bonnerjea, 1982; Coote, Harman and Hewitt, 1990, p.43; Evandrou, Falkingham and Glennerster, 1990, p.258).

It has been a primary object of policy in the 1980s to expand the role of informal provision, both for ideological and practical reasons. For example, the White Paper *Caring for People* states bluntly: 'the reality is that most care is provided by family, friends and neighbours' (Department of Health, 1989b, p.1). The idealisation of the family as a haven of supportive care was discussed in the previous chapter. The practical issues concern the cost of state provision in a time of constraint, exacerbated by the fact that much of the physical plant through which direct care was provided – institutions built in the previous century – was approaching the end of its useful life.

Calculations about dependency ratios, and the future cost of an ageing population tend to assume that the non-state sector will take the same proportionate share of provision that it has in the past. Since the numbers of elderly people will increase, this implies that a greater overall volume of care will be provided from this source. This may present problems. While the need for extra state health and social care spending may be calculated with some precision, it is not clear that the resources are available to increase the amount of informal care proportionately. There are a number of social processes that are likely to affect the available pool of carers.

First, the majority of carers are women. The Office of Population

Censuses and Surveys (OPCS) disability surveys showed that only a third of carers were male – almost all of them husbands caring for wives. Women carers included a substantial number of daughters (about a fifth of all carers) as well as a substantial group of other female relatives and non-relatives (Martin, White and Melzer, 1989, p.xii, 98). Some other studies put the proportion of men carers as high as 40 per cent, although these conclusions are disputed (Charlesworth, Wilkin and Durie, 1984). The tendency for more women of working age to move into the formal labour market discussed earlier will either reduce their availability for simultaneous informal care or construct that care-work as a 'double-shift' of formal plus informal labour. Secondly, a number of writers suggest that changes in patterns of family life, including increased rates of cohabitation (especially before marriage), of single parenthood (often associated with poverty) and of divorce and remarriage (which may complicate the relationship between elderly parents and parents-in-law and children who may be potential carers) will undermine the relationships of felt obligation on which informal care rests. Whether this will be important is at present unclear. There is no evidence of a decline in the volume of informal care, if anything the reverse.

Parker (1985, p.14), Hicks (1988, p.1) and Henwood and Wicks (1985) concur on an estimate of 1.3 million carers providing over 20 hours care a week, based on the 1980 General Household Survey and other sources. The Women and Employment survey carried out in the same year produces a slightly higher figure of 1.33 million. This refers only to women carers, and uses a more inclusive criterion – more than fifteen hours care-work a week. Perhaps 0.4 million should be added to this, to take account of men carers. An estimate attributed to the 1984 General Household Survey of 1.4 million carers providing over 20 hours care a week is quoted by the Social Services Select Committee (1990, p.vii) although this may well come from the 1985 survey, which seems to have included the relevant question in its questionnaire (OPCS, 1987, Appendix 1, Individual Questionnaire, pp.46–57). The questions asked in the 1985 survey are considerably more detailed than those of 1980.

The official Disability Survey, carried out by the Office of Population Censuses and Surveys between 1985 and 1988, with most of the relevant fieldwork between 1985 and 1986, used a rather different methodology. Instead of asking people whether they carried out care tasks, it asked people with a disability whether they received any help or care from others. This approach, which may well lead individuals to underestimate the care they receive since a positive value is attached to independence in our society, produced a figure of 1.1 million main carers, 0.7 million of them working for 20 hours a week or more. On this basis, it is difficult to speak confidently of trends in care. However, the GHS and surveys using a similar methodology indicate a slight increase in the number of carers over the early 1980s, consonant with population trends.

Changes in employment patterns indicate that the continued expansion of informal care will only be achieved with considerable difficulty. The implication is that, over the next four decades, social care will involve substantial increases in state spending – up to the quadrupling of existing social services spending estimated above – or that social care will remain outside the state sector either provided informally by people also engaged in paid employment, or through the private market. The expansion of informal care under present arrangements will throw this inequitably onto women. Social change in the family may also have an effect.

If these costs are translated into percentages of GDP they appear relatively small. Increasing the 1984–5 social services budget by a factor of four is a one-off cost of 0.3 per cent of GDP. Spread over a substantial time-period, this does not require enormous modification of the 0.16 per cent annual increase in the proportion of GDP devoted to social spending which was estimated as necessary to maintain current levels of provision by the OECD (Table 3.2). The proportion is unlikely to approach the 0.41 per cent required in France, for example. In fact, the UK personal social services budget increased by just over a fifth in real terms in the five years to 1989–90, which is about a third of the required rate. The conclusion to be drawn from arithmetical argument is that coping with the consequences of changes in family patterns for social care is likely to be a matter of political decision-making rather than of accommodation to an inexorable social force which dictates the retrenchment of policy.

The issue may also be approached from another direction. Many writers have pointed out that the inequitable distribution of social care work involves real penalties for women in terms of the obligations imposed on them (Land, 1989, p.156); their command over resources (Joshi, 1990, p.52); their social status (Coote, Harman and Hewitt, 1990, p.7); their citizenship (Lister, 1990, p.464) and their autonomy (Pateman, 1989, p.182). More equitable sharing of this work must involve either placing it in the public arena, at a reasonable rate of pay comparable with men's earnings elsewhere, or the alteration of the structures of support and opportunity costs that result in such work being identified as primarily the domain of women. The creation of services to aid this change would be an alternative use for extra public resources, again depending on political decisions. However, this question also involves moral issues, to which we will return in Chapter Eight.

Conclusion

This chapter has reviewed two lines of argument that suggest that future pressures will undermine the viability of the welfare state. The first claims that the burden of state provision acts as a brake on economic growth. It is reinforced by the second, which points to changes in age-dependency ratios as a reason why the burden of state spending will increase further, so that it is doubly important to find ways of reducing it immediately. New developments in patterns of family life suggest that the problem of providing adequate social care for increased numbers of elderly people will grow more severe. It is striking that the challenge to welfare arising from the economic burden of social spending and from change in population structure has been used to justify radical departures in policy in Britain, despite the fact that spending levels are relatively lower and the potential demographic burden less expensive than in many other countries.

There is no convincing evidence that state welfare spending on the scale of the most expansive systems damages economic growth, or that anticipated changes in the age-structure of the population will impose insuperable burdens. Attempts to show that welfare spending damages growth through specific mechanisms such as the pre-empting of resources or the erosion of work incentives are not supported by evidence. More recent analysis indicates that the development of welfare states rests on political and social factors operating in particular local contexts as well as on the level of economic development. Economic crisis has opened up divergent lines of development in welfare states over the past decade, both in spending policies, and more broadly, in response to unemployment. There is speculative evidence that this is associated with a growing divergence in the development of political economies, resulting from the break-down of the Fordist mass-production paradigm of capitalism. Since different countries have responded to economic problems in different ways there are no strong reasons for concluding that economic pressures must inevitably lead to welfare state retrenchment.

Arguments about the significance of changes in population structure are sometimes presented as the outcome of an inexorable science of demography. However, they contain implicit assumptions about the operation of social processes – that elderly people are necessarily dependent and younger people productive. Whether these assumptions are correct depends on social institutions – the nature of retirement, the level of unemployment and the structure of the family. There are good reasons for suggesting that some at least of these institutions may change as problems of dependency grow more severe and may mitigate the difficulties in maintaining the welfare system.

Other social changes imply fresh needs for welfare policy. These can only be realistically met through the extension of welfare state provision. The costs of expanding existing services, so that the level of provision is maintained in the face of new needs, and of developing new services, so that, for example, informal social care can be brought within the sphere of paid employment, are large. However, it is possible to meet them, provided governments choose to do so. The comparative analysis carried out by the OECD indicates that the UK is well-placed compared with many other advanced countries to meet the costs it will face if it chooses this path.

We move on to consider further forces ranged against the current welfare settlement, operating at the level of ideological rather than economic or demographic change.

CHAPTER 4

SOCIAL POLICY, INEQUALITY AND POLARISATION

As you know, there's no such thing as society. There are individual men and women, and there are families. And no government can do anything except through people, and people must look to themselves first. It's our **duty** to look after ourselves first . . .

Mrs Thatcher

Inequality and social cohesion

The 1980s saw an abrupt reversal of the long-term trend to greater income equality in Britain. This chapter discusses evidence on the growth of inequality and of poverty and explanations of the change. The question of whether and how much shifts in government policy have contributed to these changes and what the long-term impact on popular support for the welfare state will be is hotly contested. If the rise in inequality and poverty results from the impact of forces outside the immediate control of government, then the changes cast doubt on the effectiveness of state welfare provision. If, however, policy changes are an important factor in augmenting these trends, then government action may itself undermine support for state welfare.

From one perspective inequality in incomes poses no threat to the continued viability of the welfare state. The protection of an acceptable degree of social cohesion despite the existence of obvious inequalities may be seen as the whole point of state welfare in class society. Marshall suggested in an oft-quoted phrase that social policy provides, through the guarantee of citizenship, 'the foundations on which the structure of inequality may be built'. Thus 'citizenship has become . . . the architect of legitimate social inequality' (1950, p.117). The policy maker is engaged as a sort of under-labourer for patriarchal market capitalism. This approach underlay much of the discussion of legitimation crisis and citizenship deficit in the 1970s and early 1980s. The principal concern was that democratic governments were forced to develop new policies in response to the demands of organised sectional interests and could not restrict resulting inequalities to the level sanctioned as legitimate by the losers.

An alternative approach which has gained increasing attention in the 1980s, inverts the order of causation. Instead of social welfare being understood as underpinning cohesion in an unequal social structure, change in social structural relations is seen as a threat to the continuance of social welfare. This perspective argues that the widening gap between prosperous and impoverished people will itself threaten the viability of the welfare state. If government policy is responsible for a substantial growth in inequality, and this leads to a decline in enthusiasm for state services and a shift in allegiance to the private sector, then developments in the 1980s will provide a good test of the claim that it is possible for governments to engineer a collapse of support for state welfare. This chapter discusses changes in the level of poverty and social inequality in the 1980s. Evidence of the impact on the values that buttress the involvement of the state in an extensive system of welfare provision will be examined in Chapter Five.

Income and inequality

Two main statistical series contribute to our understanding of poverty – the Low Income Families statistics, published by the DHSS for the years 1972 to 1985 and continued up to 1987 by the independent Institute for Fiscal Studies, and the Households

Below Average Income statistics, with which the government replaced the former series, back-dating the starting point so that it covers the period from 1981 to 1987. The Low Income Families statistics give details of the numbers of people and families living at or about the supplementary benefit/income support level – the poverty line of last resort social security benefits. The second series gives information on the numbers living at various levels in relation to average income. Considerable doubt has been cast upon the utility of both series by three factors: the data are published after a considerable and unnecessary delay, so that they cannot be used to support commentary on contemporary policy developments; second, the substitution of the second for the first series appears to have been inspired by official reluctance to reveal the substantial increase in the number living at the poverty line in the late 1980s; third, errors in the second series massively over-reported the rise in the living standards of the poorest group and were used to buttress ministerial statements about the success of anti-poverty policy which were later shown to be inaccurate.

The official figures prepared by the Department of Health and Social Security for the early 1980s initially showed a substantial rise in real incomes among the bottom tenth of households. Incomes for this group were believed to have risen by over 8 per cent in real terms, as against under 5 per cent for the population as a whole over the period from 1981 to 1985 (DHSS, 1988). These statistics were used by the Prime Minister and other politicians in support of the claim that economic expansion benefited the poor, since there was a 'trickle down' of income growth from advantaged to disadvantaged groups: the Prime Minister stated that 'everyone has benefited from the increase in national prosperity – everyone' (Hansard, House of Commons, Oral Answers, vol.133, col.801, 1988). The Secretary of State for Social Services asserted: 'what the most recent published figures actually show is that . . . the poorest in our society not only shared in the general improvement in living standards, but did better than average' (Moore, 1988). However, subsequent analysis demonstrated that these claims are simply incorrect. The bottom tenth had gained a 2.6 per cent increase in real incomes – less than half the average increase of 5.4 per cent and insufficient to meet average increases in effective rents and other costs over the period (Hansard, Debates, vol.170, cols.687–88). This debacle discredited much official analysis.

In its corrected version, the Households Below Average Income series concurs with the Low-Income Families series in providing evidence of a substantial increase in poverty in the 1980s. The Low-Income Family data show that the proportion of the population living below the minimum subsistence supplementary benefit level rose from 4 per cent in 1979 to 5 per cent by 1987, whereas the proportion living at that level rose from about 8 to about 14 per cent. Supplementary benefit had risen slightly against retail prices over the period, but the increase is not sufficient to make much difference to its use as a bench mark of poverty. The real value of supplementary benefit had risen by less than 4 per cent over that period, against a rise of over 18 per cent in real average earnings (DHSS, 1988; Johnson and Webb, 1990, p.20; Oppenheim, 1990, p.19, Barr and Coulter, 1990, p.314). The Households Below Average Incomes series shows that about 19 per cent of the population were living below half national average income in 1987, a rise from some 9 per cent in 1979 (DSS, 1990). The close comparability between the estimates produced by different series and based on different methodological approaches reinforces the point that poverty has increased substantially in Britain in the past decade.

This shows a sharp contrast with the pattern in the 1970s. The Low-Income Family series shows that the increase in the proportion below the supplementary benefit level was from 3 to 4 per cent between 1972 when the series began and 1979. The corresponding increase in the proportion on supplementary benefit was from 3 to 8 per cent (DHSS, 1983; CSO, 1974, no.5, Table 80).

The poorest groups have not participated in the prosperity of the more fortunate. Average incomes have risen substantially in real terms over the 1980s – by 23 per cent between 1979 and 1987 (DSS, 1990). There have also been important changes in incomes at the top end of the distribution, and these have contributed to a substantial growth in inequality. Constraint on social benefits has contributed to this process. Table 4.1 gives details of the trends in relative household income over the past two decades for the population as a whole, and shows the proportion of household income coming from earnings and benefits. The income of the bottom tenth, dependent mainly on social security benefits for the whole period, stayed roughly constant relative to the median over the 1970s but fell behind the rest of the population in the 1980s.

Table 4.1 Inequality in Britain, 1970–90

Gross household income:
Deciles and quartiles as a percentage of the mean

	bottom decile	bottom quartile	top quartile	top decile
1970	31	60	141	194
1979	30	52	148	204
1989	25	46	164	233

The chief source of income; the percentage of household income derived from wages and salaries and social security benefits in the various income groups

	Wages	Benefits	Wages	Benefits	Wages	Benefits	Wages	Benefits
1970	3	81	48	27	85	3	72	3
1979	2	85	25	48	83	4	79	3
1989	1	89	28	36	74	5	77	2

Note: Income sources for deciles and quartiles are taken as those of the nearest income band in the published FES tables.

Sources: CSO, *Family Expenditure Survey reports for 1970, 1979 and 1989*, Tables C, 48 and 24 respectively for the first table and 26, 46 and 22 for the second.

Among the lower quartile of the income distribution dependency on benefits has increased with the rise in unemployment, so that these overtook earnings as the main source of income in the mid-1970s. The position of this group has also fallen steadily relative to the median. The incomes of the top quartile and decile, who depend mainly on labour market income, but with a rising contribution from unearned income have increased rapidly, especially in the 1980s. Thus the top quartile moved away from the median by about 5 per cent between 1970 and 1979, but by some 15 per cent between 1979 and 1989. Corresponding figures for the top tenth are 10 and 30 per cent. These statistics show how rapidly the incomes of different groups have diverged.

The evidence of growing inequality reinforces the argument that prosperity does not 'trickle down' from the prosperous to the miserable. Another side of the pattern is presented in data on the distribution of wealth in Britain. Official statistics are provided by the Inland Revenue. These show that the distribution remains extremely unequal. The long-established trend towards gradual redistribution away from the rich towards lower income groups has been brought to an end over the past decade, although there is a continued trend for the moderately rich to benefit at the expense of very rich people. The bottom half of the income distribution has lost to the more well-resourced half. The share of total wealth held by the top 1 per cent fell from 21 to 18 per cent of all marketable wealth between 1976 and 1981 and thence to 17 per cent by 1988. However, the share of the top 10 per cent remained level at 50 per cent in the 1970s but rose to 53 per cent in the 1980s. The assets of the top 25 per cent rose from 71 to 73 per cent between 1976 and 1981 and to 75 per cent by 1988. The least wealthy half of the population retained a holding of just 8 per cent of total wealth in the 1980s. This had fallen to 6 per cent by 1988 (Good, 1990, Table E, p.145). Since rich people employ skilled accountants, these figures should be viewed with detachment. They also include the value of owned housing, and a large part of the downward shift is explained by the expansion of home ownership. It is not clear to what extent this resource is comparable with the other components of marketable wealth, since the need for shelter continues if the asset is realised. Recent analysis of the redistribution of resources through inheritance indicates that asymmetry in wealth holding of this order will continue for the foreseeable future. The redistributive effect of the spread of home ownership is cancelled out by the concentration of prospects for substantial inheritance among the group who are already most wealthy (Mintel International, 1990).

Both poverty and income inequality have increased at an accelerating rate over the last decade. This poses two questions in relation to the theme of the book. First, it is uncertain whether the changes of the 1980s are due primarily to government policy, or to the operation of social forces outside the control of government. If it is mainly the result of particular government policies, policy changes could in principle remove a threat to the welfare state. If it results from social forces that operate outside the control of the government, then the resolution of this problem may require a fundamental shift in the structure of welfare provision.

The second question is linked to this and concerns social cohesion and social welfare. It is unclear whether the rise in inequality and the increase in poverty are eroding the values that have supported the growth of the welfare state since the Second

World War. If so, then the shift poses a problem for state welfare, which is the more serious if the motor of change is outside the control of social policy.

Explanations of inequality

Three factors contribute to the explanation of changes in the level of poverty: changes in employment, in family and population structure and in government policies.

In the first area, the most important factors are unemployment itself, early withdrawal from the labour market, the gap between dual- and single-earner households and the increase in part-time and insecure employment. In the second, the rising numbers of elderly and single-parent households, who often receive inadequate benefits, have already been discussed in Chapter Three. The number of those excluded from work due to disability is also increasing. In the third area are official policies which fail to curtail unemployment, cut benefit levels, increase the tax paid by poorer households and reduce industrial support.

Corresponding factors appear in accounts of the rising incomes of those who are already well off, and thus play a part in explanations of inequality. In relation to employment, earnings at the top end have increased rapidly. Changing patterns indicate a growing gap between those households which are able to support a secure standard of living on the earnings of a number of workers and those which are dependent on one or none. Government policies have cut the tax bills of those who are already well paid by large amounts.

Trends in employment patterns, population structure and official policy in the UK over the 1980s have contributed to the increase in poverty and inequality. We move on to review the available evidence and the results of various attempts to apportion responsibility between the various factors.

Changes in employment

The main factors in the labour market have been rising levels of unemployment and changes in the pattern of earnings. The oil crisis of the 1970s led to recession and a rapid increase in unemployment to the highest level since the war in many capitalist countries. One result was an increase in the numbers in poverty due to lack of work. The UK once again stands out as an unusual case among European countries. Unemployment in the UK rose from 4 per cent in 1975 to the highest level of any major EC economy by 1985 (11.7 per cent, compared with 9.6 for Italy, 10.2 for France and 8.3 for Germany, using standard OECD definitions: OECD, 1988b, Table R18). The abrupt rise in unemployment was associated with an equally sharp increase in numbers in poverty. A cross-national study shows that poverty in Britain increased more rapidly between 1975 and 1985 than in any other country of the European Community – from 6 to 12 per cent of the population. Corresponding figures for the European Community as a whole show a small increase from 12.8 to 13.9 per cent, concentrated in the 'Mediterranean rim' countries of Greece, Spain and Portugal (O'Higgins and Jenkins, 1989, p.3: poverty is here defined as disposable income under below half of average equivalent household disposable income.). Unemployment in Britain fell subsequently to 6.2 per cent by April 1990, a level substantially lower than that of France and Italy, but not Germany (National Institute for Economic and Social Research, 1991, p.104). Unfortunately, no comparable analysis of changes in poverty rates for the European Community over the late 1980s is available. As the British economy moves into recession, unemployment has again started to rise, reaching 7 per cent in the official statistics by February 1991.

There is considerable debate about the utility of British unemployment statistics. Changes in definition so that the official figures now include only those entitled to benefit by reason of unemployment have excluded many categories of unemployed people from the count over the 1980s (Halsey, 1988, p.176). Unofficial attempts to calculate figures on a consistent basis excluding the alterations give a low of 8.4 per cent in early 1990, followed by a rise to over 10 per cent (Unemployment Unit, 1991, p.11). The reduction in the number of jobless people in the late 1980s was not attended by any decrease in the numbers in poverty, indicating that the real increase in employment was accompanied by the development of new low-paid jobs.

High levels of unemployment encourage members of the groups

Table 4.2 Inequality in earnings in the 1970s and 1980s

Gross weekly earnings as a percentage of the median, 1971, 1981 and 1990

	Men			Women		
	1971	1981	1990	1971	1981	1990
Manual workers						
Top decile	147	151	159	143	143	157
Bottom decile	68	69	63	71	70	68
Non-manual workers						
Top decile	167	175	182	169	172	173
Bottom decile	60	60	55	65	68	62
All workers						
Top decile	162	168	181	165	172	179
Bottom decile	65	64	58	66	68	62

Source: Department of Employment quoted in CSO, 1990, Table 5.4 and author's calculations from Department of Employment Gazette, November 1990, p. 574.

Percentage increases in real weekly earnings after income tax, national insurance contributions and child benefit: 1971–81 and 1981–89

	1971–81			1981–89		
	Bottom decile	Median	Top decile	Bottom decile	Median	Top decile
Single man	9	10	13	17	28	40
Single woman	27	26	31	24	30	37
Married man	10	10	13	17	27	40
Married man with two children	9	9	12	16	24	37

Note: the calculations assume (unrealistically) that the man is the sole earner in married couple households. Partner's earnings probably increase the trend to inequality.

Source: Inland Revenue, quoted in CSO, 1991, Table 5.14.

that are most strongly affected to leave the labour force altogether, through early retirement, sick absence or disability. Economic activity rates among 50–59 year-old men have fallen by ten per cent and among 60 to 64 year-olds by 17 per cent between 1980 and 1989 as older workers move out of the labour force (Department of Employment, 1989, p.170; 1990, p.194).

The rise in the level of unemployment has an obvious direct

impact on incomes. There have also been changes in the overall distribution of earnings which show a pattern of increasing inequality. Table 4.2 gives statistics on weekly earnings produced by the Department of Employment and the Inland Revenue. The Department of Employment series covers gross earnings whereas the Inland Revenue series is confined to tax-payers and takes into account the impact of government policy through direct tax and child benefit over a slightly briefer period. Both tables tell the same story of rising incomes at the top end and stagnation among the low-paid.

The statistics of gross weekly earnings, which take the story up to 1990, ignore the effect of taxation, but enable the statistics to be analysed by class and gender. Working-class people and women, who earn less, also have a rather lower degree of inequality in their incomes. In the 1970s the changes in relative earnings for the different groups are not great. In the 1980s, however, the earnings of the highest paid tenth have increased rapidly (especially for manual women workers and non-manual men). In all groups the earnings of the bottom tenth have fallen relative to middle earners. When the effect of direct taxes and universal benefits on the relative growth of incomes for different households is taken into account, as it is in the Inland Revenue figures, a similar pattern emerges. The growth over the 1970s in real disposable incomes was roughly the same for the bottom tenth as for the median for the different households considered. The top tenth made moderate gains. In the 1980s, the incomes of the bottom tenth failed to share in the prosperity of other groups. Families with children fared especially badly. Incomes for the top tenth increased rapidly, especially for single and married men without children.

Divergence in the earnings commanded by different groups plays an important role in the increasing inequality of the 1980s. The Inland Revenue statistics show that government policy on tax and benefits has not countered the drift to inequality for the mass of the population.

Household change

Three changes in population structure are important: the increase in the number of retired people, the increase in numbers of low-income single parent families and changes in the numbers of earners in a household. The first two have led to an increase in the numbers of people at risk of poverty, whereas the third change has contributed to the rise in inequality. Neither old age nor single parenthood are in themselves reasons why someone should have a low income. However, the exclusion of many people over retirement age from employment, the lack of adequate childcare, the low wages commanded by many women workers and the inadequacy of state benefits for these groups combine to render them vulnerable to poverty.

Changes in the age structure of the population have been discussed in Chapter Three. The risk of poverty among pensioners has declined over the past four decades due to increases in state pensions and the expansion of private supplements. The Households Below Average Income series shows that by 1987 only a quarter of pensioners received an income that was under half the national average, as against a third of sick and disabled people and three fifths of single parents and unemployed people (Oppenheim, 1990, p.30). The Low Income series shows a decrease of 6 per cent in the numbers of pensioners at or below supplementary benefit levels between 1985 and 1987 (Johnson and Webb, 1990, pp.10–11). Large numbers of people are still involved. Pensioners made up about a quarter of supplementary benefit recipients in 1987 and nearly a third of those below supplementary benefit level. The association between old age and low income is not confined to Britain. A major European Community study covering the period up to 1986 points out that 'elderly people . . . remain in many countries the largest category who are poor or on social assistance . . .' (Room, Lawson and Laczko, 1989, p.170).

Family Expenditure Survey reports provide a different perspective on inequality among this group. The half of retired households who are mainly dependent on social security have an income that averages just under 40 per cent of that received by pensioners who have other sources of income (CSO, 1991b, Table 22). The spread of occupational pensions over the past three decades has brought little benefit to this group.

The number of single parents living at or below the supplementary benefit poverty line rose from 360 thousand in 1979 to 680 thousand by 1987. The number with an income less than 40 per cent above the rate increased from 70 to 220 thousand (Millar,

1987, p.160; Johnson and Webb, 1990, Tables 3 to 7). Almost 60 per cent fell into the bottom quarter of the income distribution in 1989 and over 90 per cent into the bottom half, as against only 2 per cent in the top quarter and 1 per cent in the top tenth (CSO, 1991b, Table 26).

The impact of the changes in the pattern of incomes from employment is compounded by changes in the distribution of workers among households. The decline in employment has reduced the average number of workers in each household slightly overall. At the lowest income levels, the decline has been dramatic, especially among those without children. The average numbers of workers in each household in the bottom seventh of the income distribution fell from 0.5 to 0.2 for single people and 0.9 to 0.6 for couples without children among people who were not retired (Piachaud, 1990, Table 7).

Changes in both patterns of work and in household structure have both contributed to an increase in poverty and in inequality. We now consider the part played by government policy. A number of policy measures, including changes in the tax system, the de-indexation of benefits from earnings indices, restrictions in entitlement and the restructuring of aspects of the system after the 1986 legislation affect both poverty and inequality in incomes. In addition, measures in the field of industrial and wages policy have had a considerable impact.

Official policies: tax and benefit changes

Tax changes have benefited those who are already prosperous. Field points out that, although 'government has refused to publish the cumulative gains of the very rich', available statistics show that in 1988–9 alone 'the richest one per cent . . . cornered £4.7 billion in tax cuts' as a result of the budget changes over the decade – nearly £23,000 each (Field, 1989, p.74). Government policy has shifted the tax burden towards lower paid people. The most important shifts are the reductions of income tax rates, so that the highest rate has been cut from 83 per cent to 40 per cent and the standard rate from 35 to 25 per cent, an increase in VAT from 7.5 to 15 per cent, a series of increases in National Insurance contributions and the substitution of the Community Charge for local authority rates from 1989 onwards in Scotland and a year later elsewhere.

Official statistics do not chart the effect of the last named change. A comparison with the impact of local authority rates carried out by the Local Government Information Unit concludes that overall about two-thirds of families lose from the switch and a third gain. The losses are concentrated at the lower end. In the bottom tenth of income earners, 83 per cent of families lose and only 16 per cent gain, whereas in the top tenth 29 per cent lose and 71 per cent gain (Local Government Information Unit, 1990). The new structure of local taxation is certain to exacerbate the trend towards greater inequality in disposable incomes charted in statistics referring to the period up to the end of the 1980s. The impact of the shift to a Council Tax is at present uncertain. It will not restore the distributional effect of the rates.

Official calculations of the impact of tax changes based on the Family Expenditure Survey are published in Hansard on an occasional basis. The series is imperfect since the effect of Value Added Tax and other indirect taxes is only included for some years, and that of the substitution of Poll Tax for rates is not calculated. The available evidence indicates that the net effect of tax reform has been to shift the burden of total taxation downwards. For a couple with two children on half national average male earnings, the tax bill had increased from 1.4 to 7.3 per cent of their earnings between 1979 and 1989, mainly as a result of increases in National Insurance contributions. For a comparable couple on three-quarters of average earnings, the increase is from 30.2 to 33.3 per cent, again mainly as a result of insurance changes. At average earnings the increase is from 34.5 to 36.9 per cent, as VAT and insurance increases wipe out a slight fall in income tax. For families above twice average earnings, data on the impact of VAT and rates is not given. At this level the policy changes make very little difference in the proportion of income paid in income tax and insurance contributions (a rise from 25.2 to 25.5 per cent). Above twice average earnings statistics show a marked fall in tax bills, which grows greater as one moves up the income scale. At five times the average, the fall is from 40 to 34.1 per cent. At ten times, it is from 50 to 37.1 per cent. At twenty times, it is from 55 to 38.6 per cent (Hansard, Written Answers, 1989, vol.144, cols.633–56; 1990, vol.176, cols.699–708). For single people and couples without children, the impact of the changes is somewhat larger. These statistics show how the overall impact of government policy has been to advance inequality by shifting tax burdens from wealthy minorities to those at the poverty-line. This reinforces the effect of the changes in earnings and in incomes charted earlier in Tables 4.1 and 4.2.

The principal changes in benefits have been the severing in 1979 of the link between pensions and wage indices (if these rose more rapidly than price indices), the 1986 Social Security Act which followed the 1985 review and a number of other minor changes designed to sharpen work incentives and constrain spending. The effect of de-indexation at a time when real earnings have been rising rapidly has been to ensure that basic rate pensions rose more slowly than they would have if the law had remained unchanged. This has had the effect of choking off the real rise in state pensions against earnings that had occurred in the 1970s. In 1970, the basic rate pension for a couple was worth 37 per cent of average earnings, net of income tax and insurance contributions. By 1979, the ratio had risen to 43 per cent, but by 1989 it had declined to 35 per cent, a figure lower than the 1970 level (DSS, 1990, Table 46.15). Thus the poorest group of pensioners – those who do not have access to substantial private pensions – have failed to share in the prosperity of the better off sections of the working population.

The 1986 Social Security Act set out a framework for restructuring last resort means-tested social security and retirement pensions. Details of the legislation are discussed elsewhere (for example, Hills, 1990, Chapter 5). Here we are concerned with the impact on living standards. The effect of the changes to means-tested benefits is hotly contested. In calculating the overall impact of the shift, the government stated that only 12 per cent of claimants would be worse off as a result of the changes. The official Social Security Advisory Committee puts the figure at 43 per cent. Independent analysis varies between the Policy Studies Institutes' 48 per cent of losers and 32 per cent of gainers and the Benefits Research Unit's claim of 60 per cent losers and 20 per cent gainers (see Svenson and Macpherson, 1988, pp.41–53 for a review of the debate). One important difference in the estimates is that the government figures do not take into account the levels of contribution to local and water rates that claimants will have to pay under the new system, but work from national average figures that are not updated.

In an attempt to resolve these differences, the House of Commons Social Services Select Committee commissioned a detailed comparison of the new income support rates for 1988–9 with the old supplementary benefit rates for the previous year, uprated to take account of inflation and the allowances to cover general rates and the water rates contributions now levied on claimants. The results show substantial losses for single people, especially those under 25, and also real falls in income for the poorest groups of pensioners, as a result of the fact that the benefits fail to cover the amounts that must be paid in rates. While couples with children made small real gains, those without did not. Single parents also suffered real losses (Social Services Select Committee, 1989). Since single parents form such a large and growing proportion of families in poverty, this is a cause of particular concern. This analysis supports the higher estimates of the numbers of losers from the reform and indicates that official calculations did not take adequate account of the effect of local tax payments.

A second approach to the impact of new government policies is based on empirical studies of the effect of new legislation on poor people. A whole series of surveys carried out in local areas have documented the effect of the social security changes and show how they have penalised claimers. For example, a study of 140 families living on income support in Tyneside in 1989 found that they spent half as much per head as the average family on food, and had lower standards of heating, clothing, domestic goods and entertainment (Bradshaw and Holmes, 1989). A study of young homeless people in London in the same year found that over 78 per cent had to sleep rough and over half had no money for food (Randall, 1989). Craig and Glendinning document the extent to which Social Fund debts force the living standards of families on benefit below income support levels in Manchester and Sheffield (1990). A study of nearly 600 children admitted to hospital in East London showed a strong link between ill-health and 'adverse social conditions'. The unemployment rate of the parents of children admitted was over twice that of the area, a third of the children lived in severely over-crowded conditions, and a quarter reported damp, inadequate heating and inadequate water supply (Carter, 1990). The denial of state benefits to 16 to 18 year olds who do not take part in Youth Training Schemes from 1987 onwards is seen by many as an important factor in the increase in destitution among this group. The number of young homeless people in London was put at about 30,000 in 1985 (O'Mahony, 1988, p.14). By 1989, the figure was estimated at somewhere between 75,000 and 125,000 (Salvation Army, July, 1989; National Federation of Housing Associations in Greve and Currie, 1990).

The changes in pensions in the 1986 Act are designed to encourage people to shift from use of the state's supplementary earnings related pension to private provision. State pension entitlements are to be cut by changing the formula on which they are based, so that the benefit is based on average life-time earnings, rather than the best twenty years, the state commitment to uprate to take account of inflation is reduced and surviving spouse's rights to inherit their partner's pension entitlements are cut by 50 per cent. Incentives to use the private sector are enhanced through moderation in regulation of the industry and cash subsidies to those who switch from state to private schemes. Over four million people – mainly young workers – transferred between 1988 and 1990 and more are expected to do so (National Audit Office, 1990). The changes will only affect the distribution of pensioners' incomes gradually since those involved will not retire until the next century. They are likely to penalise those who are low-paid in working life, since these have the least opportunity to switch, and in particular, women, who will also lose out since their inheritance rights are cut back (see Owen and Joshi, 1987, for a detailed analysis). In all, the changes are calculated to reduce the cost of the state scheme to half of what it would otherwise have been by the early years of the next century.

The effect of new policies on poverty and inequality is uncertain, since the evidence is contested. Cuts in direct taxes have benefited better off people, while increases in Value Added Tax and National Insurance contributions have caused a rise in the proportion of income paid in tax by those on below average incomes. The shift from rates to poll tax is likely to have exacerbated this change. New social security legislation has penalised some groups – especially single people on benefits. The scale of the change is uncertain, due to the inadequacy of the official figures, but it appears to be substantial. There are many small-scale surveys that document an increase in the misery of those in poverty. Policies in relation to both taxation and benefit provision have made a contribution both to inequality and to poverty. The second area of government intervention concerns industrial policy.

Official policies: industry and employment

A number of policy changes affect income distribution. The most important are in the fields of regional development and wage regulation. In both areas there have been substantial cuts in state intervention since 1979.

Regional policy had traditionally incorporated two elements – the carrot of subsidies to special areas under legislation dating back to the 1930s, and the stick of planning controls under the 1947 Town and Country Planning Act. The system of Industrial Development Certificates, part of the 1947 Act designed to channel industry in particular directions, was abolished in 1979, on the grounds that it constituted an unnecessary intervention in the free play of market forces. The advisory Regional Development Councils followed soon after. The areas covered by regional assistance were repeatedly cut back, so that by 1982 the proportion of the workforce included had fallen from 47 to 28 per cent and the level of the grants reduced (Smith, 1989, p.98). Further cutbacks took place in 1984 and 1988. In the mid-1970s, unemployment in the worst-hit regions – Scotland, the North, the North-West and Wales – was about two-thirds as high as in the South-East. By 1989 the rate in the South-East had risen by a quarter, whereas that in Scotland and the North had doubled, and in Wales and the North-West it had risen by more than two-thirds (Oppenheim, 1990, p.112). The need for regional aid grew more intense at the same time that policy was emasculated.

Wage regulation policies in Britain have never formed a co-herent whole, nor have they affected the majority of the work-force. Wage councils set minimum wages for about 2.5 million workers in traditionally low-paid service sector industries. Protection for 16–21 year olds (about half a million of those covered) was removed in 1986, and a consultation paper in 1988 proposed the abolition of the system. The elimination in 1982 of the Fair Wages Agreement, whereby government departments and local authorities adopted a uniform policy of only accepting tenders from contractors who recognised national pay agreements, continued the downward pressure on wages for these groups. Other changes in social security and trade union legislation are likely to have a further impact on low pay.

The 1986 Social Security Act changed the structure of the social assistance system in a way that effectively cut benefit levels for many people of working age, and changes in water charges and the substitution of Poll Tax for rates increased their cost of living disproportionately compared to better paid groups. Benefits for most categories of 16 to 18 year olds were abolished from 1987 onwards. More recent legislation in 1989 denied benefits to those who refuse a job on the grounds of low wages. These measures have further eroded the position of vulnerable groups in the labour market. They are an important factor in explaining the process discussed above, whereby the decline in unemployment in the latter half of the 1980s has not been accompanied by a reduction in poverty.

This brief review of the evidence indicates that changes in the labour market, in household structure and in government policy have all contributed to poverty and to inequality in the 1980s. The case for saying that official policy has played a substantial part in this development appears strong. We now turn to consider some attempts to disentangle the relative significance of government action from that of changes in patterns of demography and employment.

The balance of explanation

Economic, social and political forces interact in explaining the rise in poverty among various social groups, and the increase in social inequality. There have been two main attempts to unravel the contribution of the different factors. The first uses data from the Family Expenditure Survey to assess the relative significance of government policy on benefits and trends in market income and household size on living standards in the UK (O'Higgins, 1985). The study covers the period from 1976 to 1982. The second approach to the problem uses material from the larger but less detailed Labour Force Survey (Buck, 1989). It covers the period from 1979 to 1985. The two studies thus refer to different, but overlapping periods of time and base their conclusions on the analysis of different data sets. This goes some way in explaining their different conclusions.

O'Higgins' work demonstrates that for the late 1970s and early 1980s, changes in the pattern of market incomes were more important than shifts in the incidence of state benefits in explaining the trend towards greater inequality: 'recession rather than reaction has been the main pressure resulting in a rise in poverty and inequality' (1985, p.303). This conclusion is scarcely surprising since the analysis covers the period before the principal cuts in public spending and the policy changes discussed above occurred. In any case, many writers agree that the increase in unemployment in Britain has been a major factor contributing to poverty but that state policy has made a major contribution to the increase in unemployment (Walker and Walker, 1987; Mishra, 1990, pp.32–42, Jenkins, 1989). For example, Barr and Coulter in an analysis which is restricted to the effect of taxes and benefits on household, not individual, inequality, but covers the period from 1971 to 1986 show that state benefits are indeed redistributive, but add that 'the system became less redistributive between 1979 and 1986, allowing the share of the top quintile to rise from 40 to 44 per cent of gross income' (1990, p.326). They also point out that the average number of people in the households that fall into the poorest group has increased, since a greater proportion of these households are unemployed families rather than single or couple pensioners. Thus the trend to inequality between individuals is more marked than that to inequality between households, weakening the impression of redistribution in the statistics.

From this perspective it is the concealed effect of labour market and industrial support policies in contributing to unemployment rather than the direct effect of policies on individual benefits and services that is the main issue, and this is necessarily ignored in a re-analysis of the Family Expenditure Survey that defines unemployment as a market effect rather than the result of government policy at the outset. The study takes the division between state and market factors at face value, without considering the way in which state policy may affect the operation of markets.

It is difficult to apportion responsibility for the exceptional rise in unemployment in Britain between government policy and economic forces outside government control. One influential econometric analysis, which attempts to disentangle the impact of established trends in the economy from government action suggests a fifty-fifty split (Metcalfe, 1982, p.264). A similar division was implied in the draft of a House of Commons Select Committee Report on the 1983 budget, but deleted from the final version (Treasury and Civil Service Select Committee, 1983). Unemployment will also influence income inequality by curbing wage demands among the most vulnerable groups. These considerations imply that the impact of government policy on inequality through its effect on the market is substantial.

The second study focuses on the differential impact of the various factors on different income groups over a later period. It points to a different conclusion. For the bottom three deciles where the lion's share (some 70 per cent in 1985–6) of household incomes comes from state benefits, the main reason why incomes fell behind the median is, as might be expected, the lack of growth in those benefits. In the next two deciles, the most important factor is rising unemployment, coupled with the increase in the number of one-parent families, most of whom are on benefit. The impact of market forces in generating inequality is clearest in the top half of the population. These groups suffer relatively little from unemployment. Managerial, professional and technical salaries have risen rapidly, as the data on earnings among different social groups in Table 4.2 indicated.

These findings place much greater emphasis on the role of state policies and benefits in relation to the poor. They refer to a rather different time-period from O'Higgins' account, and one in which welfare cuts were beginning to bite, with the de-indexation of pensions from wages in 1979 and the real reductions in short-term National Insurance benefits in the early 1980s. In addition they disaggregate the experience of different population groups more clearly. The impact of the market lies in a substantial increase in real incomes for the groups most securely placed in employment, and in the denial of work to a particular group among the poor. While market forces may have a strong impact on inequality, especially through changes in the pattern of incomes at the top end, it is direct state policy which has had the most powerful effect on the increase in poverty among those on benefits at the bottom of the income distribution. State policy has also had a substantial indirect effect in reducing pay levels for the most vulnerable groups in employment.

Conclusion

The most significant cuts in state intervention have taken place since the mid-1980s when Buck's analysis ceases. The tax rates levied on high incomes have been more than halved. The contribution of market pressures to unemployment has become less significant as the recession recedes and international growth rates rise. State benefits have been restructured in a way that appears to reduce entitlements for the poorest groups. State policy has grown even more important in generating inequality in the late 1980s than it was earlier. Explanation of the striking increase in poverty in the UK in the 1980s must pay close attention to the role of government. State policies have played an important part in fostering the growth in size of the group at the bottom of the income distribution and in widening the gap between their own living standards and those of more favoured sections of society. Changes in the pattern of incomes cannot be seen as further evidence of the 'failure of the state' to guarantee a shift in the direction of greater equality as a component in a common citizenship. Government is itself an active participant in the process of inequality.

We move on to consider the implications of these changes for patterns of popular ideology. New government policies reinforce trends to greater inequality. Some writers argue that these shifts contribute to changes in popular values, which will themselves act as a further influence on policy. Endorsement of the shift will lead to a further restructuring of the welfare state, whereas disquiet may generate countervailing political forces.

CHAPTER 5

SOCIAL COHESION AND SUPPORT FOR WELFARE CITIZENSHIP

Public opinion deserves to be as much respected as despised.

G.W.F. Hegel

Let us say we are trying to understand the goals and values of a certain group, or grasp their vision of the polity: we might try to probe this by a questionnaire asking whether or not they assent to a number of propositions . . . . But how did we pick those propositions? Here we relied on our understanding of the goals, values, vision involved, but then our understanding can be challenged and hence the significance of the results questioned. Perhaps the findings of our study, the compiling of proportions of assent and dissent to those propositions is irrelevant, is without significance for understanding the agents or the polity concerned.

C. Taylor

Introduction: values and inequality

The previous chapter argued that both inequality and poverty have increased rapidly in Britain in the 1980s. Government policies – or the lack of them – have made a substantial contribution to these developments. Some writers claim that this strategy of inequality – a kind of backwards social engineering – will reverse the direction of popular support for the state as chief guardian of welfare.

Four arguments support this view: as social cleavages widen, sympathy for the poor will decline; people are less willing to pay for benefits that they see as going mainly to increasingly remote social groups; rising prosperity will enhance the opportunities for some to decamp to the private sector; as incomes grow larger, consumers will want more individual control over the services they receive.

The first argument claims that as 'comfortable Britain' becomes increasingly detached from 'miserable Britain', the better off are likely to become less sympathetic to the needy, whom they see as increasingly remote: 'a whole series of budget changes . . . have . . . redistributed income to those who are at the top end of the income scale . . . . This policy has played a prominent part in isolating the most vulnerable group at the bottom of the income pile' (Field, 1989, p.74). The second point follows from this. If those who have done well out of social change view poorer people from a comfortable isolation, they may well become less inclined to pay taxes to support benefits that are understood to flow away from themselves, across that social distance.

Third, an influential account argues that the relation between the consumer and mass services can be understood in terms of three options: Exit, Voice and Loyalty (Hirschman, 1970). Those who are dissatisfied may be able to exit from the state sector to alternative forms of provision. Alternatively, the political expression of their demands – voice – may lead to change. Those who cannot leave and cannot change things have no option but loyalty. Private sector services expanded rapidly in the 1980s, partly as a result of rising real incomes for better-off people and partly as a result of deliberate government policies which extend subsidies to this sector and cut back direct competition from state services. Hirschman's analysis raises the question of whether this development will undermine collective support for the welfare state and foster the demand for separate welfare provision: 'exit' to the private sector for the better off, leaving no option but 'loyalty' to a residual state service for the poor (see Rentoul, 1990).

Fourth, it is argued that rising income leads to a greater demand for choice, control and flexibility in consumer services in all fields, from cars to shoes, from restaurant menus to financial services. Pressure for product differentiation in welfare will generate a demand for greater consumer control over provision; this will encourage individuals to withdraw from the state and construct a package of services tailored to meet their own specific needs from the private sector.

> A standard analogy would be with the process whereby up to some income level the *quantity* of consumption increases, but thereafter attention switches to the *quality* of consumption. It is not obvious that greater affluence should produce a demand for non-mass production of food or clothes, but not of health, education or pensions (OECD, 1988, p.20).

Sidney Webb drew an analogy between the development of social policy and the clothing of a regiment of naked men. Necessity 'needs clothing too urgently to grumble that the standard sizes of the regimental contractor make all the uniforms nothing better than misfits'. However, as standards rise, government must increasingly cater for the separate demands of minorities: 'every citizen . . . has to be supplied just as every soldier in the regiment has to have his pair of marching boots' – and these must fit the individual need, not the standard pattern (Webb, 1911, quoted in Glazer, 1988, p.103).

In this chapter we will use data from attitude surveys carried out over the last decade to assess how far the pattern of popular ideas about state welfare is undergoing change as a result of the increase in income inequality. There are a number of difficulties with the use of attitude survey data which must first be addressed.

Attitude surveys and public consciousness

Attitude surveys suffer from two kinds of problem as a guide to currents in people's ideas. These result from the technical features of the method and from the logic that underlies their use. On the technical side, the method analyses data from face-to-face interviews between strangers, typically structured around an interview schedule. The development of ever quicker and cheaper computing and communications has resulted in a rapid expansion in the use of such surveys in recent years. However, there is good evidence that what people are willing to say to strangers is strongly influenced by the circumstances in which the interaction takes place (see Marsh, 1979, for a clear discussion of the limitations of opinion polling). In addition many questionnaires tend to be devised round an agenda set by the researcher – which may not bear a close relation to the way the respondent thinks about the topic. Indeed the person who is interviewed may never have seriously considered the theme, but will give a coherent series of answers out of politeness, to conceal ignorance, or to placate the importunity of the interviewer. The facility with which people will discuss non-existent policies in interviews bears witness to this. A classic example is a survey of attitudes to the 'Metallic Metals Act' carried out in the USA. Despite the fact that the Act was entirely fictitious, 70 per cent of the sample were able to give a clear verdict of approval or disapproval which could be analysed in terms of an elegant correlation with independent variables, signifying nothing about the ostensible object of the survey (Payne, 1951).

Similarly, the interpretation of results depends on the orientation of the researcher. There are many examples of reinterpretations of the same data-set to support opposing conclusions. For example, Saunders and Harris produce evidence from the 1986 British Social Attitudes survey showing high levels of support for private housing and education to challenge the survey report's conclusion that Britain contains; 'an increasing "collectivist" or "welfarist" majority' (1989, p.4); Judge, Smith and Taylor-Gooby re-analyse data from the Institute of Economic Affairs 'Choice in Welfare' surveys to 'undermine the view that support for private welfare necessarily implies opposition to the welfare state' (1983, p.477), as the authors of the original report imply.

Recognition of these technical problems has led to increasing sophistication in survey design; the use of extensive piloting to check that the questions relate to some coherent aspect of the interviewee's conceptual world; the support of conclusions with data derived from alternative methods such as group and discursive interview (often termed 'triangulation': see Cooke, 1979, Chapter 1); and the cross-checking of surveys against each other to assess consistency. Nonetheless, attitude survey remains an inexact science, and must be approached with more than the usual degree of sociological detachment, caution and irony. The method is at its strongest in charting trends over time, so that it is reasonable to argue that contextual problems of interview and question-wording are held more or less constant between repeated rounds of the survey. This approach will be used here, where possible, and the data will come mainly from the prestigious British Social Attitudes Survey, which is executed by an organisation with a reputation for high quality fieldwork.

A second set of problems with the method concerns the logic of attitude surveys, and is less tractable. The answers given in interviews show how people as individuals answer questions. The findings are used to assess the ideas of mass publics in relation to a range of public issues. Interest in such ideas usually stems from the aspiration to work out how people are likely to behave under certain circumstances. However, the relation between what an individual says and the contents of his/her mind is simply unclear, as is the relation between holding a particular idea and action in a social context (Deacon and Hyde, 1986, p.15). There is a considerable body of evidence which shows that ideas are influenced by the social context in which they are expressed, as well as a considerable body of theory which locates the genesis of popular ideology in social factors and not in isolated ratiocination, as the epigraph to the chapter indicates. Precisely similar arguments apply to the link between the independent individual's ideas and behaviour. In any case other factors, of which the most important are compulsion or notions of self-interest, may play a large part in behaviour.

The defence of the use of attitude surveys to explore the climate of popular opinion against these points operates on three levels. First, there is no other method conveniently available which enables social scientists to discuss consciousness with such precision – and this we wish to do, since consciousness is a major element in much social theory. Second, the individual interview technique mimics a major strand in democratic capitalism. The individual is conceptualised as an isolated market actor, propelled in interaction with others by the pressure of individual wants and judgements about the resources to satisfy them that might be obtained, just as the particles of early atomic theory followed paths precisely defined by the collisions and attractions of other particles. Similarly, the citizen votes as isolate, in a secret ballot. Of course, this account overlies a reality of social relations operating through group, class, gender, region and other factors which influence behaviour. However, the parallel with a strong current in ideology serves as basis for the assessment of how that ideology works in practice. Third, the technique is not entirely defenceless against the conceptual problems outlined above. A survey can explore notions of self-interest and the individual's conception of their own place in society. Theories that see attitudes as epiphenomenal to underlying currents of ideology still imply that attitude structures are not random. Investigation of the pattern of attitudes serves as a useful tool understanding the direction of ideology among different social groups. Nonetheless, attitude surveys must be treated with caution, and are used here *faute de mieux*.

Attitudes to welfare: popular endorsement for state provision

The main features of the pattern of public attitudes to welfare in the 1980s are well known. First, the welfare state is extremely popular. A large number of surveys indicate strong enthusiasm for the key institutions of state welfare and a willingness to pay increased sums in taxes to support them (for example: Mack and Lansley, 1985 and 1991; Lewis, 1980; Furnham and Lewis, 1986, Chapter 11; Heath, Jowell and Curtice, 1985, pp.137–8; Dunleavy and Husbands, 1985, pp.165–70; Jowell *et al.*, 1984–90). Few studies produce a conflicting picture, and those that do follow a questionable methodology (Harris and Seldon, 1987). There is growing evidence that support for state welfare increased among all social and political groupings and became more unified as the 1980s progressed. Rentoul reports that 'the major growth in private provision and private ownership over the past 10 years does not seem to have led to increased support for individualism' (1990, p.176). Table 5.1 summarises evidence from the British Social Attitude Survey series. Support for increased spending among professional, managerial, and intermediate workers is no longer significantly lower than that among junior non-manuals and manual workers. Conservative voters have moved substantially closer to the position held by Labour voters.

The fact that there has been a noteworthy increase in support

Table 5.1 Support for welfare state spending, 1983 and 1989

	1983	1989
Reduce taxes and spend less on health, education and social benefits:	9	3
Keep taxes and spending as now:	54	37
Increase taxes and spending:	32	56
N	1719	2930
Percentage supporting higher taxes and spending:		
Class		
I/II:	28	57
III non-manual:	35	53
III manual:	32	58
IV/V:	33	56
N	1267	2755
Party		
Conservative:	24	48
Centre parties:	36	65
Labour:	42	68
N	1481	2467

Source: Calculations from British Social Attitudes Survey (1983 and 1989).

for more welfare spending, even among supporters of the party of government, at a time when the dominant theme in welfare policy has been the concern to constrain spending on state provision gives rise to a puzzle in explaining the relation of popular attitudes to practical politics. The most plausible explanation is the one to emerge from the major election surveys: welfare is low down on the list of issues that decide how people cast their votes (Heath, Jowell and Curtice, 1985, p.174; Sarlvik and Crewe, 1983, p.172). Nonetheless, welfare issues rose up the political agenda in the 1980s and disquiet about the general direction of welfare policy must contribute to the general political climate. The impression that welfare policy – which accounts for some two-thirds of state spending – is a prime arena of solidaristic support for the 'rolling forward of the state' is however, complicated by four other points to emerge from the data.

The limits of support for state welfare

First, the welfare state is not a seamless web. A number of specialised surveys show a clear distinction in the level of support for services directed at groups seen as more or less deserving of provision (for a powerful study of attitudes to the able-bodied poor, see Golding and Middleton, 1982). There is a similar and overlapping gap in levels of support between the mass services which meet the common needs of the majority of the population – the NHS, education and pensions – and the services directed at minorities – unemployment benefit, council housing and means-tested provision. Policy changes designed to target state spending more accurately on poor minorities have sharpened this division, as has the expansion of tax concessions which go mainly to better off groups. There is evidence from more recent studies that sympathy for poorer people is growing, and this is born out in the increasing consensus in attitudes to general welfare provision noted above. For example, Mack and Lansley's study in 1990 and Townsend's Greater London survey carried out between 1985 and 1987 found a greater awareness of the needs of poorer groups and willingness to pay taxes to meet those needs than did Golding and Middleton's study in 1976 (Taylor-Gooby, 1991b). However, the evidence from the British Social Attitudes survey finds that the mass services of the NHS, education and pensions are still far and away the most popular. Cash benefits for disabled people – a group traditionally regarded as highly deserving – command more than twice the support that benefits for unemployed people and three times the support of benefits for single parents (Table 5.2). The sharp increase in popularity of the NHS as top priority has drawn support away from non-welfare areas. However, the detailed examination of priorities for social security benefits shows that enthusiasm for pensions and child benefit, which go to the mass of the population, and for the needs of the highly deserving

Table 5.2 Differences in support for different groups, 1983 and 1989

	Percentage naming the service as first or second priority for extra spending:	
	1983	1989
Main Service Areas		
NHS	63	84
Education	50	55
Housing	20	22
Social Security	12	14
N	1719	2930

Note: the question also included defence, public transport, roads, police and prisons and overseas aid, but these did not attract more than eight per cent support and so are omitted.

Social Security Benefits	1983	1989
Retired people:	64	67
Disabled people:	57	60
Unemployed people:	33	25
Child benefit:	21	30
Single parent benefit:	21	17
N	1719	2930

Source: Calculations from British Social Attitudes Survey (1983 and 1989).

group of disabled people has reduced the level of support for unemployed people and single parents.

The second complicating factor is the high level of support for the private sector which co-exists alongside support for state welfare. In much of the theoretical writing in the social policy tradition state and market are conceptualised as standing in a contradictory relation. However, many consumers see the two as complementary. This corresponds to reality: those who use private medicine for particular courses of treatment often also use the NHS for conditions for which there is no waiting list; recipients of private pensions remain entitled to a state National Insurance pension. Table 5.3 gives the pattern of answers to questions about

Table 5.3 The NHS and private medicine, 1984 and 1989

Private medical treatment should be:	1984	1989
abolished	9	12
restricted to private hospitals:	48	50
allowed in both private and NHS hospitals:	39	35
NHS GPs should be free to take on private patients	59	54
NHS dentists should be free to take on private patients:	64	59
N	1719	2930

Politics and private medicine % in the various parties willing to allow private medicine in NHS hospitals:	1984	1989
Conservative:	58	51
Centre parties:	40	25
Labour:	26	21
N	1719	2930

Source: Calculations from British Social Attitudes Survey (1984 and 1989).

the NHS. Views on this service provide the clearest test of attitudes to the role of state and private sectors. The NHS supplies a highly valued service free at the point of demand. It is often seen as an emblem of universalism. It operates in a field where there are well-known private alternatives. The question of how the two should relate was brought sharply to the forefront of political debate by the Department of Health's assertion that: 'there is already a growing partnership between the NHS and the "independent sector" ' and the 1990 Health Services Act designed to ensure that 'under these proposals . . . Health Authorities will buy services from the private sector' (Department of Health, 1989, p.68).

In an interesting study, which uses detailed discursive interviews alongside more formal questionnaires, Calnan and Cant demonstrate that there is strong ideological and practical attachment to

Table 5.4 Freedom to buy privileged treatment, 1986 and 1989

	1986	1989
Those who can afford should be allowed to buy better treatment in		
Health care:	53	49
Education:	52	46
Pensions:	61	63
N	1548	1461

Privilege and Party		Centre parties			Centre parties	
	Con	parties	Lab	Con	parties	Lab
Health care:	66	53	42	61	46	36
Education:	69	51	37	61	40	31
Pensions:	74	65	47	77	65	47
N	505	264	553	593	172	463

Source: Calculations from British Social Attitudes Survey (1986 and 1989).

the National Health Service, even among those who have access to private health insurance (1990). In any case, state and private services do not stand in simple opposition. Many of those covered by private insurance use state medicine as well, and therefore have an interest in resisting any restriction of the service that would exclude the better-off (Busfield, 1990, p.84).

Table 5.3 shows that attitudes to private medicine have changed little. If anything there is a slight shift away from support for the expansion of private provision in NHS hospitals. The real debate is not on whether the private sector as such should exist, but on whether it should be permitted to operate within the NHS. On this issue, opinion divides on party lines. The rest of the table shows that there is a clear and stable endorsement of practitioner's freedom to work in the private sector. This theme is echoed in Table 5.4 which shows that a substantial group – an outright majority in 1986 and a plurality in 1989 – assent to the view that people who can afford it should be permitted to buy privilege in welfare. This again is hotly contested between the different political parties.

Table 5.5 Moralism and welfare imagery, 1983 and 1989

Percentage agreeing that:	1983	1989
The welfare state makes people nowadays less willing to look after themselves:	52	39
The welfare state encourages people to stop helping each other:	37	32
People receiving social security are made to feel like second-class citizens:	48	53
Desert and Social Security Claims:		
Large numbers of people these days falsely claim benefits:	65	65
Large numbers of people who are eligible for benefits fail to claim them:	81	84
N	1616	2529

Source: Calculations from British Social Attitudes Survey (1983 and 1989).

The third complication in the clear pattern of support for state welfare concerns attitudes to the moral impact of state welfare on society. The view that the welfare state encourages an undesirable dependency was discussed in Chapter Two. This argument has been developed most powerfully in relation to the exploitation of social security benefits by work-shy people – 'scrounging' – but also has a wider reference to the behaviour of groups throughout the social structure (see Deacon, 1978). We have already seen that judgements on the group to whom a benefit is directed have a powerful influence on popular support for it. In addition to these material concerns, there is also evidence of moralistic disquiet. Table 5.5 shows the answers to questions about the moral impact of welfare provision and to questions focused more specifically on claims for social security benefits.

Disquiet at the extent to which state welfare is presumed to erode self-sufficiency and community spirit has declined notice-ably in the 1980s. Conversely the level of unease at the stigmatic effects of social policy has grown stronger. As we might expect, this area excites strong differences in opinion between supporters of different political parties: Conservative voters are roughly twice as likely to see the welfare state as damaging to self-help than are

Labour voters and half as likely to see stigma as a real problem. Centre party voters incline more closely to the Labour than the Conservative view.

When the focus is narrowed to the heartland of scandal – last resort social security benefits – there is virtually no shift in attitudes over time. Some two-thirds of the sample agree that there is a considerable number of false claims. However, an even larger group feel that there is an equal problem of people who are entitled failing to claim their due. In this case, the associations with party and social group are weak. Thus it seems that arguments which rely on the 'moral hazard' or perverse incentives associated with state welfare attract some support, but they do not gain the agreement of the majority of the population.

The fourth issue concerns the level of satisfaction experienced by users of state welfare services. The question just discussed shows that there is a strong popular perception that the social security system is failing to direct benefits accurately to those who most need them. Despite its high level of popularity there is also evidence of growing disquiet at provision in the NHS. The proportion who declared themselves satisfied with the NHS fell from 56 to 36 per cent between 1983 and 1989, and the proportion dissatisfied rose from a quarter to a half. These attitudes are only weakly associated with party support and social class. The response of government has been to identify the cause of the concern as a problem of management and organisation, and to respond by restructuring the service and placing greater emphasis on an internal market designed to expand the role of the private sector.

These four aspects of current popular attitudes to welfare cut across the pattern of established support for the welfare state identified by survey questions that focus simply on that one theme. The level of support for services directed at undeserving minorities is much lower than that for the heartland services that absorb the lion's share of welfare state spending and account for most of the contact with state services by the average citizen. Second, a strong current of support for the private sector runs alongside and does not contradict support for state welfare. Third, there is a substantial minority who are particularly exercised at the moral impact of state provision. Fourth, there is real dissatisfaction at the quality of some of the most highly valued state services. Although support for state expenditure as a whole has become more solidaristic over the 1980s across social groups and supporters of different political parties, attitudes in the first three of the four areas mentioned above remain divided. Beneath the surface consensus of commitment to state welfare, there is thus ample room for dispute and strong possibilities for the structuring of that dispute on political lines. The welfare state seems certain to remain an arena of controversy.

We now turn to the four currents in popular ideology that theoretical arguments suggest may threaten the security of the welfare state consensus – shifts in attitudes among different income groups in approval of welfare for poor people, in willingness to fund services for them, in support for a separate system for better-off people and in enthusiasm for a greater measure of individual control over welfare services. The analysis rests mainly on evidence from the British Social Attitude series. Much of the discussion concerns the influence of inequality on popular ideas. The survey sample displays a close comparability with the population at large along this dimension as well as the dimension of social class, age, household, tenure, employment and regional patterns customarily checked in survey analysis (Brook, Taylor and Prior, 1990). The household income of the lowest decile of the Family Expenditure Survey sample fell from 33 to 25 per cent of the median, that of the lowest quartile from 52 to 46 per cent, while the highest quartile rose from 154 to 164 per cent and that of the top decile from 214 to 233 per cent between 1983 and 1989 (CSO, 1985 and 1991b, Table 24). The corresponding statistics for the Social Attitudes survey are falls from 34 to 26 and 56 to 49 per cent of the median and increases from 152 to 158 and 213 to 233 per cent.

Attitudes to poverty

There is little evidence that people who feel better off are less sympathetic to the needy than are those on narrower incomes. Indeed the pattern of attitudes to social security claimers bears close comparison with evidence from surveys carried out in the 1960s and 1970s which show that the most punitive attitudes to claimers are held by the poor themselves (Coates and Silburn, 1973; Golding and Middleton 1982, p.169). Similarly, a major study of social class and class consciousness carried out in 1984 found routine manual workers roughly twice as likely to agree with the proposition that 'there are too many scroungers around' as non-manual workers (Marshall, Newby, Rose and Vogler, 1988, p.186).

The Social Attitudes survey includes a question which makes it possible to divide up the sample by their subjective feelings about their own living standards. The question asks whether people feel they are 'living comfortably on their present income', 'coping', 'finding it difficult', or 'finding it very difficult'. This serves as a useful expression of the division of the population into 'comfortable Britain' and 'miserable Britain' by the report of the Archbishop of Canterbury's Working Party in 1985. The pattern of answers is reasonably stable over time, with roughly a quarter of the sample falling into the comfortable group and the two bottom groups making up a further 25 per cent, leaving about half who describe themselves as 'coping'.

Table 5.6 shows how the answers to the 'social imagery' and 'scrounging' questions discussed above relate to people's views on their own circumstances. The shift in opinion away from the notion that the welfare state undermines self-reliance and towards the view that social security is stigmatic increases as one moves from prosperity to the breadline. It is most strongly endorsed by the very poorest group, who, according to the Family Expenditure Survey data quoted earlier, have lost out most markedly in the social changes of the 1980s. Endorsement of the dependency culture model has fallen by about a fifth among the better off and about a third among the poorest groups. Conversely, there has been little change over time in attitudes to desert and benefit claiming: as the earlier surveys showed, poorer people are most inclined to believe that there are large numbers of false claims, and also that there is a corresponding problem of non-takeup. The gap between the attitudes of the poorest group and those who feel better off to an increase in state welfare spending, to be financed out of increased taxation, has grown much narrower.

Perceptions of the nature of poverty have shifted little over time. When asked a series of questions about how they defined

Table 5.6 Desert, stigma and poor people, 1984 and 1989

	1984			1989		
	Comfortable	Difficult to cope	Very difficult to cope	Comfortable	Difficult to cope	Very difficult to cope
Percentage agreeing that:						
The welfare state makes people less willing to look after themselves:	53	44	42	42	37	26
The welfare state encourages people to stop helping each other:	39	42	39	33	36	27
People receiving social security are made to feel like second-class citizens:	50	68	70	51	67	74
Large numbers of people these days falsely claim benefits:						
Strongly agree:	37	36	44	39	35	45
Slightly agree:	27	26	21	28	25	26
Large numbers of people who are eligible for benefits fail to claim them:						
Strongly agree:	42	52	56	46	53	59
Slightly agree:	34	30	26	37	30	29
Welfare spending						
Percentage supporting more taxes and more welfare spending:	35	48	53	55	56	61
N	387	293	130	795	500	179
Percentage of sample:	24	18	8	27	17	6

Source: Calculations from British Social Attitudes Survey (1984 and 1989).

poverty less than a third of the sample endorsed the kind of relative definition favoured by academics ('enough to buy the things they really need, but not enough for the things other people take for granted') and the strongest support was for a strictly minimalist definition ('not enough to eat and live without getting into debt') favoured by 95 per cent of the sample. There was little difference in attitude among the different income groups.

Despite the meagreness of perceptions of what counts as real poverty a substantial majority (over two-thirds) agree that 'there is a lot of real poverty in Britain today', with little differentiation by income group. This is a noticeable increase on the level of 55 per cent agreeing with the statement in the 1983 survey. Over half those who answered the question believe that poverty in Britain will increase in the future. The evidence indicates an increase in sympathy for the poor, but one that is clearly constrained within the traditional limits of a breadline perception of poverty.

This account is supported by evidence from other studies. For example, the detailed survey of living standards in London carried out by Townsend between 1985 and 1987 found that 76 per cent of the sample of 2,703 agreed that 'there was such a thing as real poverty these days'. The survey by Marshall and his colleagues reported that

> over 70 per cent of our sample think that the distribution of wealth and income in Britain is unfair, and well over 80 per cent of all assessments as to why this is so indicate a desire to redistribute wealth down the social hierarchy . . . there is perhaps surprisingly widespread support for a more equal distribution of rewards, even among those who would on the face of it be relatively worse off as a result (1988, p.187).

If the focus of interest is widened from concern about the impact of welfare on work incentives to the general effect of state provision on self-reliance and on social values among the population at large, there is little evidence that this is seen as morally damaging. As indicated earlier, support for the expansion of state welfare has grown among those who feel comfortably off, as well as among those who live hard lives.

It does not seem that income inequality has led to a greater harshening of attitudes to the needy: if anything the reverse is true. Social polarisation is not accompanied by ideological polarisation. The second aspect of the argument about inequality and social cohesion concerns attitudes to taxation and welfare.

Taxation and state spending

Table 5.1 detailed the sharp increase in support for an expansion in welfare spending to be paid for by increased taxation. Approval for state welfare has become more general among supporters of different political parties and members of different social groups. However, as the Table 5.2 showed, the different welfare state programmes continue to command different levels of support. Table 5.7 gives the responses of the bottom 25 per cent of the distribution by household income compared with the top 25 per cent. The gap between wealthy and poor people has grown wider. The data enable us to examine whether this change has eroded support for the benefits which are commonly seen as going to poorer groups among those who are better-off.

The table shows little difference in patterns of support for the main areas of welfare spending as priorities for increased resources. The rapid increase in support for the NHS which has become if anything, more solidaristic between the top and the bottom quartile of the income distribution has not drawn support away from the other welfare areas – education, housing and social security – but from the miscellaneous unfavoured areas. In housing and social security, which are the domain of poorer people, the two groups remain as far apart as they did in the early 1980s. This picture of a continuing but not a widening gap in attitudes to the stereotypical services for poor people and for the mass is reinforced by the pattern of priorities for spending on social security benefits. Here, the answers for the two years are broadly similar, with poorer people keener on retirement pension, and better-off people shifting their support from benefits for single parents to child benefit, possibly as a response to the freezing of this benefit in cash terms in 1987, and its subsequent erosion by inflation. The level of support for the needs of unemployed people is equal among both income groups, and has tended to decline over the period covered by the survey. The mass benefits of retirement pensions and provision for the highly deserving group of disabled people continue to be top priorities.

The evidence presented in Chapter Two showed that middle-class people gain most from the education system and are – presumably – most affected by spending constraint. Health care

Table 5.7 Income inequalities and social spending, 1983 and 1989

	1983		1989	
	Lower Quartile	Upper Quartile	Lower Quartile	Upper Quartile
Percentage agreeing that taxes and welfare spending:				
should be reduced:	12	5	3	2
kept as now:	44	61	34	36
increased:	38	32	58	59
Priorities for service areas:				
Health:	59	62	81	82
Education:	40	61	40	64
Housing:	26	16	28	16
Social Security:	27	1	27	8
First or second priorities for social security benefits for different groups:				
Retirement pensioners:	68	62	72	63
Disabled people:	62	60	65	61
Unemployed people:	30	30	24	24
Child benefit:	16	19	23	29
Single parents:	18	26	14	19
Views on benefits:				
Real poverty exists in Britain:	62	51	66	58
Benefits are too low and cause hardship:	50	45	56	50
Benefits are too high and discourage job-finding:	32	36	24	26
N	415	318	671	563
Percentage of total sample:	27	21	26	22

Source: Calculations from British Social Attitudes Survey (1983 and 1989).

appears to be truly universal. Social housing and social security are directed at the poor. The pattern of support for state welfare shows no evidence of polarisation in attitudes, if anything the reverse. It does however indicate that there is room for divergence in support within the framework of statism. The degree of divergence does not seem to be growing more marked, at least over the time scale covered.

This impression is reinforced by the evidence on perceptions of poverty. Unemployed people have been regarded with considerable suspicion on the grounds that they are wilfully evading a responsibility to work. The view that benefits for those without jobs are too low and cause hardship is endorsed by increasing majorities and the gap between the income groups is small. Coupled with the evidence of a continuing but unspectacular endorsement of this group as a high priority for extra state spending in the table, consistent across time and across the better-off and worst-off quartile groups, this contradicts the view that polarisation is undermining support for welfare even for an undeserving minority.

Inequality and support for the private sector

Policy reforms in the 1980s have enhanced the attractiveness of the private sector. Lengthening NHS waiting lists coupled with growing public debate about the quality of the service and the expansion of tax reliefs in the 1990 Act have led to a tripling in the numbers covered by private medical insurance from just over two to 7.2 million between 1979 and 1990 (Laing and Buisson, 1990: CSO, 1991, p.128). The numbers purchasing private treatment directly is unknown, but certain to be substantial for some conditions. One study indicates that by 1981 one in eight patients admitted for elective surgery were treated privately, with round about a quarter of hip replacements and varicose vein operations carried out in this way (Nicholl *et al.*, 1984, p.91). Some estimates suggest that the private elective surgery had risen as high as 30 per cent of the whole by 1986 (Timmins, 1988, p.16). Total expenditure on acute private medicine in the UK rose from £111 million to £356 million between 1979 and 1986, after allowing for the effect of inflation (Laing and Buisson, 1987).

Similarly, private education has expanded, aided by the Assisted Places Scheme which was providing some 35,000 state-funded places by 1987 (Treasury, 1989, p.220). Official statistics estimate the overall increase in the proportion of school children in the private sector as unspectacular – rising from 5 to 7 per cent between 1979 and 1991 (CSO, 1991, p.52). However, this contains a high and increasing proportion of sixth-formers, rising from about a quarter to a third over the period (CSO, 1989, p.52). The repeal of legislation which linked annual state pension increases to movements in wage indices if these rose more rapidly than price indices in 1979 ensured that the value of state pensions fell sharply in relation to the living standards of the working population. The basic state pension for a couple fell from 33 to 25 per cent of average male earnings between 1978 and 1990. By 1985, private pensions were accounting for 55 per cent of the total of all cash paid in pensions and directing it to the top 37 per cent of pensioners (Barr and Coulter, 1991, p.294). In the same year, the Social Security Act set up a system of direct subsidies to those who joined private pension schemes in addition to the existing tax reliefs and allowances. This was worth £9.3 billion between 1988 and 1993 (National Audit Office, 1990).

Not surprisingly, these changes led to an increase in the use of the private sector over the period of the Social Attitudes survey. Between 1984 and 1989, the proportion of the sample covered by private medical insurance had risen from 11 to 15 per cent, and the proportion who reported that they had attended private school from 7 to 12 per cent. Information on membership of private pension schemes is not collected in the survey, but the massive switch from state to private schemes after 1988 (some four million by April 1990) is bound to be reflected in the sample. The question to be tackled in this section is whether increased access to private services erodes support for the state sector among better-off people along the lines implied by Hirschman's influential 'Exit, Voice and Loyalty' model. As before, the study uses the highly salient service of the NHS as a 'tracer' for attitudes to the private sector.

There is little evidence to support the view that prosperous people wish to forsake the state sector. Their attitudes have grown closer to those of the less fortunate. Table 5.8 shows that support for a two-tier health service, whether through the introduction of private medicine into NHS hospitals, or through the restriction of the NHS to low-income groups, so that the better off were

Table 5.8 Attitudes to the private sector, 1983 and 1989

	1983		1989	
	Lower Quartile	Upper Quartile	Lower Quartile	Upper Quartile
Percentage disagreeing that the NHS should be restricted to low-income groups only:	57	73	69	74
N	415	318	671	563
Private medicine should be allowed in private hospitals only:	54	40	47	48
in all hospitals:	32	52	34	41
N	510	587	671	563
People who can afford it should be allowed to purchase better:				
Health care:	56	58	45	49
Education:	54	55	42	47
Pensions:	56	70	54	74
N	353	309	671	563
Percentage of total sample:	26	23	26	22

Note: the income bands used in the survey for 1986 produce an upper 'quartile' of either 14% or 32% of the sample. Statistics based on 23% are estimated by interpolation. This has the effect of reducing the upper quartile statistic by 2 per cent in each case.

Source: Calculations from British Social Attitudes Survey (1983 and 1989).

compelled to purchase treatment privately was never strong. It has declined over the decade. In the earlier survey, the bottom quartile were markedly more likely to support the exclusion of better off people from the NHS. By 1989, their concern about the quality of the service had reduced their support for this policy. The firm refusal of the top quartile to countenance a 'two-tier' NHS highlights an important point: middle- and upper-class people do well out of collectively provided mass services, when these meet needs that they share with poorer groups. Material interest does not impel them to abandon state provision in such areas. We have already seen that their views on the relative priority of services which go mainly to the poor is close to that of low income people themselves (Table 5.7). The pattern of middle-class interests is further elaborated in questions on privileged access to welfare.

As remarked earlier, there is a high level of support in the population at large for the right of individuals to purchase better quality services if they so choose, and are able to do so. In respect of the mass services which have provoked considerable public disquiet in the 1980s – the NHS and education – support for privileged access has declined among both better-off and poorer groups. Despite the increased level of private health insurance and private education, most members of both groups rely on state provision in these areas. Private medical insurance is typically used to expedite treatment where there are long NHS waiting lists. By 1989 only 3 per cent of the survey sample actually had children at private school, despite the increase in numbers who had a private education at some time in the past. Only 34 per cent of the sample had children of school age, so the vast majority of the top quartile are unlikely to have a direct interest in the private sector.

In relation to private pensions, the pattern is rather different. Support has declined slightly among the less well-off and risen among the well-off group. In this field, the private sector is already well established, as a middle-class supplement to state provision. The 1986 legislation makes the service even more attractive to most people. The high level of support for private pensions as an addition to the state sector may be explained in terms of the interest and the experience of the population groups involved.

Some writers attach considerable weight to the evidence of support for the freedom to shift from state to private sectors. For example, Saunders and Harris argue that the evidence of strong support for state welfare is an artefact of the structure of social provision:

> people in Britain are obliged to pay for state health and education services through taxes . . . In such a situation of pre-empted choices it is perfectly rational . . . to express opinions which appear to support both systems . . . the private sector because it is their ideal

preference . . . the state system because this is the system on which they are obliged to depend (1989, p.10; see also Saunders, 1990, Chapter 4).

It is difficult to substantiate this view on the available data. Support for the state has grown stronger as the state sector is cut back and the role of private provision increased, even among those groups for whom private sector has become most significant. However, it is clear that those who are in a position to do so would like to retain the opportunity to use private services alongside the state system. This ambivalence in attitudes indicates that support for state welfare retains its strength, despite the enhanced opportunities and incentives to use private sector services. There are also clear differences between different social groups in what they want from government policy. The issue of flexibility and control takes this point further.

Flexibility and control

The state provides a community-wide system, designed to allocate available resources between a wide range of needs. The private service offers an individual contract, and market forces will shape this so that it meets the particular needs of the social group to whom it is directed. As a result, the private sector is likely to be in a better position to respond to the particular demands of individual consumers. Conversely, the state may be in a stronger position to guarantee provision as an individual right, rather than through a contract, available only to the consumer who can pay, and dependent on the continued commercial viability of the supplier. Part of the argument about the way in which inequality might lead to polarisation in support for welfare rests on a contrast between the responsiveness of the private sector and the guaranteed minimum standards offered by the state. The flexibility of private provision will be greatest for those who can pay most and thus income differentials will translate into differing levels of support for the state and of desire to exit to private alternatives.

A study carried out in 1984 by the author explored these issues. Many of the questions developed there have been repeated in subsequent Social Attitudes Surveys. The study focused on the

Table 5.9 Dissatisfaction and the welfare state, 1984 and 1989

Reasons for Dissatisfaction with the main State Services
(Attitudes to Welfare Survey, 1984)

	State Pensions	NHS	State education
No dissatisfaction:	32	53	43
Dissatisfaction with issues of consumer control:	7	24	11
Level of service:	61	10	32
Rudeness, inconsiderate treatment:	NA	13	NA
Discipline:	NA	NA	14
N	1362	1321	381

Notes:
1. Responses post-coded from an open-ended question.
2. Questions only asked to users of the relevant service.
3. Consumer control issues were: (pensions) ease of getting information, transferability and commutation of benefit, compulsory contribution, age of entitlement; (NHS) choice of doctor, hospital and treatment, consultation and availability of information, access to a second opinion, and issues connected with opening times, visiting hours and appointments; (education) communication with teachers, school policies over curriculum, gender and ethnicity issues, school hours and holidays, access to teachers and choice of school.

Aspects of the NHS in Need of Improvement (Social Attitudes Survey, 1989)

	Lower Quartile	Upper Quartile
Hospital services		
Hospital waiting-lists for *non-emergency* operations:	82	89
Waiting-time to see consultants:	83	89
Staffing level of nurses in hospitals:	67	82
Staffing level of doctors in hospitals:	66	81
Hospital casualty departments:	45	68
Condition of hospital buildings:	48	76
Quality of hospital medical treatment:	23	45
Quality of nursing care in hospitals:	19	32
GP services		
GP appointments systems:	35	43
GP consultation time:	31	42
Being able to choose which GP to see:	20	38
Quality of GP medical treatment:	21	26
N	671	563

Source: Calculations from British Social Attitudes Survey (1989) and Attitudes to Welfare Survey (1984).

three chief areas where state and private provision are well established – pensions, education and medical care. A series of questions covered the main aspects of the services. The work showed that, for most aspects, private services were seen by the sample as superior in quality to what was offered by the state. In response to an open-ended question: 'are you satisfied with the treatment you received from [the relevant service] . . . ?', sizeable groups indicated no dissatisfaction (Table 5.9). Those who expressed dissatisfaction gave a wide variety of reasons. These were grouped into those that indicated concern about the extent to which the consumer had control over the service offered, and those that simply reflected the level of provision. The overwhelming cause for dissatisfaction with state pensions was simply the low level of the pension offered. In relation to the NHS, relatively little dissatisfaction was expressed, and about a quarter of the sample raised issues to do with the extent to which the service responded to their individual needs. Complaints in respect of state education were mainly concerned with issues of quality, in particular, staffing levels. There was very little variation by income group in people's satisfaction or dissatisfaction with state services.

The Social Attitudes Survey provides few questions by which attitudes in this area can be assessed. In 1989 a series of questions about which aspects of the NHS were seen as most in need of improvement was included. Unfortunately, this provides little scope for comparison over time since the earliest occasion on which a similar question was put was only two years earlier in 1987. The pattern of answers between the two years is broadly similar. The answers show that better-off people are more inclined to question the quality of state provision, consistently over all aspects of the service. This is a common finding of surveys in this field (see, for example, Cartwright, 1967; Heidenheimer, Heclo and Adams, 1990, pp.354–5). The hospital service gives rise to stronger dissatisfaction than the family doctor service. This may be because hospitals, unlike general practitioners, have been cash limited since the early 1980s. Concern about levels of provision has been expressed most strongly in relation to hospitals in public debate.

The issues which give rise to the strongest concern all involve levels of spending: waiting lists, staffing levels, casualty departments, and the condition of buildings. Taken together with the evidence of strong endorsement of a policy of increased public spending and of the identification of the NHS as a major priority area, these show that public concern is much more clearly directed at the basic level of quantity of provision, rather than at the more sophisticated demands for flexibility and individualised provision. There is little evidence of differences between income groups on this issue. These findings correspond to those of the 1984 'Attitudes to Welfare' survey which asked a broadly comparable question (Taylor-Gooby, 1989, p.211).

The evidence of the surveys lends a limited support to the contention of the government of the 1980s – that welfare reforms are justified by popular demands for change. However, they indicate that the new regime offers entirely the wrong cure for the right disease. Dissatisfaction with services like the NHS is to be dealt with not by reorganisation, an admixture of the private sector and spending constraint, but by the expansion of spending on the state sector.

The argument presented so far indicates that there is no support for the view that growing income inequality in Britain in the 1980s has reduced support for the welfare state, especially among the more contented groups in society. The evidence points in an entirely contrary direction. However, there is some indication that better-off people express stronger preferences for a system which would give them access to private welfare alongside citizen rights to state services. The appeal of privilege is scarcely surprising. In this sense there may be some limited support for the polarisation thesis, but it is at the expense of admitting that it is nothing new. The interests of income groups have always differed. The survey evidence indicates that the expression of this difference in divergent patterns of support in the field of welfare has grown less marked in the 1980s. Income polarisation has not led to social division.

Some cross-national evidence

These surveys indicate that the sharp growth in social inequality has not subverted support for social welfare in Britain in the 1980s. British experience may be compared with that in a number of other countries. The 1985 International Social Survey Project

Table 5.10 Attitudes to state welfare in selected countries, 1985

	Austria	W Germany	Italy	Britain	Australia	USA
Governments should reduce income differences between those with high and low incomes:						
Bottom Quartile:	70	63	79	58	51	49
Top Quartile:	64	52	64	37	30	22
Interquartile gap:	8	11	15	21	21	27
The government should spend more on:						
Health Care:						
Bottom Quartile:	73	54	82	90	69	66
Top Quartile:	59	33	78	84	55	54
Interquartile gap:	14	21	4	6	14	12
Unemployment Benefits:						
Bottom Quartile:	27	41	63	59	19	47
Top Quartile:	13	19	52	25	7	14
Interquartile gap:	14	22	11	34	12	33
Percentage of sample						
Bottom Quartile:	22	23	18	28	26	25
Top Quartile:	23	24	19	24	26	24
Total sample (N):	987	1048	1580	1530	1528	677

Notes:
1. Germany refers to West Germany.
2. Income data for Germany was not collected on a household basis. Respondent's income is used as a proxy.
3. Income was banded in the data-set. Quartiles use the nearest approximation.
Source: Calculations from International Social Attitudes Survey (1989).

focused on attitudes to the role of government. Unfortunately, there is at present no high-quality survey that enables cross-national comparisons over time to be made.

Table 5.10 gives some key findings from the survey on people's ideas about the proper role of the state in welfare. These show interesting differences in the pattern of attitudes that cannot be explained simply in terms of the levels of need and of service provision. In response to a general question about whether government should attempt to reduce income differences, people in countries with a strong corporatist history of 'top-down' welfare policy – Austria and Germany – show both high levels of support for the policy, and relatively little disagreement between income groups. Italy is described by Leibfried as a 'Mediterranean rim' aspiring welfare state, because it shares some features of the corporatist model, but has developed social policy more recently and displays substantial differences in living standards, most strongly evident on a regional basis (1990). Support for redistribution is even stronger here and the income differences slightly greater. The regimes which Esping-Anderson characterises as 'liberal' – Australia and the USA – display a lower level of commitment to such a policy and much stronger differences of opinion (see also Papadakis, 1990, p.14). The lower quartile of households by income is roughly twice as likely to favour radical income distribution policies as the better off group. Britain occupies a position midway between the corporatist and the liberal group.

A similar pattern emerges in analysis of questions about attitudes to inequality asked in the 1987 round of the International Social Survey, which covered a wider group of countries: 'public support for welfare spending is highest among the Hungarians (average of nearly 80 per cent), followed closely by the Italians and – rather less enthusiastically – by the citizens of the other three social democracies of West Germany, Britain and the Netherlands . . . the gap between these countries and the . . . capitalist democracies [Australia and the USA] is widest' (Smith, 1989, p.61). An earlier study carried out in Britain, Germany, the Netherlands and the USA in 1974 shows a similar picture: the level of 'agenda support' for state intervention in the form of health care, education, housing, pension and employment policies is noticeably higher in the first three countries than the fourth (Barnes and Kaase, 1979, p.413; see also Heidenheimer, Heclo and Adams, 1990, pp.354–6).

In relation to specific policies, current political issues and perceptions of the level of provision on offer are likely to play a stronger role. The table shows the level of enthusiasm for more state spending on health care and unemployment benefits, representing a mass service for which the collective need is widely acknowledged and provision for a minority, often regarded with suspicion. In all countries there is both a higher absolute level of support for health care spending and a higher degree of consensus between income groups on it than for spending on unemployed people, except in the case of Australia. The small interquartile gap in the case of support for unemployment benefits in this country reflects the modest support among any group for such benefits.

These data show that mass needs, such as health care are more popular than the minority needs of unemployed people as areas for extra state spending in both liberal and conservative regimes, despite the wide variations in current levels of provision for these needs. The high level of concern for extra health spending in Britain among both better off and less well-off people is hardly surprising, given the urgency with which the problems of NHS funding are viewed. At the time of the survey, Britain had the highest level of unemployment of the countries (and indeed of any OECD country – 11 per cent against 10 for Italy, 8 for Australia, 7 for Germany and the USA and 4 for Austria: OECD, 1988b). Nonetheless, support for more spending on this group is not remarkably high and the interquartile gap is the highest of any of the countries studied. The cross-national data throw into relief the level of support for state welfare in Britain and the extent to which different welfare services are seen by consumers in different ways. Unlike the question on priorities for social security benefit spending asked in the British Social Attitude Survey, which showed a low but consensual priority for the needs of this group, the international survey question about extra spending, asked separately for this benefit, shows a substantial divergence in opinion. The needs of unemployed people are low on everyone's priority list, but less well-off people are rather more likely than comfortable people to think that something should be done for them. This may indicate that there is an undercurrent of polarisation in relation to attitudes for minority benefits, despite the overall approval of the welfare state.

Conclusion

This chapter has presented evidence which shows a substantial increase in income inequalities in Britain in the 1980s. Poorer groups have stood still while the better off have enjoyed substantial increases in living standards. A number of writers have suggested that such a sharp rise in inequality will threaten the consensual support for government policy on which the welfare state is assumed to rest. Evidence from the British Social Attitudes Survey and elsewhere demonstrates that there has been no increase in disapproval of the welfare state over the decade, in fact the reverse is true. Nor is there any evidence of a shift in support towards the private sector.

However, this does not imply that the welfare state is endorsed unquestioningly or in its entirety. There is a markedly lower level of support for services directed at the needs of poorer minorities and a substantial demand for the opportunity to use private sector services alongside state provision. There is a strong current of moralistic concern about the poor. These attitudes do display large differences between different income groups. Income polarisation is not reflected simply in the pattern of popular attitudes to state welfare. There is also a substantial demand for access to privileged services for better-off groups. This corresponds to the evidence of Chapter Two, where it was shown that the welfare state has always encompassed inequalities in service for unequal social groups. The chief virtue of state welfare in class society is this capacity to contain the interests of different classes. On the evidence of attitude surveys, it appears sufficiently elastic to persist in performing this act of reconciliation under altered circumstances. One and a half cheers for the welfare state!

CHAPTER 6

SOCIAL SCIENCE AND DISENCHANTMENT

It is a general popular error to imagine the loudest complainers for the public to be the most anxious for its welfare.

E. Burke

Introduction: the realignment of theory

In this chapter we move on to consider approaches to the role of the state in welfare implicit in recent developments in sociology. The main tradition in post-war sociology of welfare assumed that government could provide agreed levels of service to cater for a limited range of needs as an accepted component in a common citizenship. In the 1980s, this assumption was rejected at the practical level by the reality of government policy. Welfare sociology had emerged from the comfortable consensus of statism to be buffeted by new theoretical approaches and by the hard fact of a government and a political climate (extending to opposition parties) no longer ready to be convinced that more is necessarily better. At the same time, the main theoretical currents in the discipline of sociology also began to express disquiet at the capacity of the state to serve the end of human welfare. Inconvenient empirical evidence indicated that social policy had not been conspicuously successful in meeting the needs of the most disadvantaged.

The realignment of theory is particularly interesting for two reasons. First, the processes of polarisation outlined in Chapter Four have ensured that the need for welfare provision at the most basic level in British cities is obvious, although the best way of meeting these needs may not be so clear. Second, the discussion of cross-national data in Chapters Three and Four drew attention to the paradox that the UK has been exceptionally hasty to control its level of welfare spending and has pursued policies that produce the sharpest increases in poverty and unemployment in any European country at a time when the pressures on the future development of welfare are mild compared with most other developed nations. The UK is the only country out of the seven major capitalist economies in which the aged dependency ratio falls by the end of the century. Recent work indicates that official concern about dependency in the next century may be over stated; the official analysis fails to take into account the possibility of economic growth, the increased participation in the work-force of married women and the likelihood of a reduction in the historically high levels of unemployment of the mid-1980s. From this viewpoint, the crisis of the welfare state in the UK is the outcome not of inexorable social forces, but of political choices. The perversity of policy indicates a current in ideology set firmly against welfare statism. It is of interest that this shift finds an echo in the broad sweep of higher level theories of welfare.

The impact of the new approaches

Despite their apparent differences in method, assumptions, provenance and direction, the new approaches to the role of the state in welfare share a number of key features. In the early 1970s, the view that the current configuration of democratic welfare capitalism contained a tendency to crisis was advanced on different premises by writers on the left and the right of the political spectrum. The work of O'Connor, integrating the US normative public policy tradition (best summarised in Galbraith's antinomy of private affluence and public squalor) and a Marxist class logic implied that the conflict between the limitations on state revenues resulting from the private property system and the burgeoning demands of organised private interests made it impossible for the state to deliver the policy demanded of it. Democratic capitalist states tended inevitably towards fiscal crisis, since the political system generates interest-group pressure for the redeployment of resources by government, although government's control over resources must of necessity be limited by the system of private property ownership that is central to western capitalism (O'Connor, 1973).

Similar arguments are advanced from different standpoints. Bell analyses the expansionary citizenship demands of status groups and power-blocs, which the state finds increasing difficulty in containing (1976). The arguments of public choice theorists claim that state services tend to inefficiency, due to the tendency of politicians to acquiesce in the demands of electorally important groups, so that the state tends to take over areas of economic life which it is ill-fitted to manage (Dunleavy and O'Leary, 1987, pp.326–7). A harder-nosed variant, derived from Hayek's rigorous methodological individualism points to the logical impossibility of a centralised intelligence meeting needs and allocating resources which are divided up among a large number of private individuals.

These arguments have been reinforced by empirical claims about a crisis of citizen confidence expressed in taxpayer revolt. A series of writers in the late 1960s and early 1970s developed notions of allegiance deficit and legitimation crisis: the modern state maintains its legitimacy by the democratic promise to satisfy all legitimate interests, yet is imprisoned within the conflict of opposed interests, which appear equally legitimate to those who hold them. The failure of the state to deliver what citizens see as their right may ultimately undermine the logic of collective action at the cultural level – what Habermas refers to as 'motivation crisis' (1976, pages 50 and 75; see Taylor-Gooby, 1985, pp.8–13 for a more detailed discussion of the implications of these ideas for the sociology of welfare).

The crisis thesis has been undermined by events. Governments in a number of western democracies retain citizen allegiance while discriminating vigorously between interest groups. The balance of reward between social classes, unemployed and employed people, trade unionists and capital, state sector workers and others has been redressed in the UK and the USA. Similarly the challenges of groups previously excluded from the bargaining system – principally women and ethnic minorities – are readily contained in accommodation to the existing class hierarchy. Crisis in western capitalism generated by (among other things) the operation of an interventionist welfare state has been resolved by transferring the burden of crisis to groups of welfare state consumers. As apprehension of crisis is blunted by a more sober reality, a calmer critique has emerged – the critique summed up in the notions of 'transition' or 'modernisation' referred to in Chapter One.

The distrust of the state

The central theme running through the contemporary sociology of welfare is distrust of the state. In the 1970s and 1980s the theme of state crisis corresponded to a politics of cuts, privatisation and contraction of the role of government. Now a sociology of disquiet accompanies a politics which views the deployment of state power with suspicion, and advocates the discipline of government through a more extensive use of non-state agencies – or simply (and more crushingly) claims that the time of the welfare state is past. There are four main aspects to this in recent sociological work. These are: a growing awareness of the multiplicity and interaction of the sources of social identity and motivation in consumption patterns, gender, family and kinship relations, community networks and the other bases of common culture; a renewed emphasis on ideologies of privatism and of familism in official and academic discussion of social and economic life; the development of a new political sociology of consumption sectors as a substitute for analyses based on production cleavages; and a political and economic sociology based on the restatement of the theme of 'civil society' against the power of the state.

These themes are linked together in two over-arching sets of ideas – the decline of social class as a basis for objective or subjective divisions in society, and, linked to this, an emphasis on the complexity of social divisions. First, the previous tradition relied heavily on the notion that welfare could be advanced by the simple reallocation of social resources through tax and social benefit policies, coupled with a range of health, social care, education and housing services. It saw social class divisions as both the primary structures of welfare need and the sources of political pressure for welfare state action. One leading writer argues: 'the decline of the welfare state may be associated with the historical decline of the organised working class and class-based communities' (Turner, 1990, p.195). The new emphases in sociological work undermine the tradition of welfare statism by pointing out that human welfare is more complex and multifaceted than this approach can hope to encompass.

Second, the new approaches place more weight on family relationships, private property and market position as sources of social identity. This erodes the link between class and welfare statism and emphasises the point that action through the market and through family and kinship networks is a major component of welfare. We will discuss the four areas of sociological work and the two themes that draw them together in more detail, before attempting to assess them and to draw conclusions about the implications for the future of welfare statism.

Welfare and the sources of social identity

An important influence on the general argument that individual social identity is strongly influenced by culturally-ascribed position in the status order is Turner's work on citizenship and the role of social movements in articulating the demands that individuals make of the state. Not surprisingly, this approach minimises the influence of economic class position (see Turner, 1986). His starting point is the Weberian analysis which distinguishes between class, status and party as separate elements in stratification. Weber wrote: 'whereas the genuine place of "classes" is within the economic order, the place of "status groups" is within the social order, that is within the sphere of the distribution of honour. From within these spheres, classes and status groups influence one other, and they influence the legal order and are in turn influenced by it. But "parties" live in a house of power.' (Gerth and Mills, 1948, p.194).

Weber's analysis of stratification is often distinguished from

Marx's on the grounds that the former placed less emphasis on market relations and more on status position than the latter. Whether this is justified is open to doubt. Weber certainly adopted a rigorous and deterministic 'description of capitalism as an "iron cage" and there is a close relationship between the [Weberian] concept of rationalisation and the [Marxist] concept of alienation' (Abercrombie, Hill, Turner, 1988, p.268).

Turner's own contribution to the debate derives from an interest in the construction of citizenship in the context of the modern interventionist state. He builds on Weberian analysis, to stress the significance of status, drawing on Bourdieu's conception of status as cultural life-style (1984). This approach is used to undermine the traditional emphasis on class in the production order as the principal determinant of stratification, whether or not this may be modified to a limited extent by status position. For example, he claims that relations driven by sentiments of solidarity and common feeling (*gemeinschaft*) rather than simple mechanistic association (*gesellschaft*) are characteristic of the labour market, so that collectivities based primarily on status enter the temple of the market order of class.

> The organisation of class systems and economic relations in terms of status and cultural divisions also represents a major deviation away from Weber's conception of a rationally organised market place and Marx's concept of capitalism in which labour power is freely bought and sold like any other commodity (1989, p.594).

The way is now open to place status ordering in a central position, alongside class in a theory of stratification. Culturally ascribed statuses, such as ethnicity, or age-divisions between the young, the mature and the elderly can enter the analysis:

> the social stratification system is structured by an economic dimension (the ownership and control of the means of production), by a political and legal dimension (the control of various political and legal resources, which structure the distribution of rights and obligations) and by a cultural dimension (the monopolisation of various forms of cultural capital which at the level of life-style differentiate and demarcate social groups). The relationship between these three dimensions of social stratification is historically contingent and the dominance of any particular dimension can only be ascertained by historical and empirical research (p.590).

The precise importance of cultural issues is uncertain and Weberian theory, approached from this standpoint, is rendered sufficiently plastic to accomodate almost any analysis of social relations.

A good illustration of the implications of this perspective is Turner's analysis of age-groupings as a dimension in stratification in welfare state societies. He argues in developing a 'multi-dimensional model of stratification which considers ageing in relation to economic class, political entitlement, or citizenship, and cultural life-styles' that 'the theory of social ageing can be located in the core of sociological theory, because it is connected fundamentally to the conditions of social solidarity' (1989, p.588). The problem of locating age-divisions in social theory is comparable to that of finding a satisfactory analytic place for the location of ethnic patterns. The divisions implied by both principles cut across the pattern of established inequalities due to divisions of power, wealth, labour market position, education and so on, in a way that is difficult to analyse coherently. The extended Weberian model provides a framework in which the construction of old age is a cultural artefact, not a product of the operation of the labour market. 'Ageing and age-groups are demarcated not only by economic and political practices, but also by specific life-styles, a cultural habitus and by dispositions which differentiate them from other competing social groups' (1989, p.590).

Turner points out that in welfare states, the position of the elderly is one of the major issues in the allocation of citizen entitlements – the biggest single group of state welfare beneficiaries are those defined as elderly, principally through pension, disability benefit, health care and social care services. This gives rise to concern about the implications of population ageing for future expenditure patterns discussed in Chapter Three. At the same time, the elderly come to constitute an organised interest group capable of defending entitlements and cutting across traditional divisions of class and party – the paradigm being the Gray Panthers in the USA. Turner's own account of the social ascription of ageing is to do with people's capacity to maintain relations of reciprocity. As citizens progress from childhood to maturity they take on more and more responsibilities that extend the network of social relations with others. As they move towards old age, their families grown up, they move out of formal employment and their net-work of relationship grows thinner. It is this cultural process of disengagement that leads to the low status of elderly people and entails their exclusion from work and their relatively high risk of social disadvantage and poverty.

This account may be challenged on empirical grounds. First it is clear that other dimensions of stratification cut across old age in determining the stratification position of old people. Poverty is overwhelmingly the lot of those who have been poor in their life-times – it is closely linked to class, as Piachaud points out (1990). Second, relations of reciprocity appear to be more complex than this analysis allows – poorer people are as well able to maintain reciprocity as those who are better off. In any case reciprocity may be maintained on an inter-generational basis, the young helping the old in expectation of a return when they grow old themselves (Finch, 1989). However, such points are the stuff of empirical debate. The real significance of Turner's discussion of ageing is that it illustrates the way in which accounts of the cultural ascription of status can be inter-woven with conventional discussion of welfare state citizenship and market oriented class to provide insight into the complexity of social order and of the pattern of interests which individuals experience in relation to the state. This complexity is substantially greater than that envisaged in the traditional theories that link class interest to state power, and which use market inequalities as the grist for state intervention.

However, the neo-Weberian approach does not undermine the justification for welfare statism, since the linkage between inequalities in the market and in cultural orders may itself imply a role for state intervention. This is well illustrated in a recent study, which pays particular attention to the cultural meanings ascribed to different forms of work and the contribution that participation in work makes to people's social identity within a community.

Social identity and work

The starting point for an in-depth study of social relations on the Isle of Sheppey (R. Pahl, 1984) is a rigorous analysis of all forms of work, including formal employment and self-employment, paid work that is not officially acknowledged (usually in order to evade taxes), unpaid work for others, and the informal work carried out to enhance living standards in the home, on the allotment or on the physical structure of the dwelling. The analysis draws on Gershuny's argument that the capacity to carry out labour to one's own advantage outside the structure of formal employment is an increasingly important aspect of people's capacity to control and improve their standard of living. Gershuny points out that modern capitalism has enabled economies to be achieved in the organised production of commodities through the co-ordinated division of labour. It simply does not make sense for an individual to produce autonomously the things that he or she might need, such as a bicycle, refined sugar, a carpet or a washing machine. However, in some service industries corresponding economies of scale have not been realised by the substitution of capital goods for labour, so that it is entirely sensible to paint or improve your own house, drive and service your own car, mend your own bicycle tyres and wash your own clothes. People can purchase capital goods – houses, cars, washing-machines – and produce their own services – shelter, transport, cleanliness – provided, of course, they have the wherewithal and the relevant skills (Gershuny and Miles, 1983). Thus the explosion in purchase of commodities which enable people to develop an individually run self-service economy: DIY tools, videos and other forms of home entertainment, cars for private transport and so on.

Pahl's contribution builds on the point that participation in the self-service economy requires cash and skills. In analysis of detailed data on the work carried out both formally and informally by households on Sheppey, and on the social relationships involved with work, he demonstrates a growing structural division between those with access to formal employment, which enables the purchase of the relevant capital goods, from privately-owned housing to cars to home-freezers, but also often furnishes skills, contacts and tools, and those excluded from participation in this peculiarly modern arena of combined consumption and production. Self-servicing extends beyond the sphere of home, family and immediate dependents to include the possibility of informal exchange-relationships with those with access to other skills and services. As government policies extend the notion of active citizenship to include participation in the management of schools, hospital trusts and the development of voluntary social care, it is the 'insiders' who are included in a world of vigorous social participation, from which others are excluded. 'Insiders' progress on a virtuous spiral of production and consumption, aided by developments in welfare policy and the labour market. In addition, social security rules make it rational for spouses to work when their partner is in employment, but penalise those who work while their partner is on benefit, since their earned income will be set against the benefit entitlement (Cooke, 1987, p.371). The division between core work, providing stable and secure income, and peripheral work, only able to sustain normal living standards for those who share in the wage of a core worker is growing stricter (Hakim, 1989, p.491). 'Outsiders' remain dependent on static state benefits, increasingly expensive rented housing and uncertain access to paid work. The outcome is a society in which a majority flourish while a social minority are increasingly divided from them in interests and in living standards.

This account mirrors Townsend's analysis of poverty with its central theme of inclusion/exclusion based on access to the means of consumption considered normal in society (1979). Townsend's principal contribution to work on poverty is to develop a rigorous empirical analysis of the components of living standards experienced by social groups at different levels of income. This is used to demonstrate a radical discontinuity in access to the elements of mass consumption. Just as Pahl sees the inability to participate in all forms of work as leading to a social exclusion, Townsend understands poverty as a denial of the capacity to share in a common level of consumption.

This approach has been criticised on the grounds that consumption patterns reflect individual choices as well as the financial means to purchase the relevant goods, and that these choices may be conditioned by taste or culture (Piachaud, 1981, p.419). However, this argument misses the point of Townsend's exercise – to find an empirical basis for the notion of social solidarity that has underlain much discussion of social policy and is often embodied in references to integration, community, stigma and citizenship. The demonstration that exclusion from normal consumption may be linked to income thus substantiates the claim that the damage of poverty is not simply to do with the brute fact of not being able to buy certain goods. It is also a matter of social relations. The poor cannot afford to participate in the activities that enhance, support and assert social identity in our society and are thereby

diminished. Similarly, Pahl suggests that access to secure employment, the capability for satisfactory self-provisioning and the use
of private means of welfare consumption not only constitute a
particular production and consumption location, but also, beyond
that, place an individual on one side or other of a major fault-line
of social division.

The point that the division between insiders and outsiders does
not rest simply on differences in the sphere of production – social
class – but on the interaction of class and activity in the sphere of
consumption – the status order – can be understood in terms of
Turner's (1988) analysis of the triple foundations of stratification.
What this approach does not do is suggest any justification for a
diminution in state intervention. State policies involving welfare
cut-backs widen the division by making it more difficult for
outsiders to acquire the means to become insiders. The significance of the gulf suggests an additional importance for interventionism to mitigate the bleakness of exclusion. The new sources of
social identity do not necessarily supplant the case for the welfare
state.

Social identity and kinship obligation

A further illustration of the implications of neo-Weberian
approaches is provided in analysis of kinship systems. Recent work
on patterns of family support has led to an enhanced understanding of how such structures operate to meet a need for social care
which government agencies do not fulfil. However, the fact of
kinship support – a central element in any account of the status
system – does not offer a satisfactory and universal alternative
service which could justify a reduction in state support for
dependent groups.

The role of family and kinship networks as sources both of
obligation and individual support is analysed by Finch (1989). In
summarising the detailed examination of the literature contained
in her book, she makes three basic points: 'assistance from
relatives still is of considerable importance to many people – in
some respects more so than is often imagined, for example the use
of kin networks to help in finding jobs'.

Second 'the lives of some people (most of them women) are

dominated by the assistance which they give to a relative, especially people who are the main carer for someone who is handicapped and infirm'. Third 'kin support in many ways is unpredictable . . . we cannot simply predict from knowing that someone has a sister, or a father, or five grandchildren, what assistance if any is passing between them now, or has ever done. It all depends on their particular circumstances' (1989, p.238).

Finch is at pains to emphasise the significance and also the complexity of kin relationships in determining support and contribution as elements in the social identity of the individuals bound by them. Kin is certainly important – of supreme importance in determining the sheer quantity of work done by some people for the welfare of others as, for example, Lewis and Meredith's study of domestic care-work carried out by women shows (1988). The contribution of kinship obligation to identity is mediated crucially by gender: 'women are more involved than men because they need to be: the division of labour in our society accords them a range of domestic and caring responsibilities for which they need the support of others' (p.239; see also Lewis' historical review, 1984, p.222).

Detailed review of the literature indicates that the structure of kin obligation is mediated by complex rules. The two most important are: first, a division between an 'inner circle' and an 'outer circle' of relationships, in which the ties of the former will tend to take precedence over the ties of the latter – immediate family demands typically receiving a more substantial response than those of more distant kin, such as cousins. Second, a loose principle of reciprocity affects many kin relationships, so that individuals achieve a rough balance between their contribution to and their receipt of care from others over time, although this may not apply to the obligation felt by parents towards children, which often seems to function on an intergenerational basis.

This brief summary shows that kinship patterns operate to structure relations of dependency and aid that cut across systems of economic inequality. These patterns retain their significance in modern industrial society. However, the architecture of kinship is governed by rules that operate in complex and uncertain ways, so that it is difficult to use them to predict the precise levels of linkage between individuals. Finch uses this point to show that attempts by politicians to base welfare systems on family aid are simply misguided: we cannot argue with sufficient certainty that people will help each other on the basis of kinship to use family relationship as an acceptable substitute for state-guaranteed services. The neo-Weberian analysis applied to the family does not undermine the role of the government in welfare provision.

Privatism, familism and the state

The link between state and private sphere has been one of the strongest issues in social policy discussion in the 1980s. At the level of immediate politics, all major political parties seek to represent themselves as champions of the family. As the UK's economic malaise proves impervious to the palliatives proposed from left and right, the cultural sphere has gained greater importance as the arena in which the struggle for the 'middle ground of politics' will be fought out. Central to this territory are the values represented by the family. Family life has been a central theme in social policy since its inception, implicit in the system of aggregation of partners' income for means-testing, the definition of dependency for benefit additions for spouse and children, the dividing lines drawn between collectively managed and private health and social care, the pattern of housing forms and of employment and education policy (Smart, 1987; Watson, 1987).

Recent developments make these assumptions explicit. The Conservative approach is well summarised in the passage in the 1987 election manifesto which defined commitment to the family in terms of extending people's freedom of choice about 'what they do for themselves, for their families and for others less fortunate' by reducing the role of an 'over-powerful State' (1987, p.27). In practice, this has meant a reduction in state provision and an assumption that families, and very often women in them will bear the resulting burden (Abbott and Wallace, 1989, p.79; Deakin, 1987, p.99). It has also been linked to specific policies designed to increase incentives for individuals to live in couple-headed households, where children are assumed dependent on parents until they enter the world of work. Penalties for those who contradict this ideal are correspondingly increased. Child benefit was frozen in 1987. Its value has fallen steadily behind all other benefits. Support for single parents has risen at a rate no faster than that of price-inflation, so that the living standards of this group steadily fall behind those of the population at large. Benefits for young people have been truncated with the result that family dependency for those not in the labour market continues to the age of 18 rather than 16.

The Labour party's response is informed by a positive notion of freedom (Hattersley, 1987). This defends state provision because it enhances individual choice by extending opportunities. However, until recently, the party has been unwilling to develop policies that recognise the diversity of existing family forms. A speech at the 1990 Party Conference by the leader, heavily influenced by a report from the Labour party think-tank, the Institute for Public Policy Studies (Coote, Harman and Hewitt, 1990) signalled a positive commitment to develop policies that gave real support to single parent as well as couple-headed families, both through benefits and in access to paid work, and which demanded a real extension of support for those with children, through the improvement and extended availability of child-care. Change in the form of the family has entered politics as a live issue.

In this political context, much of the sociological analysis of the early 1980s emphasised the significance of the defence of the private sphere as a foundation of individual consciousness among working-class people. It was argued that the private sphere of home, hearth and family forms a defensive bulwark in times of economic uncertainty. The focus of popular interests shifted away from the collective sphere of class struggle through political organisation and participation in efforts to advance the working class as a whole and thereby serve the ends of each worker. Unemployment levels appeared out of control, British economic prospects were increasingly subject to decisions taken elsewhere, trade unions had grown visibly weaker in legal rights and in membership. Under conditions of endemic uncertainty 'a sound pragmatic strategy for . . . people, concerned to get by as comfortably as possible, is to put their resources of time energy and skill into making their domestic world more secure. At least in that sphere they have some control' (Pahl and Wallace, 1986, p.382). People *en masse* turn away from civic or political collectivism to the consolations of a 'retreat into the privatised world of home and family' (Marshall, Rose, Vogler and Newby, 1985, p.274).

Nationalism displaces political citizenship as a unifying bond, influences from the cultural level of status making a major contribution to power and party in the language of the modified Weberian model discussed earlier. Just as Goldthorpe and his colleagues argued in one of the seminal works of post-war sociology that stability and security engendered a mood of privatised consciousness among affluent workers (1969), so current analysis locates the genesis of a similar ideology in the experience of the bankruptcy of collectivism (see also: Alt, 1979, p.272; Seabrook, 1984, for studies of the 'mood of the British people' from radically different perspectives, which reach broadly comparable conclusions).

This analysis had a substantial influence in the sociology of the mid-1980s. This is illustrated in contributions to the prestigious Economic and Social Research Council-financed symposium on the theme of class (see Roberts *et al.*, 1986; Newby *et al.*, 1986). It shows clear links with the neo-Weberian conception of the social order as more complex than that captured by one-dimensional models of social class. As a corollary, welfare statism is less likely to be capable of accommodating the intricacies of human welfare. Academic concern with the fragmentation and political quietism (as Newby and his colleagues sometimes put it, the stoicism) of the working class is clearly influenced by the success of the Conservative party in three national elections. However, by the end of the decade, the sociology of stratification had shifted its ground. The most influential single piece of work is undoubtedly the detailed study of class imagery and social location carried out by Newby and his colleagues (Marshall *et al.*, 1988).

This study originated as part of a cross-national attempt to provide an empirical test of Wright's neo-Marxist schema, alongside Goldthorpe's categorisation of occupational positions. The analysis concludes that 'the class structure is not polarised in the manner suggested by Wright . . . a more reliable and empirically convincing class analysis reveals 'intermediate' categories which are, both demographically and socio-politically located between the working- and the service-classes' (1988, p.266). Goldthorpe's neo-Weberian analysis is largely endorsed, although the authors point out its inadequacies in the categorisation of women as workers. In relation to the earlier discussion of a pragmatic decline in social class as an organisational category, however, they conclude that 'there is no evidence of a decomposition of class', although 'it is true that individualism, consumerism and privatism are readily apparent' (p.273). The solution to the apparent paradox is that socio-political consciousness in Britain contains a powerful ambivalence. What is more, it always has. 'A historical perspective suggests that sectionalism, privatism and instrumentalism have always been close to the surface of working-class life' (p.267). At the same time there are powerful currents of working-class collective identity, resentment at social inequality and perceptions of injustice. Different strands come to the fore in different contexts: in the mid-1980s, cultural themes associated with the exhaustion of political action for citizenship may cut across class difference. By the end of the decade, political unity may appear to have more point. Similarly, a study of a working-class suburb of Coventry shows 'a considerable degree of communal sociability in an (apparently) unlikely context' and concludes that both sociability and privatisation are 'recurring features of working-class life' (Procter, 1990, pp.157 and 175).

This account is entirely compatible with the neo-Weberian emphasis of the tripartite plasticity of the sources of social consciousness. It also allows considerable room for the strands of citizenship, market position and status to interweave in different ways, and provides an account of why the cultural order of status should command attention in the 1980s. The analysis offers a convincing explanation of the retreat to the private individual sphere from the apparently futile world of politically-oriented collective action. This is the theme to which the politician's concern with family values is attuned.

However, the evidence of a decline in working-class engagement in class politics does not imply that class is no longer a central component of people's ideas about their social locations. The earlier shift to a sociology of stratification based on a status order diverted attention from the continued importance of class and of associated state interventionism. Marshall and his colleagues are able to demonstrate that the recognition of class inequality as injustice and the demand for corrective government action remain as central elements in popular citizenship:

> a substantial majority in each class are convinced that rewards are
> distributed unfairly . . . these findings can be considered alongside

those...where it was reported that 70 per cent of our sample think that the distribution of wealth and income in Britain is unfair, and well over 80 per cent of all assessments as to why this is so indicated a desire to redistribute wealth down the social hierarchy (1988, pp.185-7).

Privatism does not contradict support for the welfare state.

A further strand in political sociology has taken the themes of status order emphasized in the neo-Weberian approach and political privatism in the analysis of class imagery to generate a new model of political consciousness and behaviour. This has developed into a self-conscious account of political ideas as structured by cleavages originating in the sphere of consumption rather than the production divisions that underlie conventional accounts of social class. Since this approach in its strongest form seeks to supplant market position (except insofar as it is able to influence consumption choices) it may come into conflict with neo-Weberian accounts of social location which operate in terms of an empirically determined interaction of class and status.

Consumption sector and the politics of welfare

The argument that it is people's location in relation to the means of consumption (which in Weberian terms is likely to be heavily influenced by economic class, but also to be affected by status-group membership) that is the crucial determinant of political consciousness and thereby of voting emerged in the work of a number of writers at the end of the 1970s (Dunleavy, 1979; Duke and Edgell, 1984; Saunders, 1984). In fact it gained so great an influence, fostered by the desire to explain why working-class people should vote in large numbers for the Conservative party (which has traditionally identified with the interests of the higher economic groups) that some commentators complained that it had become the 'new orthodoxy' (Franklin and Page, 1984).

The relevance to discussion of the welfare state is again that the pattern of interests in society is shown to be complex so that it is difficult to see how state policy can cover a wide range of social needs. In this sense the political sociology of consumption complements the neo-Weberian sociology of status – the latter explains how people conceive of the social structure in which they find themselves and which their actions reproduce, while the former explains how that consciousness is translated into collective action through state citizenship. The approach has received the fullest development from a political science perspective in the work of Dunleavy and his collaborators, and from a sociological viewpoint in the analyses of Saunders. Both writers have applied their ideas empirically in the analysis of large-scale surveys.

Sectoral cleavages and voting behaviour

Dunleavy used the 'sectoral cleavage' approach in analysis of the 1979 General Election Survey in order to assess the importance of two divisions associated with the growth of the welfare state in voting behaviour. The divisions are between those with access to private forms of consumption, particularly in the use of services like transport and housing, and those who are restricted to use of state-subsidised public transport and council housing on the one hand, and those who are employed in the state sector, the civil service and state education and health care in particular, and those who work in the private sector on the other. The application of the idea of sectoral divisions to employment was not empirically successful. Work by others focuses almost entirely on consumption sector. The range of services where a division between state and private provision is relevant was extended by Duke and Edgell to include health and social care and pensions. In analysis of a specially commissioned survey of the 1983 election, Dunleavy terms his approach the 'radical approach' in distinction to the traditions of party identification – the view that people simplify the problem of choosing between competing programmes by developing customary allegiance to one or other party (see for example Butler and Stokes, 1969) – and the issue voting approach – based on the assumption that the electorate make more or less rational choices based on assessment of the cost-benefit of the different programmes (see for example Mueller, 1979, Chapters 3 to 7). The analysis moves beyond the original notion of consumption sector in two ways. First, the basic influence upon people's political alignment is seen as individual position 'in a complex structure of social inequalities and conflicts of interest' (Dunleavy and Husbands, 1985, p.18) which include both 'production influences (such as social class, economic activity status, sectoral location, unionisation and gender) and consumption influences'. Thus the role of consumption is softened and diffused. Stratification by production position – class – re-enters analysis. Second, ideological messages structured crucially through the operation of the mass media interact with the notions of interest resulting from social structural location to produce perceptions of group interest which then underlie both attitudes to particular issues and general patterns of voter alignment in elections.

The analysis of the election campaign and of the way political messages mediated by the media influenced popular perceptions of political interest provides some empirical support for the model. The attention paid to the role of newspapers and television in structuring popular ideas is a valuable development in the main stream of British voting studies. The examination of consumption sector effects shows that the use of individual services has a comparatively weak relation with voting behaviour. It is only when access to private services is cumulated over five consumption processes – home ownership, use of a private car, private medical care, family use of an old person's home and past, present or prospective use of private schooling – that a strong relationship is obtained. However, this is at the expense of substantially reducing the proportion of the sample who fall into the relevant category – using four or five private services. The approach offers no substantial advance over class theory in explaining mass behaviour.

The question of whether consumption sector in itself exerts a major independent influence on voting behaviour is further illuminated in a separate study of the 1983 Election. Heath and his colleagues consider the most powerful sectoral division (that between the state and private housing) in some detail, and are able to show two things: first the shifts in home-ownership over the 1960s and 1970s are comparable to the shifts in patterns of social class formation, so that the proportion of home-owners in the various class groups stay roughly constant over time. It is therefore difficult to see changes in patterns of home ownership as a major source of change that cannot with equal logic be attributed to changes in the patterns of social class (Heath, Jowell and Curtice,

1985, pp.52–3). Second, they are able to cross-reference voters between different rounds of the British Election Study and trace the voting patterns of tenants who have recently become home-owners. Analysis of party support shows that a change of consumption sector in housing is not accompanied by a substantial change in the voting behaviour between recent elections.

The outcome of this discussion is to throw some doubt on the usefulness of the consumption sector approach as a tool to be used in the analysis of electoral survey data – which has been the central concern of the British political science tradition. However, Dunleavy's radical approach does offer some valuable insights into electoral behaviour, particularly in terms of the operation of the mass media, and the incorporation of production and consumption into a model which explains the contribution of both aspects of social life to the moulding of political choice. This is achieved, as in the neo-Weberian analysis of the influence of status, at the expense of reducing the theory to a plasticity which can interpret the data from both class and status perspectives. The extent to which the theory can tell us which is the predominant influence in a particular context is limited. This becomes a matter for empirical research. However, there is no clear evidence that consumption divisions are sufficient to undermine support for the welfare state. The empirical studies of both Dunleavy and Heath, with their colleagues, indicates a continuing support for state welfare along traditional lines. The former show stronger support for statements endorsing the welfare state than for those calling for privatisation (Dunleavy and Husbands, 1985, p.165); the latter write that: 'in the case of welfare state spending there has been increased opposition to cut-backs' (Heath, Jowell and Curtice, 1985, p.138).

Consumption sector and housing classes

Saunders' work originates in the development of the logic of housing classes as an alternative system of stratification to production classes. In a much quoted paper (1984) he argues that housing has a peculiar relationship to its users, an 'ontological significance' which ensures that home-ownership has a meaning beyond that implied by the subsidy arrangements and means of access to shelter in a given society. He takes this argument further in a major theoretical work, which is a self-conscious attempt to rewrite the new urban sociology in terms of the sociology of consumption rather than of production sectors. In summary, his argument traces the development of collective consumption in advanced market societies through three stages: market-orientation, which is the paradigm of the Victorian *laissez-faire* era, socialised consumption (the heyday of the organisation of consumption through the interventionist welfare state) and the newly-emerging form of privatised consumption. This refers to the provision of state-subsidised welfare according to market forms for the mass of the population, while the minority who are unable to command this are 'cast adrift on the water-logged raft of what remains of the welfare state' (1986, p.318).

Burrows and Butler develop four lines of criticism (1989). The account is ethnocentric: research in other societies indicates that the social meaning of housing as a source of personal identity under different institutional arrangements is of less significance than in the UK. It over-simplifies history, both in terms of the periodisation of state interventionism and in terms of the assumed contrast between *laissez-faire* and welfare statism. It attempts to erect a theoretical edifice on the peculiar circumstances surrounding the UK housing market, which contains an unusual mix of tenures and system of state subsidies and financial institutions, and it pays too little attention to the political and economic factors that mould policy. The state-organised collective consumption of the welfare state can be seen as just as much the outcome of the demand for control over the means of consumption to advance individual interest, as can the system of private ownership. It is an empirical question whether council housing gives most members of the working class more secure housing than private landlordism, or whether state medicine gives the consumer as much control over access to health care as does a fee-for-service doctor.

Nonetheless, Saunders' account provides an interesting analysis of the transition from socialised to privatised consumption that is a feature of recent welfare policy. Rather than simply pointing to the complexity of the social order with which the state must deal, his approach is more directly critical of state intervention. The crisis in support for the welfare state derives from four factors: the failure of the state policy to achieve the ends laid down for it, amply illustrated in Le Grand's analysis of the inegalitarian outcomes of many components in the 'strategy of equality' discussed in Chapter Two; the increasing demand for private services due to the escalating cost of state provision and to the real popular preference for direct individual control over services; the fact that rising real incomes enable people to put their suppressed demand for greater choice into practice; and the claim that the expansion of the private sector creates a self-propelling dynamic. As Hirschman argues, the option of Exit from the state places greater strains on Loyalty to the services it provides (1970).

The force of the argument is rather different from that of the neo-Weberian political sociology which made a regretful case for a working-class withdrawal of support for the welfare state, and then discovered through empirical survey that this was not in fact the case. For Saunders the move out of the state sector is a positive and liberating escape. The arguments are developed in greater detail in ˌa recent empirical survey of popular attitudes to the provision of housing through state systems and through the private market.

The study of the social and moral meaning of home-ownership starts out from the premise that private property is basic to human society: 'private property and human society have evolved and developed in tandem' (1990, p.11). Following the account of the development of consumption outlined above, the spread of home-ownership and access to private pensions is seen as a revolution in the means of collective consumption – the coming of age of the state-managed privatised system, after the brief interlude of the directly interventionist welfare state – comparable in significance to the domination of the means of production by industrial capitalism some two centuries earlier. This revolution was accomplished without bloodshed and to such universal assent that, to most people it was 'normal and inevitable' (p.13). The study demonstrates that the expansion of home-ownership in the inter-war period took place for the most part without substantial state subsidy, and uses this point to support the argument that the movement was driven by popular preference rather than by state planning. A survey of owners and tenants in three towns demonstrates that ownership is the universally preferred form of tenure, and that most owners conceive of their housing as conferring a sense of 'psychological well-being' that goes beyond the financial advantages (Chapter 5).

The arguments that privatised housing is associated with a privatisation of life-style in the sense of a retreat into the domestic nest (see for example Lockwood, 1966, or more recently, Newby *et al.*, 1986, p.95) or with a life-style that implies oppressive domestic gender-roles for women (for example, Allan, 1985, p.56; Davidoff, L'Esperance and Newby, 1976, p.173) are challenged on the basis of contrary evidence: home-owners are actually more inclined to take part in social life outside the home and more inclined to engage in diverse patterns of domestic roles than tenants. However, the sample is relatively small, and the analysis is not controlled by age, so that these different patterns of activity may be as much the function of different stages in family life-cycle as of tenure. A larger sample analysed in the British Social Attitudes series indicates that age and the presence of young children are the most important factors in influencing domestic work arrangements (Ashford, 1987, pp.127–31, see also Martin and Roberts, 1984). Pahl's work draws attention to the point that people need money to participate in a social life outside the home. Control of Saunders' data by income shows that resources are an important factor in life-style. For example: 'home owners tend to go out more than tenants . . . this difference can mainly be explained by differences in income' (1990, p.288).

The psychological benefits are understood in terms of the 'ontological security' referred to above – the sense of attachment to the home, in contrast to the 'alienation' experienced by tenants, the greater opportunities for self-expression through the DIY labour of home-improvement, and for family continuity through inheritance of a real and appreciating asset. More than that, it generates a sturdy independence: 'a home-owning society is likely to be one where people are quietly proud of their achievements and fiercely jealous of their rights and privileges . . . it is almost as if the vanished independent yeomanry of England [sic] is gradually being remade behind the hedgerows of Acacia Avenue' (p.313).

Whether the institutions of state-subsidised home-ownership actually generate such a powerful sense of collective self-interest is unclear from the data presented by Saunders. However, it does seem that ownership may have a social meaning that motivates people to some extent in addition to the financial advantages. This motivation may not extend far beyond a particular national culture nor be particularly strong: although incomes are substantially higher, less than a third of the population of Switzerland, two-fifths of the population of West Germany (before reunification) and half the population of France were home-owners by 1981 (Boleat, 1985). In any case, it is not clear what evidence of a cleavage in preferences between state and private sector would imply, if it could be established unequivocally. Sullivan points out that 'it is insufficient to claim that, when apparent social differentiation occurs along any axis which is not directly consti- tuted on class lines, that this axis is therefore constructed independently of class' (1989, p.197). There is a strong association between social class and tenure in the UK. In 1987, 31 per cent of heads of households among the population were non-manual workers, but only 8 per cent among council tenants (OPCS, 1989, p.23). Arguments about the role of tenure cleavages must establish not only the significance of the divisions, but also their independence from class differences. This Saunders' analysis does not do.

The book opposes the ontological security of private property to the collectivism of the welfare state. The analysis thus leads to a powerful argument against state welfare provision that parallels the political sociology of consumption sector in linking the use of private services to support for the political party which asserts the aim of reducing state power. This is to miss the point of the organisation of state intervention in the British housing market. Despite the cuts in state spending on council housing, the average subsidy for a home-buyer in 1988–9 was £733, for a council tenant, £624, and for a private tenant, £243 (National Federation of Housing Associations, 1991). The force of the distinction between independent private owner and state-subsidised tenant collapses. The evidence of housing preferences does not imply any rejection of state intervention as such, just as the consumption sectoral arguments failed to root political cleavages in the logic of divisions between state and private consumption.

We have reviewed a number of approaches which draw on the key themes of a neo-Weberian sociology of stratification – the complexity of social order, the increased emphasis on privatism and the retreat into the domestic sphere, the political sociology of consumption sector – to suggest that social change renders the state less important as a bearer of welfare. Government is no longer a central focus of political demands, and at the same time the pattern of social need is too complex for the state to meet.

Evidence from empirical studies of class imagery, the significance of kinship, stratification and political consciousness and behaviour fails to sustain these contentions. Support for the welfare state is if anything stronger than it was three decades ago, when sociological confidence in welfare institutions was at its peak.

A further strand in political sociology, confined mainly to the left, questions the state approach to welfare from a different direction. This is based on an opposition between state and 'civil society' rather than state and stratification order. To this we now turn.

Civil society and state welfare

The notion of civil society as a sphere over and above the state has a substantial history in the political theory of the modern era. To the thinkers of the seventeenth and eighteenth centuries, writing in a social context dominated by the unleashing of the progressive dynamic of market capitalism, civil society was 'coterminous with the private sector – a realm of personal autonomy in which people could be free to develop their own methods of moral accounting' (Wolfe, 1989, p.15). For Rousseau, just as for the liberals of the Scottish enlightenment, this realm was incorporated in the market and founded on the principle of private property: 'the first man, who after enclosing a piece of ground, bethought himself of saying "this is mine", and found people simple enough to believe him, was the true founder of civil society' (Rousseau, 1973, p.76). The market provided the citizen with a bastion against the absolutist power of the monarchy, or the dead hand of the feudal order. It is this battle against the state that Saunders is still fighting, under rather different historical circumstances. For these thinkers, the extension of markets through human affairs relied on a moral framework: 'in proportion as men extend their dealings and render their intercourse with others more complicated, they always comprehend in their schemes of life a greater variety of voluntary actions which they expect from the proper motives to cooperate with their own' (Hume, 1963, p.89). Hegel summed up the notion of a free civil society under market capitalism in the claim that the individual energies released by the market create 'a system of complete interdependence wherein the livelihood, happiness and legal status of one man is interwoven with the livelihood, happiness and legal status of all' (1942, p.123).

As the nineteenth century progressed the capacity of the operation of markets to shatter and assimilate the moral order in which they inhered became more evident. This gave rise to perspectives which distinguish between the market system and normative order. Comte stressed the contribution of belief and ritual to social solidarity in his notion of a 'religion of humanity'. Durkheim developed analysis of the role of religion in inducing participation in social life. Hirsch, in a more recent analysis of the self-stultifying effects of the unrestricted operation of markets, points to the dependence of the market on principles that originate outside itself: 'the principle of self-interest is incomplete as a social organising device. It operates effectively only in tandem with some supporting social principle' (1977, p.12).

The recognition of the failure of the market to serve as the basis for a moral order of freedom led to a shift from what Wolfe terms a bipartite to a tripartite notion of civil society. The opposition of market freedom to state power is supplanted by an appeal to a moral order outside both state and market expressed in the early sociologists' notion of *gemeinschaft*, or Habermas' more recent conception of the 'life-world' (1976, pp.4–8). This approach bears a close analogy to the ideas of status-order and cultural location discussed above. However, the idea of civil society goes beyond the assertion that elements beyond the market and political power enter into stratification. It postulates an explicitly moral order and consciously opposes this to the dominion of the state.

Sociological interest in civil society faded during the great period of expansion of both capitalism and state intervention after the second world war. However the notion has re-emerged, due to 'an increased feeling that modernity's two great instruments – the market and the state – have become more problematic' (Wolfe, 1989, p.17). Attention is again directed to civil society, set in opposition to the capitalist state.

Keane is the most significant contemporary writer in the UK to draw together these concerns. His approach is self-consciously socialist in inspiration: 'west European socialism must break with its defensive and statist character, and become synonymous with the vitalisation of civil society and the democratic reform of state power' (1988, p.25). Four factors account for the strong appeal of his case for the foundation of democracy on the institutions of civil society rather than the state. The first is the disillusion of the left, engendered by the failure of left-wing governments to respond to the demands of the labour movement (Sheffield Group, 1989), to make significant advances in welfare distribution (Walker, 1984, Wicks, 1987) or to offer a satisfactory role for the new social movements which embody radical protest over women's, environmental, peace, imperial and world development issues (Rowbotham, Segal and Wainwright, 1979).

Second, the development of citizenship through the welfare state has lead to what Turner describes as a paradox: citizenship is about individual freedom, but the creation of institutions to mass-produce it involves individuation, categorisation and regulation – the imprisonment of the individual in the 'iron cage of bureaucracy'. 'Citizenship must necessarily breed the social and political conditions which undermine it' (1986, p.109). Third, many feminist perspectives have expressed ambivalence at welfare statism: while state power may be the only way to guarantee women's rights, welfare state policies have advanced the interests of men at the cost of women (Dale and Foster, 1986, p.179).

Fourth, the suppression of civil society as a means of destroying the possibility of opposition to central government in Eastern Europe has been echoed in minor key in the policies of the Conservative government of the 1980s. Michnik wrote of the Solidarity labour movement in Poland: 'the essence of the . . . spontaneously growing independent and self-governing Labour Union Solidarity lay in the restoration of social ties, self-organisation . . . civil and national rights . . . 'civil society' was being restored' (1985, p.124). In Britain, the government has challenged many civil society institutions, seeking to achieve greater regulation of newspapers and television, of the trade union movement, restricting the right to stand for political office, instituting more stringent control of education, of voluntary associations and of local government, extending state control of family life, sexuality and child-rearing, and, in a move unparalleled in the political history of this century, engaging in active confrontation with the church and the Royal Family over social issues. The exemplar of the East and concern about developments in the West led to a strong desire, particularly on the left to safeguard the institutions of civil society.

In this context, Keane develops the argument for a socialism based on the institutions of civil society, rather than on party and state, in the grand tradition of labour movement socialism. His arguments have strong implications for welfare statism – in fact, two of his four examples of pre-figurative forms of socialism are in the sphere of welfare policy – West German Green Movement proposals for the redistribution of formal employment and British feminist and local government initiatives in the sphere of child care (1988, Chapter 1). Since welfare represents the lion's share of state intervention in terms of taxation and state spending and also legislative restriction, any critique of the state must involve welfare. However, his analysis does not lead finally to a rejection of the perspective of the state, but to a strengthening of it.

Keane's conception of civil society involves virtually all extra-state activity:

> in the most abstract sense, civil society can be conceived as an aggregate of institutions whose members are engaged primarily in a complex of non-state activities – economic and cultural production, household life and voluntary associations – and who in this way preserve and transform their identity by exercising all sorts of pressures or controls on state institutions (1988, p.14).

The argument distinguishes Keane's analysis from the neo-conservative conception of a legally-guaranteed sphere dominated by capitalist organisations and patriarchal families – the bipartite approach of the early Liberals, discussed earlier, who saw civil society as the moralising context in which markets inhered, and were concerned to use civil society to challenge the oppressive operation of state power. Keane's approach stands distinct from both economic and state citizenship orders. The challenge is to widen the definition of civil society to embrace a 'vitalized non-state sphere comprising a plurality of public spheres – productive units, households, voluntary organisations and community-based services.' This requires major social changes.

First 'the power not only of private capital and the state, but also of heterosexual white male citizens over what remains of civil society would need to be curtailed through social struggles and public policy initiatives that enabled citizens acting together in "sociable" public spheres to strive for equal power'; second, 'state institutions would have to be made more accountable to civil society by having their functions as protectors, co-ordinators and regulators of citizens' lives recast' (Keane, 1989, p.14), in a framework reminiscent of the principle of separation of state power and civil society espoused by the early European writers on political democracy, such as Paine, de Toqueville and J.S. Mill.

Despite its attractions in the current British context, the devising of a programme to put this approach into practice presents serious problems. The notion of a greater role for civil society contains much that would find a responsive echo in right-wing demands for a more active citizenship, the extension of market institutions, and the withering of state power. The key difference lies in Keane's appeal for a restructuring of civil society to defuse the power of class and patriarchy. It is clear that the only agency capable of deploying authority on the scale required to challenge the major buttresses of privilege is the state. In neo-Weberian terms, Keane is calling for the use of citizenship power against the vested interests of economic class and the status-order of the patriarchal family system. The problem now is that the approach seems likely to tumble into a paradox analogous to Turner's paradox of citizenship. Just as the struggle for citizenship autonomy leads to the imposition of state bureaucracy, so the regeneration of civil society as the locus for individual control requires the exercise of state authority against the principal forces in the divided civil society that exists today. As is clearly recognised in work like that of the Sheffield Group, making the work safe for individual power must rest on a politics of the state. Presumably, the state in question will have a major welfare component since an active interventionist policy in the sphere of redistribution, the extension of work and educational opportunities and the guarantee of social and child care will be necessary to confront the power of patriarchy and class. Civil society socialism goes hand-in-hand with the enlarging of the welfare state.

Conclusions: sociology and social welfare

This chapter has been concerned to review some of the principal developments in recent sociological approaches to stratification, political consciousness and behaviour and the relationship of civil society to the state. It has identified two themes that command widespread assent. First, there is a renewed emphasis on the complexity of social order, as constructed by its members, which leads to a recognition of the utility of three-dimensional approaches, emphasising the independent roles of market order, systems of social status and the use of political authority in constructing social locations. This leads to the development of neo-Weberian models in which the relationship between the three dimensions in any political context is a matter of empirical investigation. The complexity of patterns of inequality undermines a welfare statism based simply on a strategy of economic class equality. Second, there is the suggestion that the current in popular political ideas is set firmly against the idea of welfare statism, as economic class declines in relevance and the capacity for individual control through the private sector assumes greater significance.

These approaches have often been taken to imply a reduced role for central government, as individual citizens demand greater control over their own lives. However, detailed investigation based on empirical research does not bear this out. The interaction of class and status in generating opportunities for informal work to enhance living standards and act as a basis for social identity furnishes an additional arena of social inclusion and exclusion in which state intervention is necessary. Renewed emphasis on the significance of family obligation has led to studies which show that family support is incapable of offering a satisfactory substitute for reliable government services. The retreat to the domestic nest is simply the privatised side of an ambivalence in class consciousness that also recognizes the class basis of inequality and injustice. State intervention to mitigate these is vigorously endorsed by most people.

The renewed significance of the status order in generating the cleavages of age, ethnicity and gender may function as a real basis for collective identity, but one that is directed at citizenship struggles in relation to the state. Similarly consumption sectoral cleavages are one element in the production of popular conscious-ness, but one that can function as much to generate demands for state provision as for privatisation. The metaphysical quest for an 'ontological significance' in private ownership of the means of consumption appears to be bounded by the blinkers of a particular cultural location. Finally, the analysis of civil society in the work of thinkers like Keane demonstrates that the regeneration of a moral order external to state and market must depend centrally on the exercise of state authority.

A simple model of state welfare as the redistributive politics of the working class may be discarded as class divisions appear to lose their central importance in stratification theory. However, the interaction of the multiple elements in stratification provides a justification for a major role for the state in welfare as powerful as that provided by class inequalities. Political consciousness contains ambivalences that allow for both privatisation and support for state intervention to secure different conceptions of justice. New departures in sociology do not substantiate the view that the welfare state is irrelevant, nor that it will be abandoned by mass publics.

CHAPTER 7

NEED, RIGHTS AND WELFARE

O, reason not the need! Our basest beggars
are in the poorest things superfluous.
Allow not nature more than nature needs,
man's life is cheap as beasts.

W. Shakespeare

Introduction

Previous chapters show that the case against the welfare state
based on appeal to the experience of past short-comings, shifts in
the policy environment that increase future welfare burdens and
the subjective implications of a growing division between prosperity
and poverty, is not compelling. New developments in sociological
theory do not justify academic disillusion with state welfare. The
remainder of the book attempts to construct a positive argument.
The discussion falls into two parts. This chapter shows that human
needs involve moral obligations. However, it is perfectly possible
to accept that welfare provision is morally good (as does Barry,
1990, pp.101–2) or meritorious (as does Murray, 1984, p.229)
without agreeing that it is an appropriate area for state involvement.
Even if the state is involved the right may be formal rather than
substantive. For example, Minford concedes that need implies
right but argues that it is the role of the state to enforce the right,

168

but not to supply the need: 'if a family has a handicapped child, they should expect to look after and equip him or her for life as best they can . . . those who violate the rights of dependants must be punished and forced to respect them' (Minford, 1987, p.81). This is bad news for poor people who have dependent children – and for their dependants, whose arena of support is circumscribed to the family. The next chapter will consider whether welfare needs involve claims against the state, so that the right to welfare must be accepted as an essential part of citizenship.

Welfare policy and social change

Normative argument becomes more complicated when social change is taken into account because the institutions which define need are themselves subject to change. Welfare policy is trying to hit a moving target. One response to the dilemma is to reverse the order of analysis so that the moral order is defined in terms of the existing structure of institutions and change itself becomes the problem. This approach is given an added twist in arguments which refer back to a 'golden age' located conveniently in some period which is inaccessible to the direct experience of the audience.

Callaghan, Labour Prime Minister in the late 1970s, claimed that: 'the family is the place where we care for each other, where we practise consideration for each other. Caring families are the basis of a society that cares'. Finch comments tersely:

> There is a long history in Britain of politicians describing family life as they would like it to be, but presenting that description as if it were a simple account of how most people live in reality. The implication is clear of course: if we don't live like this, then we ought to (1989, p.236).

In fact, people do a good deal else as well as care for each other within families, and they do a good deal of caring outside them. The politician's statement elides aspiration into reality and then into the normative objective to be defended by policy.

Other examples of this process are to be found in discussion of the development of the welfare state. In a keynote speech to

Conservative party constituency associations, the Secretary of State for Social Security pointed out that social care in Britain predated the Beveridge reforms by a considerable period, and that in any case, a considerable proportion of care takes place outside the state and in the family. He then moved from these observations to justify new policies that cut back the role of government and expand the part played by the private sector:

> this then is the way forward for the welfare state: to build on the tradition that has been created over centuries in Britain of caring for people in genuine need, but to make provisions that fit the country we have now become. It is nonsense to pretend that our ancient tradition of social care started in 1945, and it is equally nonsense to say that it will be ended by the changes of the 1980s. A 'welfare state' worthy of the name works for the *real* welfare of its citizens. This means that while accepting its obligation to care for the distressed and needy, it also works to encourage the resourcefulness and enterprise that are the true foundation of both personal and national success (Moore, 1988, p.13).

The analysis compresses the term of the mature welfare state between a vague heritage of caring and a current reality depicted as progress. Present changes are justified in terms of claims about past traditions and the diversity of these traditions used to support the argument that cutting back the state is increasing *real* welfare.

A leading article in *The Economist* pursues a similar logic. It opens with the statement: 'Britain's middle classes, so long demoralised and impoverished, are about to grow rich once more'. The two foundations for new wealth are the inheritance of the assets of owner-occupation and the reductions in taxation, especially for the higher income groups. However, this account of the forces making for greater inequality and increased concentration of wealth leads to a critique of the role of the state in welfare: 'the new British bourgeois are setting out on the road to riches mocked by "brahmins" who think that only the state should pay for a revival of culture, urban redevelopment, better education and new hospitals. For new rich and old, the coming challenge is to prove them wrong' (*Economist*, 1988). In the previous example, claims about the past justified policy in the present. In this one, claims about present developments are used to justify particular policy directions in the future, as if the fact of change ruled out political debate about what might be the most desirable state of affairs. In both cases empirical descriptions serve as the support for normative judgements.

This style of argument undermines its own logic. It is hard to see how one can justify taking an account of arrangements at one point in time and endow it with superior status as the basis for judgements about how policy in the future ought to develop, even if one could succeed in securing agreement on what is actually happening in the present, or on what happened in the past. It is possible to produce forceful arguments to support claims about the developments that are likely to follow. However, in order to convert such claims into moral arguments about what the future direction of welfare policy should be, it is essential to include an account of why the circumstances that one wishes to preserve or the changes one wishes to foster are in themselves desirable. This returns us to our starting point, since such an account must involve some discussion of what the ends of policy should be. Aspirations masquerading as description do not provide an escape from normative argument.

Need and social policy

The object of welfare policy is to meet human needs. The most obvious problem is that there is little agreement on how need should be understood and on which needs should be given the highest priority. This undermines the status of need as a justification for state involvement in welfare, since it is difficult to make progress with the claim that welfare states are desirable because they pursue some wide-ranging and ill-defined end. Attempts to construct lists of human needs, of which the most widely-canvassed is Maslow's hierarchy of 'basic needs . . . physiological, safety, love, esteem and self-actualization' (1943, p.395), run into unresolved dispute about the status of particular suggested items, for example, esteem or self-actualization. If the evidence that some suggested needs do not seem to be pressing for some people is taken seriously, then the universality of the listing is eroded and the force of the claim that needs provide the basis for a statement of the moral ends of welfare policy is undermined.

In practice, many of the discussions of need in the social policy literature rest on observation of the use of the notion by policy-makers and professionals. For example, Bradshaw includes normative need defined in terms of expert judgement in his much-quoted 'taxonomy of social need' (1972). Smith rests his account of need on the way in which needs are socially constructed and prioritised in the discourses and practices of professionals (G. Smith, 1988). The problem of finding a secure foundation for the notion of need as the end of welfare policy remains.

Debates about needs often lead to apparently irresolvable conflicts. This has led some writers to see need as an 'essentially contestable concept' in the sense discussed by Gallie (1956) – a concept whose use involves conflict between different political positions (see for example Plant, Lesser and Taylor-Gooby, 1980, p.6). However, a number of approaches seek to establish principles which can be based on aspects of social life which are not contestable in this way. In the field of needs as goals for social welfare policy, a basic principle which has been identified in this way is human freedom. Autonomy is regarded as an essential component in any account of human welfare by a substantial number of writers (see, for example, Plant (1985), Doyal and Gough (1984), Galtung (1980), Soper (1981)).

One weakness of the method pursued in the dominant post-war Anglo-Saxon tradition of conceptual analysis is that it is possible to develop arguments about relationships between ideas without taking into account the social context of the institutions to which those arguments refer. Recent discussion of need may be traced through three stages. The first pursues a purely conceptual argument. The second develops this to take into account the fact that people experience needs and respond to them through social institutions. The third takes this point to its logical conclusion by acknowledging that people not only act through social institutions, but that their own existence as social beings is closely influenced by the social relations in which they participate. The social context of need is therefore double as is implied by the tradition of social theory summed up in Giddens' rules of sociological method: 'structures can always in principle be explained in terms of their *structuration* as a series of reproduced practices. To enquire into the structuration of social practices is to seek to explain how it comes about that structures are constituted through action, and reciprocally how action is constituted structurally' (1976, p.161, rule B2).

All three accounts start out from the principle of respect for persons which underlies Kant's analysis of the prerequisites of a moral life in *Foundations of the Metaphysics of Morals*. Kant conceived of people as citizens of the 'universal realm of ends-in-themselves' (1959, p.82). The idea that morality implied the treatment of people as ends in themselves underlies the second formulation of the categorical imperative:

> now I say man and in general every rational being exists as an end in himself and not merely as a means to be arbitrarily used by this or that will . . . the practical imperative therefore is the following: Act so that you treat humanity, whether in your own person or in that of another always as an end and never as a means only' (pp.46–7).

There is an over-riding obligation to take the ends of others as seriously as you take your own. Insofar as is possible, people should strive to organise social relations so that the basic needs which may underlie the manifold ends of others may be met. The first stage of the development of the theory of needs identifies needs that are essential to any theory of political obligation. More detailed analysis of how these needs might be met in a social context demonstrates that a commitment to redistribute resources against the market is necessary to secure basic needs for the weakest social groups. In short, meeting need presupposes action to guarantee a measure of equality. The third stage takes into account the point that modern individual life is only possible for humans constituted as members of a social organisation which provides them with systems of production, reproduction, authority and culture. The problem now is how to provide a criterion for judging between the vast variety of conceivable systems of social organisation, in order to decide which is most successful in meeting human needs. This problem is resolved by appeal to a Hegelian notion of emancipation.

Human needs I: political theory and conceptual analysis

This approach emerges in a number of discussions of need, which find their natural home in the tradition of political theory that seeks to determine the obligations of state to citizen and citizen to state at the most abstract level. A lucid exposition is provided by Weale. His central concern is to answer one of the basic questions of political philosophy by identifying 'the responsibilities that governments have for securing a particular form of social and economic organisation . . . what government should do to secure the conditions of the good for individual citizens' (1983, p.42). Different theories propose different roles for government. The problem is how to judge between them. The solution is to identify a principle that is basic to any normative political theory, a principle that must be included in a theory of this kind if it is to function as such. Political theory has the task of supplying justifications for political actions – of explaining why citizens should conduct their affairs in a particular way. In order to establish this:

> citizens must be capable of understanding the reasons contained in a political theory, deliberating upon their significance and framing their own plans and actions in accordance with those reasons they judge to be valid . . . autonomous persons are capable of planning and deliberation concerning their actions and projects. Unless a political theory assumed that persons were autonomous in this sense, there would be no point in taking the trouble to construct such a theory (p.45).

Thus all political theory assumes autonomy, whether it likes it or not. This must then be a basic goal of human institutions, for our political understanding to have any relevance to human action within those institutions. Indeed, as Weale points out later, those who reject the idea of autonomy, reject the possibility of the justification of political institutions to their members, and this includes the possibility of their being able to enter into discussion of the legitimacy of the exercise of political power against themselves. It is no good protesting at tyranny, if you don't think people should be free to discuss political arrangements. Those who fail to recognise a basic need for autonomy in effect assent to tyranny.

Weale goes on to present a sophisticated analysis of the implications of this defence of autonomy as a necessary component of any political system capable of justification to the community it embodies. Essentially, he identifies two components of autonomy – that people should regulate 'their conduct in accordance with a public set of principles' and that 'they should be capable of formulating their own projects' within such restrictions and acting to pursue them (pp.50–51). His conclusion is that such principles imply a duty to ensure individual freedom that is stronger than the assertion of negative liberty – freedom from deliberate constraint – identified as the primary obstacle to liberty by many proponents of the free market. However, the obligation is not so strong as to involve a duty on government to ensure absolute equality.

The argument that suggests that negative freedom is inadequate is based on the idea that social and economic circumstances that are not the outcome of deliberate actions by any identifiable individual may nonetheless constrain people's capacity to form and execute life-plans. This leaves such individuals open to coercion by others. For example, poverty deprives many people of access to adequate shelter, heating, nutrition and education, and these are essential to many plausible life-plans in societies which have sufficient resources to provide these things. Such individuals are vulnerable to exploitation because the urgency of hunger leaves few alternatives. Delphy's analysis of the exploitation of women's unpaid domestic work through the ownership of their labour by men in marriage rests on the claim that women are forced to submit to such an arrangement because, for the most part, they can only command a relatively low standard of living through their own employment (1984, p.71–4). However, it is not clear that autonomy in Weale's sense requires economic equality. It is acceptable for individuals to have different levels of economic power, provided the position of the worst off is not so miserable that the more fortunate are in a position to coerce them.

From this perspective the question of how far the state should intervene in the allocation of resources becomes very much an issue dependent on empirical analysis of the operation of the social system in question. A system of free and independent producers – for example the model envisaged by Marx in some of his earlier writings (Marx and Engels, 1976, p.54) – might require little state involvement, since each individual would command the resources sufficient to guarantee autonomy – although there would presumably be a role in guaranteeing allocation within households if these were to be the producer units. However, in advanced capitalist societies, there is a strong role for the state, since economic inequalities often enable capital to coerce unemployed people, and differences in social and economic power enable adults to coerce children and men to coerce women. Thus it is possible to argue for state intervention on the grounds pursued by such writers as Furniss and Tilton (1979), Pateman (1989) and Tawney (1935) – that it enhances individual liberty – and to strengthen the claim by arguing that it is a moral obligation.

Weale develops his argument to make a powerful case for the provision of a basic level of income security and an education system that placed a high priority on equality of opportunity as essential components in a modern welfare state.

Human needs II: conceptual analysis in a social context

The second stage in discussion of basic needs starts out from a comparable position – the Kantian principle of 'respect for persons' as the basis of understanding social need – and develops a similar argument. However, it pursues a route that is concerned more with the conceptual analysis of the requirements that must be met in order for needs to be satisfied than with the unexamined presumptions of any political theory that might be used to justify social arrangements. Such a course involves paying greater attention to the social context in which individual claims to resources based on need are developed. As a result, the argument arrives at a stronger egalitarian position as the proper role for government. Plant has developed and expanded such an approach in work that provides the single most influential analysis of social need among the social policy community.

The starting point of the argument is that needs are not ends in themselves, but may be thought of as means to particular goals. People need resources, services, help in order to achieve the projects that they lay down for themselves. An immediate problem concerns how we are to evaluate the different goals that people may choose – a difficulty analogous to the political theorist's problem of constructing a basic criterion to apply to different models of social arrangements. If we cannot provide some way of producing a morally defensible list of needs, the whole project of constructing a foundation for the welfare state as a social system to meet need collapses into relativism. Anybody's conception of need is as good as anybody else's.

The solution follows the arguments of the preceding section.

Basic human needs are identified on the grounds that these are essential prerequisites of any goal-directed behaviour, regardless of what the goal might be. 'These needs might be regarded generally as physical well-being and autonomy; an individual would have to be able to function efficiently as a physical entity and have freedom to deliberate and choose between alternatives if he is to pursue any conception of the good' (1985, p.18). The social context in which individuals meet needs now enters into the argument: these notions immediately imply access to health-care and education. Survival does not enable people to make sensible choices if there is no attempt to guarantee a reasonable level of physical functioning, and choice demands knowledge of one's own capacities and of relevant alternatives.

Thus far there is a close comparability between this argument and Weale's position. Plant emphasises the issue of physical survival, which does not figure in Weale's account. However, it seems reasonable to assume that the pursuit of autonomy in Weale's model implies survival on the grounds that dead people are not free to pursue plans, and indeed the point may seem so obvious as to hardly merit discussion. In addition, survival is not specifically a prerequisite of moral action, such as making the choices implied by acceptance of political obligation or pursuing a conception of the good life. It is equally essential for any technical activity such as making curtains, or playing draughts. Thus it may be thought of as a secondary issue in this debate. However, substantial numbers of people fail to survive who otherwise might and the quality of individual survival varies considerably. When these points, which become apparent from the social context in which needs are met are highlighted, the level of survival becomes a matter of interest. This leads to a strong case for access to medical and social care.

The analysis goes on to offer an account of autonomy that implies a stronger commitment to equality than the previous version. The negative notion of freedom is rejected for two further reasons in addition to the argument developed above. This pointed out that constraint by both impersonal social forces and the deliberate actions of identifiable individuals may infringe personal freedom. The first argument turns on a distinction between the foreseeable and the intended consequences of actions.

It is not unreasonable to expect people to anticipate the likely consequences of their actions, whether they intend them or not. These depend, among other things, on institutional structure. For example, a consumer may not intend to exploit the labour of Californian 'wet-backs', yet that may be the unintended consequences of the choices made at the supermarket. Universities who impose qualification hurdles may not intend to discriminate against working-class people in access to courses. Employers who fail to provide child-care may not intend to bias recruitment against mothers. However, such discrimination is likely to be the result of their policies. Once we know that social class is related to educational attainment (Halsey, Heath and Ridge, 1980, pp.55–65), or that mothers of young children who do not have child-care available are much less likely to be engaged in paid work (Martin and Roberts, 1984, p.19) this result is foreseeable.

Plant argues that foreseeable constraint is just as much an infringement of autonomy as intended constraint, since it has precisely the same effect. The goal of autonomy requires that government should seek to eradicate it. This consideration enlarges the scope of state activity substantially, since there are many transactions in which inequality leads to foreseeable constraint although it is not intended, as the examples seek to illustrate.

The second argument that there should be a positive effort to achieve equality in the satisfaction of need is more direct.

> . . . an unequal distribution of the resources required to meet such needs could only be justified if the state took the view that the goals and purposes of some persons were of so much less value than those of others that they should have a lesser share in the resources, or more extremely that some persons are so clearly of intrinsically less worth than others that they deserve a lesser share (p.19).

Both these principles are in direct contravention of the notion of 'respect for persons'. The advocate of the limitation of state welfare in a way that advances inequality is required to explain why some people counted for less or for more in resource allocation.

Moral arguments may be produced in particular cases to show why this might be so. For example, the author of an influential book on freedom and equality points out:

'To each according to his need' . . . this is in itself an egalitarian principle . . . if some people have special needs, special provision should be made for them so as to bring them as close as possible to the general standard enjoyed by their fellows (Norman, 1987, p.114).

The example discussed is a person who is disabled and requires much greater medical and social care resources than someone who is not, to enjoy a worthwhile life. The principle of meeting human need turns into a principle of equality, justifying unequal allocation to ensure an equal worth of life. Similarly, it is argued that systematically disadvantaged groups (for example, women) require extra resources to be able to exercise autonomy to the same extent as others (Pateman, 1989, p.197) although the exact level required is hard to establish in practice. There may also be practical arguments that justify a degree of inequality on the grounds that this will foster growth and enable a higher (though still unequal) level of need satisfaction all round (Rawls, 1973). However, such arguments are extremely difficult to develop in a way that is not subject to conflict. The appropriate levels of equality and inequality cannot be prejudged by appeal to analysis of the notion of needs.

Plant argues that for this reason such dispute is the stuff of political debate. Any attempt to de-politicise it is idle. The result then is a presumption in favour of state intervention to provide equal satisfaction of basic needs, unless good reason can be shown why this should not be so.

Human needs III: the social construction of social need

Human life is doubly structured by the social context of individual existence. Individuals make choices, and experience the social circumstances in which they find themselves as constraint, as moulding the opportunities available to them. At the same time, the mass of human action in interaction with nature contributes to the construction of the social circumstances in which agency is located. The third stage in accounts of basic human need acknowledges the double structure of the social context. It attempts to take into account not only the differential influence of

social circumstances on different people's capacity to live autonomously, but also the way in which social institutions contribute
to the production of individuals as social animals. This has
substantial implications both in terms of the way in which need is
conceptualised and of the obligations on governments to meet it.

A good example of this approach is a recent study by Doyal and
Gough. Their argument acknowledges its roots in the work of
Kant on personhood and moral agency as developed by Plant *et al.*
(1980) and Galtung (1980), and starts out from a similar account of
human action.

> In order to act successfully, people . . . need physically to survive
> and need enough sense of their own identity or autonomy to initiate
> actions on the basis of their deliberations. Survival and autonomy
> are therefore basic needs: they are both conceptual and empirical
> preconditions for the achievement of *other* goals (1984, p.15).

Following a road similar to that traversed by Plant, Doyal and
Gough go on to expand the notion of survival to embrace good
health, and that of autonomy to include a process of learning
which will enable individuals to practise their autonomy successfully.
They recognise the problems inherent in cultural definitions of
health and successful learning but argue that there exist minimum
levels of functioning and awareness both of one's own potential
and of social conditions below which successful autonomous action
is not possible. Thus the needs for health and education are
initially established at a basic level.

At this stage the argument departs from the logic of previous
approaches. The difference is that society is understood not just as
the context in which autonomous action will take place, but as the
set of institutions which constitute individuals as choosing agents.
In this sense, basic needs are socially constructed. People do not
exist as independent and autonomous Robinson Crusoes. This is
true in at least two ways. First as empirical fact: action and
learning involve highly sophisticated inter-personal communication
skills. They involve operation within a context where social
interaction is essential to make available the resources needed for
survival and the pursuit of individual projects.

The identification of the essential elements of the social context
of human life has been one of the basic enterprises of academic
sociology. The argument draws on the functionalism of Parsons,

dynamised in the systems theory of Luhman and Habermas to distinguish four basic categories of social institution. Material production involving the organised activity of many people is essential to survival. We exist in time, and the reproduction of society through the up-bringing and education of a new generation of adults involves the co-ordination of a whole range of individual activities. Notions of communication, socialisation and tradition presuppose a culture at the level of values which admits of debate and consent. Political authority is essential for the co-ordination of human interaction and acceptance of the operation of these systems. In complex societies, material production, the reproduction and socialisation of the young and the process of recognition and justification of authority are all collective activities. Thus individual needs for survival and autonomy generate needs for systems of production, reproduction, communication and authority that are organised on a social basis.

The argument develops these points through conceptual analysis. Selfhood is the starting point for the account of basic needs, for these are the essential prerequisites of action by the self. Our whole notion of self and of the self as acting autonomously involves a range of collective activities. The language which we use for communication is a social phenomenon. This is true not simply in the empirical sense that language use is a social activity. Since the later work of Wittgenstein, it is widely accepted that the notion of a purely private language is self-contradictory, since there is no way in which a single consciousness could check the accuracy of the rules by which the reference of words to things in the world is established. If the use of a rule cannot be checked, it makes no sense to describe it as a rule (Wittgenstein, 1958, sections 265–9). There is no natural force which sticks descriptors onto the objects to which they apply, in the way magnets hold play-letters on the fridge door to tell my child: 'this is a fridge'. The reference of terms can only be established through the social activity of their successful shared use in communication. The system of roles through which we define ourselves by rejecting, accepting and modifying is a collective cultural artefact, not an individual product. In societies involving division of labour, material production (which makes possible the generation of a surplus above the requirements of mere physical survival to finance the whole system of allocation according to need) involves co-ordinated social activity. Similarly the reproduction of the existing generation is carried out in the context of cultural traditions and shared or questioned systems of norms. The operation of complex production systems and the maintenance of culture presupposes a measure of obedience to an overall authority.

These categories of social needs – production, reproduction, communication and authority – follow the lists of essential features of society developed by analysts operating at the most general level – for example, Talcott Parson's production, socialisation, value and pattern maintenance systems, or Habermas' identification of economic, social and political levels with inputs of factors of production, values and collective goals, and outputs of material goods, motivations and authority respectively. Individual existence implies the satisfaction of needs derived from social existence. The argument now seeks to go beyond the location of individual needs in a social context to evaluate the success of different social arrangements in satisfying human needs. The social context is not simply a formal requirement, but something that enters directly into the moral delineation of needs, so that there is an obligation to provide the most satisfactory social arrangements. This poses a number of problems. Most significant is the fact that the approach now requires a criterion for the success of social systems that is not rooted itself in a particular system. It must avoid the problem of cultural relativism. Without such a criterion, the satisfaction of needs will ultimately have to be judged in terms of criteria that are relative to a particular society. The problem is analogous to the much-discussed pitfall of functionalism – that it represents individual action as the passive product of a particular pattern of social systems and writes human agency out of history. This would be a troubled conclusion for an approach that sought to identify the normative preconditions for human agency in a social context.

Hegel and the need for emancipation

The argument identifies a universal human need for *liberation*, which can be defined in a way independent from the arrangements of a particular social system. Liberation is defined as 'the process of learning and the ability to put it into practice' (Doyal and Gough, 1984, p.23).

This approach draws on the notions of human need and human liberation expressed in Hegel's account of self-transformation through action on the physical world as the gateway to freedom, refracted through Marx's analysis of human social labour. In a celebrated passage in the *Phenomenology of Spirit*, which Marx regarded as the 'true birthplace and secret of Hegelian philosophy', Hegel discusses the social development of human self-consciousness in interaction with the natural world through an account of the relationship between an abstracted and generalised Master and Slave. This is a relationship in which dependence and independence are not simply separated – the Slave being the dependant of the Master – but are intertwined and finally reversed:

> just when the master has effectively achieved lordship, he finds that something has come about quite different from an independent consciousness. It is not an independent, but rather a dependent consciousness that he has achieved . . . . The truth of the independent consciousness is accordingly the consciousness of the bondsman (1976, p.47).

Although the master has political power, he or she is dependent on the servant for access to the means of enjoyment from the physical world, whereas the servant must interact with nature and defines his or her own self in relation to it through this process. 'Through work and labour, however, this consciousness of the bondsman comes to itself . . . the consciousness that toils and serves attains by this means the direct apprehension of that independent being as itself' (pp.48–9). It is through work on the physical world that it is possible to attain knowledge of what one can achieve, of one's potential and limitations. If this is generalised, it is the labour of the human race through the investigations of science and philosophy that reveals human potential. The grand project of Hegel's philosophical opus is to trace out the trajectory of the development of the human spirit until it attains the liberation of Absolute Spirit. 'Man forms himself, comes to realize his own essence in the attempt to dominate and transform nature . . . for Hegel the role of work and its products is mainly to create and sustain a universal consciousness in man' (Taylor, 1979, p.50).

This analysis operates entirely at the level of ideas. For Hegel, emancipatory work was concerned primarily with the generation of knowledge through science and philosophy, and it was progress at this level that would liberate humanity. Following the young

Hegelian movement, Marx emphasised the role of physical work on the natural world as the core of humanity's emancipatory task. Material, rather than intellectual production was the key to analysing the progress of humanity. Social formations were to be understood in terms of the development of the means of production and (later Marxists would add) reproduction. This is the primary determinant of patterns of political authority and of culture.

Exploitation and emancipation

Marx went on to develop an account of the social impact of collective human labour that redoubled the force of the negative moment in Hegel's dialectic. Just as emancipation from brute want can be attained through the development of human productive activity, so can the mechanism of oppression be remade in the institutions of social labour that people construct to enhance their productivity. In most societies, the mechanism of exploitation is more or less explicit – slavery, feudal labour obligations, the corvee-system. In market capitalism however, exploitation takes place through a system of apparently free exchange of labour and goods, where wages and prices are not imposed externally, but decided by market forces. The reduction of goods to the status of commodities obscures the relation of individuals as consumers to the collective productive activity of humanity. All that really matters to the consumer is getting the goods they want at the best price. The relation between purchaser as individual and item purchased takes the foreground and diverts attention from the fact that purchase places that individual in relationship with the community that produced it, so that attention to the working conditions of the person who picks the tea you buy, for example, requires a theoretical effort. The market system enables enormous progress to be made at the material level by the advanced capitalist societies. This is at the cost of the exploitation of the members of those societies through their participation in the apparatus of progress.

The opportunities for exploitation involved in the expansion of humanity's collective productive activity indicate that work cannot be understood as simply and effortlessly liberating. The intellectual level of analysis emphasised by Hegel is also required to enable people to understand the social institutions they have created and to use them for their own liberation. Doyal and Gough already face the problem of how the best knowledge is to be identified and applied in meeting human needs in the most emancipating way, since their social perspective requires that people have access to the best method of meeting the needs. Marx's analysis adds the difficulty that the world of work contains a concealed reality of the conflict of class interests. Efficient production technologies may carry with them real costs in the social arrangements they foster.

Marx himself used the idealised criterion of the organisation of a future socialist society of abundance in order to assess current social arrangements, but the road to such a society seems longer now than when he wrote. The obstacles on the way have grown more severe with the loss of confidence in the capacity of science to develop material production to an adequate level without transgressing ecological limits. Thus the application of an account of basic human need that rests on the extension of needs from the individual to the social level and the dynamising of social accounts by appeal to notions of emancipation and progress seems unable to produce an unambiguous criterion for the identification of social changes which will enable people to satisfy their needs more effectively.

These considerations may seem to imply that any attempt to relate human needs to social order is doomed to failure, since we have no sure way of identifying the social order which is most successful in meeting its members' needs in the long term. This is unfortunate. Once we acknowledge that the satisfaction of human needs is dependent on social factors, we can make little progress without finding a way of discussing these issues. However, the key idea of the approach – the Hegelian argument that the more we learn about what we are capable of doing, the more we learn about ourselves – carries considerable force. The dialectic of the Master–Servant relationship is resolved in the process whereby the Servant through working on nature and discovering how to pursue successful creativity in that work is able to develop an authentic independence. As Doyal and Gough put it 'we discover what is arbitrary about the social and natural world (e.g. slavery or supernaturalistic accounts of killer diseases) and what is not arbitrary (e.g. the need for literacy to have access to different cultural traditions, or the necessity to drink unpolluted water to stay healthy)' (1984, p.23 – see Norman, 1976, Chapters 5 and 6). Unless we are to capitulate to a relativism that makes certainty impossible, it seems there must be levels of understanding which are superior to others, because they work better. Progress can then be understood in terms of the movement towards superior accounts. The problem lies in deciding what they are.

A partial solution lies in the application of reason and scientific method to the understanding of causal processes, as in the examples in the last paragraph. These may lead to what many would construe as progress in a way that challenges relativistic accounts of knowledge. For example, consider a 'characteristic disease of underdevelopment that could be cured or prevented by the application of western technology' (Doyal and Gough, 1984, p.24). Access to such technology then becomes a need because the disease damages both survival and autonomy and somewhere on the planet, the human race has found a way to cope with it. If political, cultural or production limitations prevent people learning of or applying such knowledge then there is a liberational need to overstep the boundaries of the culture.

This of course does not guarantee that particular accounts – for example, those based on western science – will always be superior, nor that such approaches can always be translated into practice without producing further problems. However, there are real liberational needs defined by the possibility of such knowledge. The core argument is that people will always be in a better position if they have access to such knowledge than if they do not. Then they are at least in a position to discuss the consequences of applying it.

Individual need-satisfaction requires the satisfaction of social needs at the optimum level to enable progress in the direction defined by the need for liberation to take place, as far as can be achieved at the level of development of the society. The success of a society in meeting human needs may be judged by its ability to organise production, reproduction, communication and authority systems in a way that maximises the opportunity to develop and apply emancipatory knowledge in satisfying the basic needs of survival and autonomy. Thus the notion of human need is at once made social and dynamic. Doyal and Gough go on to discuss the constitutional arrangements most likely to achieve this and the communicational requirements implied by the need for technical progress.

This argument leads to the conclusion that any account of human need must also include analysis of the organisational and constitutional arrangements of society, in particular, provisions for the application of available knowledge. This leads to a notion of liberation similar to that developed by Habermas (see especially 1970 and 1973, postscript). Communication should be unbiased by social interests which distort the expression and application of knowledge – as, for example, the interests of men against women have succeeded in limiting the discussion of and access to liberating reproductive technology.

These arguments operate purely at the level of constitutional form. While requirements for the process whereby decisions should be made can be stated, there is no analogous process for stipulating the substance of the decisions. The perspective on human needs in the social context leads through an account of the significance of social institutions in the production of individual social life to the conclusion that emancipatory learning is a human need, and that it can only be realised through political debate under social forms which allow the maximum of freedom.

Conclusion: the social basis of human need

The work of the writers discussed above starts out from the notion that there are human needs which are basic in the sense that they are prerequisite to any moral life. Further analysis shows that such needs must include the principle of autonomy, as the cornerstone of a social order in which political authority admits of legitimation. It then demonstrates that the category of needs must include access to services which will advance survival and good health to ensure equal respect for the 'plans of life' advanced by different people. Finally, the social context of the argument is developed to show that the satisfaction of individual needs presumes a social need for liberation through progress and through the development of institutions that enable such progress to be maximised. The normative notion of need may be used as a criterion for assessing social policy arrangements.

These approaches leave the actual arrangements for meeting

need very much up to the operation of the political system. Weale writes, 'ultimately, persons are the best judges of their own welfare' (1983, p.28).

The basic principle in the theory we have been developing . . . requires that the material conditions for autonomy be secured for all persons . . . . No significance is attached to the common goals of the political community . . . such common goals as there are emerge from the process whereby individuals form their own social identity and develop their own projects and plans (1983, p.198).

For Plant: 'there are clear limits to what can be settled by philosophical argument – and in the case of both civil and welfare rights this limit is reached once we have established that the state has a duty to protect both sorts of rights . . . . All the rest is politics' (1985, p.29). For Doyal and Gough: 'universal human liberation has been shown to be a cogent though open-ended concept . . . the struggle for liberation . . . will entail critical and democratic communication which is directed towards this end and no other' (1984, p.32).

Clearly, there are strict limits to how far those who rest their case on a basic human need for autonomy can go in specifying the needs that individuals should pursue, whether they see the collective political level as simply the sum of the individual plans, as does Weale, the medium in which interest-groups struggle, as does Plant, or as an essential part of the cluster of social institutions which constitutes individuals as beings who are able to make plans, as do Doyal and Gough. Once needs are established as carrying moral force, it is necessary to consider what this implies for individual rights against the government. Otherwise, it is perfectly possible to accept the case that human needs are an essential and morally compelling component of human welfare, but to suggest that this carries no implications at all for the practice of the welfare state.

The argument that moral obligation embraces not only the satisfaction of basic need, but also policy to ensure an equality of provision, so that the equal worth of the life-plans of different individuals is respected equally, implies a substantial role for government. Basic needs may be fulfilled through market systems with the state guaranteeing, subsidising and regulating services. It is in principle possible to imagine arrangements that will nudge the mixed economy in the direction of greater equality, for example through vouchers, or the mandation of benefits for weaker groups on employers. These are arguments that chime in tune with the sociological disquiet at the extent of state intervention described in Chapter Six. However, intervention that relies on the use of market mechanisms must continually struggle against the pressure of the pattern of unequal interests that exists in patriarchal, market society. In addition, the argument that social needs include a need for emancipatory political arrangements requires that the state should guarantee the existence of a policy-making forum in which citizens may debate the pattern of provision, with conditions as to access to knowledge and freedom of speech that are not trivial. The presumption of the discussion of social need is therefore in favour of the retention and extension of the system of direct welfare state provision. In the next chapter we consider arguments about the scope and practice of welfare rights derived from discussion of social citizenship.

CHAPTER 8

CITIZENSHIP AND MORAL HAZARD

The liberty of the individual must be thus far limited: he must not make himself a nuisance to other people.

J.S. Mill

Citizenship and welfare rights

Basic human needs are established as human rights by the argument of the previous chapter. This chapter considers the question of whether they are to be seen as rights against the state – as components of citizenship. The history of the welfare state is the story of the development and defence of citizenship welfare rights. This chapter discusses whether theoretical arguments provide a justification for direct state intervention in pursuit of welfare.

The notion of citizenship has been approached in varying ways by commentators from a left, right and more recently a feminist perspective. A basic distinction is between *substantive* and *procedural* approaches and this cuts across the different political standpoints. Substantive theories conceive of citizenship in terms of participation in the communal and political life of society. The status of citizen ultimately derives from shared values and the enjoyment of opportunities to take part in organic communal activities. The role of government is to enhance such opportunities. Marshall, for example, argues that citizenship: 'requires a direct sense of community membership based on loyalty to a civilisation which is a common possession' (1950, p.92). Such an approach finds roots in the paradigm of Athenian participative democracy and is developed in the work of Rousseau and more recently syndicalists such as Cole, feminists such as Benton and Pateman and egalitarians such as Norman.

Procedural approaches tend to define citizenship in terms of a bundle of basic rights possessed by the individual by virtue of being a citizen, and defended by government. This view was initially developed by British empiricist philosophers, such as Locke. The role of government is circumscribed to the defence of a limited range of rights. Any attempt to move beyond this is seen as *ultra vires*, and often as a damaging infringement of the liberty of the individual. The implications of a radical version of this approach are spelt out by Nozick in a famous passage:

> Our main conclusions about the state are that a minimal state, limited to the narrow functions of protection against force, theft, fraud, enforcement of contracts, and so on, is justified; and that the minimal state is inspiring as well as right. Two noteworthy implications are that the state may not use its coercive apparatus for the purpose of getting some citizens to aid others, or in order to prohibit activities to people for their *own* good or protection (1974, p.ix).

Some defenders of state welfare take a more wide-ranging view of the appropriate list of obligations incumbent on government. However, their analysis shares the notion that citizenship is a matter of claiming rights, not of participation in a collectivity (see for example, Weale, 1983, pp.132–8). Since welfare rights have often been seen as resting on a notion of social solidarity and cohesion and differential access to particular welfare services and benefits acts as a membership badge for citizenship, we will first consider the way in which substantive approaches define citizenship rights.

Substantive rights and political analysis

The political right has approached substantive notions of citizenship from two directions. First, a number of writers define citizenship in terms of participation in shared values – without them an individual cannot be a full citizen. In practical politics this view appears most clearly in the demand that immigrant groups abandon their own cultural values and undergo a process of assimilation in order to be accepted as full members of the host community. Such an approach has a long history in British social policy, summed up for example in the 1962 statement of the Commonwealth Immigration Advisory Service that: 'a national [education] system cannot be expected to perpetuate the different values of immigrant groups' (Lynch, 1986, p.44). In a similar vein, a recent prime minister stated: 'we are a British nation with British characteristics. Every nation can take some minorities . . . but the moment a minority threatens to become a big one, people get frightened . . . people are really rather afraid that this country might be swamped by people of a different culture' (Thatcher, 1978). In other words, membership of the club requires that you wear the right colour tie.

A second more positive approach develops the notion of 'active citizenship' defined as 'local people working together to improve their own quality of life and to provide conditions for others to enjoy the fruits of a more affluent society' (R. Pahl, 1990, p.8). Citizenship is something to be 'encouraged' rather than taken as of right (Speaker's Commission on Citizenship, 1990). This perspective implies that individual citizenship may be a matter of degree. It depends on the extent to which the individual participates in and contributes to the life of the community: 'the active citizen can be defined as someone who cares, but who gives expression to their caring in a quantifiable way' (Patten, 1988 quoted in Lister, 1990, p.456). Those who help most are most strongly included; those who do not have the weakest hold on citizenship and, by implication, are least deserving of access to common services. Since the caring must be a deliberate expression of personal choice, a gift to charity counts for more than paying a compulsorily exacted tax.

Left wing approaches to substantive citizenship are concerned with the extent to which a common culture can be generated and expressed through collective activity. There are strong demands for political participation so that individuals may have the opportunity to shape and contribute to the expression of this culture. Some traditions of socialism, especially those most strongly informed by the notion that political dominion by a cohesive working class was a likely outcome of the organization of workers through large-scale manufacture in capitalist production systems, express this idea. Others contend that the articulation of working-class community requires a more active programme. Gramsci argued that a proletarian movement 'must be organized as a "counter-hegemonic" project: as an alternative society, countering and replacing bourgeois ideas and practices in all aspects of life' (Dunleavy and O'Leary, 1987, p.233). The appeal to solidarity is also embodied in the 'English' socialism of Benn (1980) and others which draws on the tradition of social movements such as the Levellers with their commitment to communality, and finds its recent philosophical expression in the work of writers such as Norman. For Marquand 'citizenship is nothing if it is not public. The notion of the citizen implies a notion of the city – of the *polis*, of the public realm' (1988). In this realm, the citizen must act to further the common good.

Feminist writers have been extremely active in developing substantive notions of citizenship, for two reasons. First, women are excluded from many social and political activities either through direct discrimination or indirectly, by low income and by the demands that domestic tasks make on their time (Benton, 1988). Full social participation is an essential feature of citizenship for both men and women. Equal participation depends on the recognition that women's unpaid work is as essential to the attainment of the basic social goals of production and reproduction as men's paid employment. Rights and obligations must be redefined, especially in the field of social care, to enable women to play an equal social role (Pateman, 1989, pp.202–3). Similarly, the institutions of democracy in local government, trade unions and political parties must be restructured to allow women to play a full role in what have been predominantly male preserves (Rowbotham, Segal and Wainwright, 1979).

The second feminist argument extends the scope of debate by re-examining notions of dependence and independence. The procedural notion of citizenship offers a model of rights which permits women to gain access to services and which imposes obligations on men, so that equal individual citizenship is achieved. As Mouffe argues 'we must promote a new awareness of rights to be secured by all citizens independently of their location in the production process . . . thus establishing that *qua* citizens we do not have only political rights but also economic and social rights' (1988). The next question concerns how independence is to be used. For writers like Lister this involves consideration of power: 'ultimately the question of dependency and citizenship cannot be divorced from that of power, for true citizenship will mean women operating as subjects and not objects' (1990, p.464). Substantive feminist critiques of the traditional literature argue that equal rights will allow citizens of both sexes to achieve an interdependence in which neither is dominant and both are valued equally.

Substantive notions of citizenship are essentially ambivalent in their implications for the practice of state welfare. Some inter-pretations support the participative and interventionist welfare policy advocated by Marquand, whereas others justify a citizenship active in the sphere of neighbourliness and charity rather than in collective welfare channelled through government. The question now arises of how far the approach can be developed to give an account of welfare citizenship.

Dilemmas of substantive rights

Norman develops an ingenious argument in support of the view that a participatory democracy would support measures designed to foster social equality (1987, Chapter 5). The initial starting point is the basic theme of co-operation expressed in Rawls' theory of justice: 'since everybody's well-being depends on a scheme of co-operation without which no one could have a satisfactory life, the division of advantages should be such as to draw forth the willing co-operation of everyone taking part in it' (Rawls, 1973, p.15).

Rawls' own analysis of the notion of willing co-operation operates at the level of abstract theory through an attempt to second-guess the content of a hypothetical contract drawn up without benefit of vested interests behind a 'veil of ignorance'. The argument tries to envisage the pattern of advantage and disad-vantage that people would attach to different social roles if they were ignorant of which roles they would themselves come to occupy. His solution to the problem has been extensively criticised, because he assumes a fundamental caution, which he equates with rationality:

looking at the situation from the standpoint of one person . . . it is not reasonable for him to expect more than an equal share in the division of social goods, and since it is not rational for him to agree to less, the sensible thing for him to do is to acknowledge as the first principle of social justice one requiring an equal distribution. Indeed this principle is so obvious that we would expect it to occur to anyone immediately (1973, p.151).

Unfortunately, it is not unreasonable to be selfish and to gamble, provided the odds are right (as the experience of privatisation share issues demonstrates). For example, one could legislate for luxury for half the population (or women, or blacks), and slavery for the rest in the hope that one will end up in the advantaged group when social roles are shared out (see Barry, 1973, p.17; Dennis, 1975, pp.263–5). The abstract approach forfeits the use of arguments about how people might choose to act in an existing co-operative arrangement. Norman chooses for his analysis a paradigm case based in the real world:

imagine, for instance, a number of people who have decided to share a house and who have to decide on the apportioning of the tasks necessary to keep the house in good order – who is to do the cooking, who the cleaning and so on . . . we need only assume that they are genuinely and fully committed to working in co-operation (1987, p.69).

The crucial difference from Rawls' perspective is that in this case tasks and benefits are shared out between participants in a world they actually inhabit. There is no veil of ignorance: people are deciding which roles they will occupy in relation to each other, taking into account existing preferences. Norman's conclusion is that, *provided they are committed to co-operation*, people will decide by making sure that all views are taken into account: 'if all the members of the group are committed to working together co-operatively, they will see to it that everyone's interests are taken into account and no-one's interests are sacrificed to those of others' (p.70).

Such a situation is very different from the context of interactions about the distribution of resources in welfare state societies where political debates especially those concerning citizenship are often acrimonious, and where political groupings devote considerable efforts to excluding others from decision making. It is a probable outcome in a community where notions of membership extend beyond the defence of a bundle of purely individual rights to notions of mutuality and sharing – a commitment to participation. This is surely what a substantive notion of citizenship implies.

The object of the exercise is to highlight the significance of co-operation in social arrangements. The net result is a presumption in favour of equality: 'everyone carries an equal share of the burdens necessary for producing these collective goods. No-one benefits disproportionately by enjoying the collective benefits plus the additional benefit of not having to contribute their share of time and effort'. The Kantian principle of respect for persons requires an active involvement in discussion of contribution and preference. This exercise mirrors many of the features of Doyal and Gough's account of need. It moves from the basic notion of respect for others to the constitutional and communicative requirements of achieving a context in which a genuine and co-operative discussion is possible without the detailed analysis of social arrangements to facilitate the meeting of individual needs.

Citizenship in the co-operative community involves participative democracy. The commitment to co-operate will lead to a substantial measure of equality in the policies that are collectively pursued. When translated to a broader context, this argument suggests a major role for government in the direct provision of welfare, because states are likely to be better than non-state systems at moving in the direction of equality, as the argument of Chapter Six and the evidence presented in Chapter Two showed. However, the case is not entirely compelling. Co-operators could always choose to express citizenship through a commitment to the central regulation and supervision of private arrangements. While substantive arguments make a strong case for a high degree of citizen involvement in policy making and for the egalitarian distribution of burdens and benefits, they do not show that government needs to be directly concerned with the supply of services. We move on to consider procedural arguments.

Procedural analysis: civil and political versus social and economic rights

Many liberals argue that social and economic rights are different in kind from other categories of right. The argument is a head-on attack on rights-based citizenship theories of welfare entitlement: this perspective rules welfare rights out of court. Arguments against the assimilation of welfare to the traditional positive civil and political rights may be summed up under three headings. These concern the obligations that the recognition of welfare rights imposes on others, their indeterminacy, and the problems of incentive and responsibility associated with them.

The first objection claims that traditional civil rights are negative in the sense that they involve no *obligation* for action by others. They merely insist that others refrain from action, for example, from theft of one's property, denial of freedom of speech, false imprisonment and the like. Welfare rights imply that others must act in a positive way, typically through the payment of taxes and the allocation of the revenue raised to the needy (Cranston, 1976, p.141). However, it is not clear that this distinction withstands close examination, as a prominent liberal critic of the welfare state points out (Barry, 1990, p.79). Even negative political and civil rights can involve a substantial commitment of state expenditure. Government must act to ensure that some groups do not trample the rights of others. It is utopian to imagine that an agreement to maintain civil rights by refraining from action will stand when it is against the interests of the powerful, as the gingerbread man discovered. The maintenance of law and order at an admittedly unsatisfactory level in the UK costs more than twice as much as child benefit, and defence costs more than schools (HM Treasury, 1990).

In addition, the equal enjoyment of civil and political rights depends on social and economic rights in an unequal society. If some groups are better educated than others they will be better able to exercise their vote. If poorer people have access to a minimal standard of living, they will be less vulnerable to crass electoral bribery. Feminist writers have drawn particular attention to the extra demands made on women's time by the double-shift of care-work and paid-work and argued that this contributes to women's lower political participation (Nelson, 1984, p.217). Lower income mitigates against the use of civil rights at law in a market system where the best lawyers are not free.

The second problem of welfare rights – *indeterminacy* – is clearly stated by Barry: 'if one believes in the incommensurability and diversity of values it is strictly impossible to incorporate the various "well-beings" into one authoritative pattern' (1990, p.80).

However, this is precisely the problem that the discussion of need in Chapter Seven was designed to solve. The answer has two parts: first there are basic needs to survival and autonomy that can be established because they are preconditions of any moral life and derive from the requirement that people should be treated as ends in themselves – as moral agents. Secondly, the argument established that individual liberation involved the organisation of society to give people access to the best possible knowledge, yet also showed that it was impossible to establish *a priori* what this might be. The theory thus requires constitutional arrangements to enable the democratic discussion of different approaches, without being able to specify in advance the outcome of that discussion. This is unsatisfactory for those who look for a definitive list of the welfare obligations of government, but that does not make it incoherent. In any case, welfare rights are not necessarily any less consistent than civil rights. The basis of the right is firmly established in both cases. It is the level at which need should be met that is the subject for political dispute, as are methods for guaranteeing access to the law.

Finally, it is claimed that the granting of positive rights to welfare generates problems of *incentive and moral hazard*. To give someone a right to welfare assumes entitlement, regardless of how the need emerges. This opens up the road to scroungers who will exercise welfare rights rather than toil in order to subsist, and will speedily bankrupt the collective purse to the detriment of all. Empirical evidence indicates that the problem of moral hazard is less severe than many liberals imply. The most striking example is the American Seattle and Denver Income Maintenance Experiments in the 1970s which made social dividend benefits available to individuals without a work test in a society where last resort welfare is normally dispensed under the most stringent conditions. Analysis of the results is not without controversy, but even the most pessimistic accounts indicate that poor groups with guaranteed access to benefit were only slightly less likely to seek paid work than those without (Wilson, 1987, pp.184–5). More generally, George and Wilding conclude from an extensive review of the evidence that 'social services are only one of many factors that affect people's willingness to work, and the same volume of social spending can be found in countries with high, medium and low rates of economic growth . . . . Excessive concern with the possible disincentive effects of social policy distracts attention from its positive aspects and creates a climate of opinion for reductions in social service provision' (1984, p.186; see also Ringen, 1987). An authoritative review of the evidence is provided by Atkinson (1987, Section 5.3).

This defence provides an empirical rather than a theoretical answer to the problem and as such is not entirely satisfactory. The low incidence of counterproductive incentive may be due to the relatively low rate of the benefits paid in most systems, in comparison with wages, and the severity with which welfare rights are policed. It is difficult to convince the determined critic of the right to welfare that the availability of non-market income in a market society will not have some effect on people's willingness to undergo the pain of labour. The problem is particularly pressing for those who justify welfare on grounds of need and go on to make a strong egalitarian case, since it seems reasonable to assume that the higher the rate of benefit compared with wages, the greater the risk of disincentive. Those who want to lay the foundations of a watertight theory of welfare rights run the risk of digging a pitfall for their own feet.

An alternative solution adopted in practice in most welfare systems is to sort claimers into able-bodied and others, and to ensure that rights to welfare for the former are dependent on a test of social contribution, through efforts to find work, family care responsibility or some such behaviour (see Gewirth, 1987). Moral hazard arguments do appear to establish a real distinction between welfare rights and civil and political rights, although the difference is not of great practical significance in modern welfare systems because they provide relatively meagre benefits in deference to the work ethic. Proponents of welfare rights may counter-attack by suggesting that analogous issues arise in relation to other rights, so that the problem is not unique. For example, it is necessary to regulate the irresponsible use of a right to free speech through the criminalisation of slander. This point is not entirely convincing, since there seems to be no analogue in relation to the core political right to participate in democracy, or the core civil right of equality before the law. It is not clear what would count as feckless abuse of these components of citizenship.

Discussion of these arguments indicates that there is no compelling reason why welfare rights founded on basic need cannot be included alongside civil and political rights as necessary ingredients in citizenship, which government is constrained to guarantee provided that measures are taken to resolve the problem of moral hazard. Indeed, social and political rights are essential to the exercise of civil and political rights by disadvantaged groups. This is part of what disadvantage means. Thus it seems reasonable to suggest that the basic needs discussed earlier can become duties of government, and can be included in the range of activities of the welfare state.

Moral hazard: the limits of the right to welfare

The argument that social policy may supply incentives to engage in unwelcome behaviour carries an especial force in much discussion of social welfare. The reason for this is that modern notions of citizenship are at root based on ideas of contribution to the collectivity through work. This is the basis of Hegel's original analysis of the different levels of political participation to be accorded to the various orders and estates in the *Philosophy of Right*: 'individuals have duties to the state in proportion as they have rights as members of it' (1942, p.169). Such differential citizenship leads to disparities in obligation, seen as appropriate to the various stations in the division of labour. The centrality of work to citizenship re-emerges in Marshall's analysis of modern citizenship and in the work of Dahrendorf. It is neatly summarised in Ignatieff's remark: 'the basis of citizenship of entitlement was the insurance principle and universality of benefit: everyone contributed and everyone benefited' (1989, p.71). National insurance contribution, of course, is organised through employment. If the link between work and citizenship is so fundamental, it can hardly be satisfactory to dissolve the problem of moral hazard through the protestation that it does not happen very much in practice. If there is a substantial risk that it might, a wedge may be driven between civil and political rights on the one hand and social rights on the other. This is sufficient to undermine the claim that involvement in welfare is a necessary aspect of citizenship in the modern state.

The problem can easily be made more serious. A strong and erudite strand in recent feminist debate points out that unpaid care-work (which is the especial province of women) has been ignored in many discussions of work and citizenship. Here the problem of moral hazard returns with doubled force. All studies show that care-work is predominantly carried out by women. This is true in liberal, corporatist and social democratic capitalist welfare states, and in those which it is hard to place in any category. It is also true in state socialist countries and in developing countries. It is true irrespective of the employment status of partners, and irrespective of their declared aspirations for the division of labour.

An authoritative study by Cass reviews evidence on the gendered division of care-work for 'the liberal market societies of Britain, Australia and the US (Land and Rose, 1985; Land, 1989; Balbo, 1987; Nelson, 1984); the social democratic Scandinavian welfare states (Waerness, 1989; Borchorst and Siim, 1987) and the (post) command economies of Eastern Europe (Scott, 1975)'. The study shows that: 'in each case, the obligation to provide care, to take care of consumption work and to provide private welfare is closely related to employment status and types of employment activity . . . and to the capacity to participate fully in the politics of the state and the authority structures of the work-place' (1990, pp.1–2). (See Langan and Ostner, 1991, for recent evidence.)

Studies focusing primarily on women's participation in paid work for the UK (Martin and Roberts, 1984), for Europe (Balbo and Novotny, 1986; Epstein, 1986; Chamberlayne, 1990, p.6) for the US (Hartmann, 1987, p.45; Dex and Shaw, 1986) and for Australia (Bryson, 1988) show that the time spent in domestic work by women exceeds that spent by men by a substantial margin even when the partners' involvement in paid employment is also taken into account. Co-ordinated international attitude surveys carried out in Germany, Hungary, Ireland, the UK and the US in 1988 reinforce the conclusion of a British survey of 1986: that the idea of an equal division of domestic work is popular among single people, but that once people form couples, women carry out most of the child-care and care for the sick in the family (Jowell, Witherspoon and Brook, 1989; Ashford, 1987; Witherspoon, 1988). There is a strong prima-facie case for adopting a convergence model of the gender distribution of unpaid labour.

Care-work, reproductive labour, is vital to the continuance of society. Even those who are prepared to disallow the claims of the frail elderly and others who are incapable of contributing to future productivity must see the upbringing of the new generation as indispensable to social existence through time. On the other hand, many roles within the system of paid employment appear to bear only a tenuous relation to socially necessary production. The point is that men absent themselves from an equal contribution to socially necessary care and women carry out the relevant labour. The whole sexual division of labour appears to function as a vast engine of moral hazard, in which perverse incentives encourage one sex to refuse to participate in a major division of the totality of social labour. If welfare rights discourage a small number of people of limited employability from seeking paid employment, that is one thing. If the operation of the welfare state discourages the male half of the population from playing an equal role in the fundamental task of social care it is a much more serious problem.

   The roots of an almost universal sexual division of labour are hard to trace. Explanations offered include: women's unique adaptation to care-tasks in the tradition established by Wollstonecraft (1970, p.68); the active subordination of women to men by a system of violence (Brownmiller, 1975, Chapter 1) or material relationships (Delphy, 1984, Chapters 4 and 5); the process of socialisation into gender roles (Chodorow, 1978); the confluence of class and gender (Sayers, 1982, Chapter 1); the rational choice of women given the low wages and meagre opportunities available to them outside the domestic sphere (Scott, 1991, p.1; Barker and Allen, 1976, pp.47–69); and the assumptions of others that such tasks fall 'naturally' to women (Finch, 1989, pp.158–9). Given the mountain of available accounts, some conflicting, some mutually reinforcing, it would be inappropriate to lay responsibility for the problem entirely at the door of the partial welfare systems of some western countries. In any case the division of labour appears equally marked in countries which do not claim to be welfare states. However, it is not necessary to establish that state welfare is the sole cause of women's double shift in the social division of necessary labour in order to maintain that there is a problem of moral hazard to which welfare policies contribute.

State welfare and social care

State welfare systems act as a transmission mechanism for inequalities in incentives that originate elsewhere. Their practice may be one among several causal factors. Nonetheless, so long as it can be shown that state welfare policy makes a substantial contribution to the pattern of differential incentives that encourages men to evade unpaid care-work, the welfare state must be seen as an apparatus of moral hazard in a centrally important area of social life. This strengthens the arguments which point to a cleavage between welfare and civil and political rights and undermine the status of the former as proper areas for state intervention.

Three lines of argument are relevant. These concern: the income differences between men and women in paid employment, which function as incentives in determining the work strategy of the household; the extent to which policies pursued by government allow women good access to alternatives to care-work compared with men; and the differential availability of state services which substitute for informal care when the carer is a woman or a man.

In spite of equal pay legislation, women continue to be paid substantially less than men. Women's average gross hourly earnings in Britain in the 1980s remained at just under 75 per cent of those of men, although equal pay legislation had been in force for some 15 years (Johnson, 1990, p.211; see also Scott, 1991). Esping-Anderson's analysis of the complex shifts in the labour markets of Germany, Sweden and the US over the past three decades concludes that, in all three cases: 'women . . . remain heavily over-represented in the less desirable jobs' (1990, p.215). Land, in a review of the social processes that make women dependent on men and therefore available for unpaid care-work, delineates 'the material pressures on women to care' (1989, p.157). The point is simply that, if men can earn more for the same amount of paid employment than women can, it involves a real and substantial financial sacrifice for traditional gender roles to be reversed. If government fails to secure an effective equal pay and equal opportunities policy for women, basic economic stringencies will encourage women to become carers, or (to look at it from the other direction) encourage men to evade domestic care-work.

The evidence suggests that ideological pressures reinforce practical considerations. Graham shrewdly remarks that:

> caring defines both the identity and the activity of women in Western society. It defines what it feels like to be a woman in a male-dominated and capitalist social order. Men negotiate their

> social position through something recognised as 'doing' . . . .
> Women's social position is negotiated through a different kind of
> activity called 'caring' . . . informed by 'intuition' through which
> women find their way into unskilled jobs (in Finch and Groves,
> eds., 1983, p.30)

Land and Rose describe the dominant climate of ideas which
defines care as a peculiarly appropriate role for women as the
vocation of 'compulsory altruism' – 'altruistic practices are
structured into women's lives as they are structured out of men's'
(1985, p.93). Many writers have pointed out that social welfare
policy has always assumed that women will provide care in
circumstances when men will not, as the evidence reviewed in
Chapters Two and Three shows. The same assumption – that care
is a peculiarly female calling – is implicit in much of the policy
discussion about community care, to the extent that Finch and
Groves describe the pursuit of this policy alongside a commitment
to equal opportunities for women as governmental hypocrisy
(1980).

Through their lack of commitment to genuine equal opportunity
policies that might make alternatives more acceptable and through
the discrimination practised in the allocation of social support,
welfare states play an important role in enabling men to avoid
care-work and in encouraging women to do it for them. Substitute
care is more readily available for men than for women. Working
women find child-care difficult to obtain, thus making their
participation in paid employment more difficult. Perhaps most
important of all, there are substantial differences between the
incomes of men and women in work, so that the incentives all lie in
the direction of a gender division of paid and unpaid work as the
rational strategy for the household.

This issue has been examined by feminists who seek to
demonstrate that discussions of work and citizenship ignore the
problem of the unpaid labour that typically falls to women, and
that the welfare state colludes in permitting men to avoid.
Pateman argues that women become 'exiles in society' as a result
of the sexual division of unpaid labour and of its implications for
women when citizenship is based on participation in paid
employment (1989, p.182). Lister analyses the problem in terms of
the 'paradox of dependency' whereby, because they are assumed
to be dependents of men, women become the docile and available

workforce for the labour that men escape (Lister, 1990, p.464). Women then become second-rate citizens because they are less able to be directly involved in paid employment. These issues lead to a dilemma in feminist strategy.

One approach associated historically with Wollstonecraft argues that women have particular citizenship claims because 'their unpaid work as carers and providers of welfare provides the moral basis for the conferral of citizenship rights' (Pateman, 1989, p.202). This condemns women to the role of carers in a 'separate-but-equal' subordination. A strategy which seeks credit for such work, by bringing it into the structure of paid employment through a wage for housework channelled through the state, may fail to emancipate women. Paid care-work becomes a female ghetto in an enlarged sphere of formal employment if men refuse to give up control of the areas that they currently dominate. Accordingly, Cass insists that caring work should be recognised in policy as a responsibility for both sexes. The objective is an equal participation in this area of social labour, so that a common citizenship may rest on contribution to the 'caring obligations of private life' (1990, p.15) as well as paid employment in the public arena. Lister argues that the issue rests on inequality in political power. Only when women have equal political power with men will they be able to escape the prison of dependency. Thus the realisation of rights in the political sphere must be the foundation for enhanced social and economic rights. However, it is unclear what strategy is available to make this demand effective against the interests it seeks to damage.

The problem with both these perspectives is that they imply an idealist approach to resolving a real social dilemma. Until they are put into practice, the ingenious critic of welfare statism can always point to a gaping hole in the defence offered by the proponent of welfare citizenship against the charge of moral hazard. Problems of moral hazard require government action to limit access to entitlement under particular circumstances. This is why a discrepancy between welfare rights and civil and political rights appears. To make social rights strictly analogous to civil rights it is necessary to find a good reason why government should restrict the enjoyment of an entitlement. After all an entitlement is an entitlement, and it seems nonsensical to offer it with one hand and then deny it with the other.

Here the traditional liberal argument that one person's freedom should be curtailed if it encroaches on another individual's enjoyment of freedom is relevant. It is on these grounds that limits on civil and political rights are generally accepted, even by those who wish to restrict rights to this sphere. After all the right to vote does not permit the majority to pass a law enslaving voters for the minority party. To claim otherwise would deny the universality characteristic of rights, since one individual would then be able to use the right as a means to deny the same right to another. Similarly, it is legitimate to restrict a right to welfare if it is used in such a way that the welfare rights of others are diminished. This insight offers a possible solution to the problem of moral hazard that strengthens the case for state welfare provision.

The right to welfare as the solution to perverse incentives

The possibility that welfare rights may nourish perverse incentives is seen as a flaw in the case for the welfare state because the notion of moral hazard is typically used from a particular methodological perspective. The standpoint is usually termed 'methodological individualism'. It has received its most coherent and forceful recent expression in the work of Hayek (1948), Popper (1962) and Eysenck (1954). The relevance of the approach to social policy is discussed at length elsewhere (Taylor-Gooby and Dale, 1981, Chapter 3). Methodological individualism applies Occam's Razor to abstract entities and seeks to describe the social world exclusively in terms of individual people, their behaviour and their attributes. Social relations and collectivities are ruled out of the court of possible explanations. Such abstemiousness makes it impossible to construct theories that operate, for example, in terms of social classes, or patterns of ideas operating as ideology. This is a serious limitation on its utility. In discussion of moral hazard and public policy, it focuses attention exclusively on the behaviour of the individual who is encouraged to evade responsibilities, and distracts attention from the social impact of that person's behaviour in relation to others. The central problem of moral hazard is conceived as the fecklessness of the scrounger in question.

Once a social perspective is adopted (and with it the argument that social rights are founded in human needs for survival and autonomy) the problem is seen in different terms. From this standpoint, the problem of moral hazard is not that it undermines a person's work ethic in the paid or the unpaid sphere. It is rather that such behaviour damages the autonomy of others. In the sphere of paid employment this results from the lack of resources to enable them to pursue their plans of life at the highest level available. In relation to the larger sphere of unpaid care, the threat is more obvious. The substantial amounts of time spent by women in this sphere restrict their freedom because that time is not available to do other things.

The problem of moral hazard is most commonly emphasised by libertarians who wish to see the role of government in welfare pared to the minimum and played down by protagonists of state welfare. However, it turns out to be the surest plank in the moral case for the welfare state. Welfare rights become exactly analogous to civil and political rights, since countering perverse incentives involves no more than the kind of activity that is essential to the secure possession of all rights – namely the limitation of the exercise of a right by one person to hamper another's enjoyment of the same right. The notion of the universality of moral claims implicit in this contention returns the argument to the Kantian premise of the case for human needs set out at the beginning of the previous chapter. The categorical imperative and the principle of respect for persons were established as a result of the universalisability of moral norms. The point also draws attention to another important feature of the welfare state.

Argument that seeks to establish a moral case for the welfare state must do two things. First it must develop a compelling case for collective obligation towards particular groups. Then it must demonstrate that this obligation falls on the political entity of government. Recent discussion has centred on the first enterprise rather than the second. Arguments using human need (like those presented in the previous chapter), vulnerability (Goodin, 1985; Pemberton, 1990) and freedom (Jones, 1982) as a foundation all develop a powerful case for collective obligation. The problem is that the obligation is not directed convincingly at government. Even those extensions of the argument which use the argument for greater equality as a ground for government involvement are not entirely compelling. It is always possible in principle for governments to structure and regulate the private and voluntary sectors to enhance equality, and for the state to pursue welfare citizenship ends by indirect means.

The virtue of the citizenship argument for welfare is that it directs attention to one of the core functions of the state. Many definitions of the state do not pay much attention to the meeting of citizen needs, but all put the 'monopoly on the legitimate use of violence within a given territory', in Weber's terminology, at their heart (Dunleavy and O'Leary, 1987, Chapter 1). Welfare states are not simply about doing good to individuals by meeting their needs, they are about sanctioning, controlling and directing people's behaviour as well. The approach to citizenship rights that does not lose sight of this point is able to present a far stronger case for the view that meeting human need must be a core function of the state than the perspective which obscures the dark side of welfare.

Solutions to the problem of perverse incentives demand that welfare rights involve not only benefits but sanctions. As we have seen the pattern of incentives in the case of the gender division of care-work includes the operation of the formal labour market as well as the structure of direct state services. Accordingly, a resolution of the problem will require a substantial state intervention in pay, employment opportunities and access to training and qualifications, as well as the reform of direct state services. Equal enjoyment of rights requires that some people should be prevented from infringing the human need for freedom of others by not participating in the paid and unpaid work that is necessary to the continuance of society. The argument that the provision of social benefits can be mandated to employers or facilitated by subsidy to the private sector has some force. It is weakened when the claim that such rights must be enjoyed equally by all is advanced, since it is difficult to prevent market institutions responding to the inequalities of effective demand. However, it is possible to imagine systems of regulation for the private sector that propel it in a more or less egalitarian direction (Friedman, 1962, Chapter 8; Le Grand and Estrin, 1989, Chapter 1). It is far more difficult to conceive of methods for applying sanctions on undesirable behaviour through private systems. The state is defined as the repository of authority in all definitions and such a practice is a core activity of government. When pursued to its logical conclusion, the problem of moral hazard provides a powerful justification for the welfare state.

Moral hazard and the environmental crisis

Moral hazard arguments can also be developed in relation to other issues in public policy. Perhaps the most pressing at the present time concerns the ecological threat from human activity. The central message of the Brundtland report to the World Commission on Environment and Development (1987) was simply that current activities may make it impossible for future generations to meet their needs. The global imbalance between North and South in their contribution to environmental pollution, the depletion of irreplaceable stocks of raw material and the 'greenhouse effect' (Pearce, 1989; Jacobs, 1990, pp.26–8) point the issue forcefully at the advanced industrial nations. There are two separate problems involved. State policies may generate moral hazards in both areas. First, Brundtland's notion of 'sustainable growth' draws attention to the point that the current privileged rate of economic expansion cannot be pursued indefinitely. Self-interested incentives may lead this generation to damage the planet irreparably, so that future generations suffer environmental penalties handed down by an irresponsible present (Gribbin, 1988). The second issue concerns the extent to which some individuals and nations find it advantageous to act in ways that damage the present interests of others. The dumping of nuclear waste, or cross-border atmospheric pollution provide obvious examples.

Both kinds of damage can be seen as infringements of autonomy, of the pattern of rights which Kant's core idea of the universalisability of moral rules demands. To the extent that state policy provides incentives to act in harmful ways, a problem of moral hazard and public policy is involved that is exactly analogous to the process whereby policy colludes in the imposition of care-work on women, as we argued above. This is also a problem which demands substantial state involvement. Individual action is unlikely to help the future, because a clean environment is a public good. If one person refrains from damaging activity on the grounds of the kind of moral obligation that the theory of needs implies, that in itself does not prevent another more self-interested person from benefiting self at the cost of others in the future. Those who wish to meet such obligations face a 'prisoner's dilemma'. The problem can only be resolved through action applied to the whole community, and this must involve a central role for government (Jacobs, 1990, p.10). This issue has a special relevance for Britain: 'the national economic and political interest may suggest a strategy of imposing the costs of solution upon others by refusing extensively to control national emissions, thus 'hijacking' others into bearing the burden . . . . This is a strategy which Britain has pursued over dumping in the North Sea, sulphur dioxide pollution and the production of chiorofluorocarbons' (Ward, Samways and Benton, 1990, p.240: see also Taylor and Ward, 1982). It is only state action at the cross-national level of the European Community that is able to exert pressure on British policy.

The major difficulty in pursuing these arguments lies in the uncertainty attached to discussion of the ecological effects of human industry. It is clear that state policies in the fields of housing, transport, fuel policy, agriculture and elsewhere do contribute to ecological problems to some extent. Ward, Samways and Benton (1990, pp.242–5) give a concise review of the way new British policies in transport deregulation, the privatisation of electricity and the subsidy of agriculture have failed to pay any serious attention to environmental issues. However, it is simply impossible to say with any certainty how serious the infringement on the rights of others resulting from particular actions may be. For this reason, the issue of ecology and moral hazard will not be discussed at length here, except to point out that another powerful argument for state intervention lies in this arena. The arguments about gender and work detailed above are sufficient to provide a compelling case for direct state activity on their own. In both cases, the point must be that rights entail sanctions and this is the province of government.

Conclusion: the ambiguous excellence of the welfare state

The previous chapter pointed to the flaws in arguments that base claims about desirable social policies on simple descriptions of social circumstances. There is always a choice to be made in issues of welfare. We cannot simply read off the appropriate policy response from accounts of the present, still less from value-laden reports of the virtues of past social order. The argument goes on to point out that a secure normative basis for the goals of welfare intervention can be found in the human needs for autonomy and survival. This derives ultimately from the Kantian principle of 'Respect for Persons'. Such a principle does not enable us to develop argument very far since it is unclear to what extent we should respect the different needs of particular individuals in concrete terms. This critique opens the way to a consideration of the social basis of individual need. The argument shows that evaluation of the success of societies in meeting their members' needs must depend on the Hegelian criterion of the capacity of social arrangements to advance human emancipation. The problem now is to decide how to identify successful social patterns.

This plunges the approach into the controversies surrounding the notion of social progress. It is impossible to set up a criterion for what is to count for liberating knowledge with certainty, and even more difficult to do so when evidence on the outcome of innovations in some fields will not be available for many years. However, social and political institutions which allow open and democratic communication are most likely to secure the unbiased exploration of that goal. Democracy is thus a human need.

Arguments about needs carry the implication that an obligation rests on government to advance equality in need-satisfaction between different social groups. This chapter considers whether the case for state welfare can be strengthened by the claim that social needs constitute rights against government. Both Plant and Weale argue that welfare rights have the same status as civil and political rights. There is no reason to suppose that they are not equally capable of enforcement by government. Critics point to a number of difficulties, the most intractable of which is the problem of how welfare rights are to be limited to minimise the dilution of work-incentives. In practice, there is little evidence of any difficulty, because benefit levels are so low. However, in a more equal society, the question might become more pressing. In addition, more substantial problems arise in ensuring that men take on their share of the unpaid caring tasks necessary to guarantee the survival and socialisation of the next generation and the maintenance of dependent members of this one. This issue would present no serious problems under the ideal circumstances of a genuine commitment to co-operation. People would then not wish to evade responsibility to others. That commitment is not available in the conflict of different interests in patriarchal, capitalist society. The pursuit of a policy based on respect for persons is prefigurative of social arrangements which stretch beyond the division of interest into the realm of ends. In Doyal and Gough's sense, state commitment to the guarantee of welfare is emancipatory in that it allows citizens to respect others in a way that the market and the patriarchal system do not.

None of this, strictly speaking, entails the state provision of welfare services. What it does do is suggest that there is a strong moral case for government involvement in the guarantee of welfare provision as an equal community right, whether through state, market, family or some combination of them. There is in addition a strong practical case for direct state provision, as the most effective way of securing a shift in the direction of greater equality. The argument goes on to point out that the application of the sanctions necessary to stop the rights enjoyed by some threatening the enjoyment of rights by others through the operation of perverse incentives must be a key role for government. Since the gender division of incentives for unpaid care-work involves many aspects of welfare provision, government has a major part to play. The growing importance of care deriving from changes in patterns of population structure, family life and employment is certain to make the issue even more important in the future. Since the problem of male avoidance of care-work appears in all welfare state societies, the issue provides a peculiarly wide-ranging justification for state intervention.

The use of the moral hazard argument – filched from the marketeers by the defenders of the state – brings welfare citizenship home to the core responsibility of government. This task is the legitimate use of violence. The welfare state does not simply seek to add the extra chore of meeting human needs to the list of legitimate areas of government involvement, but contends that a moral obligation resting on the community can only be satisfactorily discharged if the state's central gift to the community – legitimate authority – is deployed. Thus welfare citizenship unites the two aspects of the discussion of rights. Substantive arguments demonstrate a human need for democratic institutions as part of a participative community. Procedural arguments demonstrate that citizenship must include state intervention to guarantee equality in the face of the problem of damaging counter-incentives.

In Chapter Two it was argued that welfare policy had considerable success in containing the diverse interests of an unequal social order within the structure of common provision, despite the fact that class and gender inequalities still remained. The end result was a substantial advance in the direction of equality. The apparent failure of the strategy of equality made the case for defending that strategy, once the context of the inequalities in power between different social groups was taken into account. Chapters Four and Five showed that public services still receive the endorsement of the mass of the population. The moral argument for the extension of state intervention to tackle the problem of moral hazard strengthens this case. Here too the index of success should not be the achievement of equality, but the extent to which social policy succeeds in moving towards that goal.

The first part of this book showed that the arguments which characterise the welfare state as obsolete are incorrect. Those strands in sociology which seek to dismiss the state as a principal agent of welfare are not convincing. The concluding chapters show that rights against the state in the area of welfare must include participatory citizenship as well as the procedural rights which require interventionist social policy. The onus is on critics of the welfare state to suggest better ways of guaranteeing the satisfaction of human needs in face of the problem of moral hazard, rather than on the proponents of state welfare to justify their position further. The cost of adopting this position is that it brings home to the proponent of the welfare state the ambiguous excellence of state welfare. The welfare state is not just about the kindliness of meeting need. It is also about the exercise of state power to stop some people doing what they would otherwise do, in the interests of equal rights. Appropriation of the moral hazard argument for the defence of the welfare state is not without irony. Why should the devil have all the good tunes?

BIBLIOGRAPHY

Abbott, P. and Wallace, C. (1989) 'The family' in Brown and Sparks (eds.), *Beyond Thatcherism: Social Policy, Politics and Society* (Milton Keynes: Open University Press)

Abel-Smith, B. (1958) 'Whose welfare state?' in MacKenzie N. (ed.) *Conviction* (London: MacGibbon Kee)

Abercrombie, N., Hill, S. and Turner, B. (1988) *The Penguin Dictionary of Sociology* (Harmondsworth: Penguin)

Aglietta, M. (1976) *A Theory of Capitalist Regulation* (London: New Left Books)

Allan, G. (1985) *Family Life* (Oxford: Basil Blackwell)

Alt, A. (1979) *The Politics of Economic Decline* (Cambridge: Cambridge University Press)

Amenta, E. and Skocpol, T. (1989) 'Taking exception: Explaining the distinctiveness of American public policies in the last century' in F. Castles (ed.), *The Comparative History of Public Policy* (Oxford: Polity Press)

Arber, S., Gilbert, N. and Evandrou, M. (1988) 'Gender, household composition and receipt of domiciliary services by the elderly disabled' *Journal of Social Policy*, vol.17, no.2, pp.127–52

Archbishop of Canterbury's Commission on Urban Priority Areas (1985) *Faith in the City: a call for action by church and nation* (London: Church House Publishing for the General Synod of the Church of England)

Ashford, S. (1987) 'Family matters' in Jowell, R., Witherspoon, S., Brook, L. (eds.), *British Social Attitudes – the 1987 Report* (Aldershot: Gower)

Atkinson, A. (1987) 'Income maintenance and social insurance' in

Auerbach, A. and Feldstein, M. (eds.), *Handbook of Public Economics*, vol.II, (Amsterdam: North Holland)

Bacon, R. and Eltis, W. (1978) *Britain's Economic Problem: Too few producers* (London: Macmillan)

Balbo, L. (1987) 'Crazy quilts: rethinking the welfare state debate from a women's point of view' in Sassoon, A. Showstack, (ed.), *Women and the State* (London: Hutchinson)

Balbo, L. and Novotny, H. (eds.) (1986) *Time to Care in Tomorrow's Welfare Systems* (Vienna: European Centre for Social Welfare, Teaching and Research)

Baldock, C. and Cass, B. (1988) *Women, Social Welfare and the State* (Sydney: Allen and Unwin)

Ball, M., Gray, F. and McDowell, L. (1989) *The Transformation of Britain* (London: Fontana)

Barbalet, J. (1988) *Citizenship* (Milton Keynes: Open University Press)

Barker, D. and Allen, S. (eds.) (1976) *Dependence and Exploitation in Work and Marriage* (London: Longman)

Barnes, S. and Kaase, M. (eds.) (1979) *Political Action* (Beverly Hills: Sage Publications)

Barr, N. and Coulter, F. (1990) 'Social security: solution or problem?' in Hills, J. (ed.), *The State of Welfare* (Oxford: Clarendon Press)

Barry, B. (1973) *The Liberal Theory of Justice* (Oxford: Clarendon Press)

Barry, N. (1988) *The Invisible Hand in Economics and Politics: a study in two conflicting explanations of society* (London: Hobart Paper no. 111, Institute of Economic Affairs)

Barry, N. (1990) *Welfare* (Milton Keynes: Open University Press)

Bean, P., Ferris, J. and Whynes, D. (eds.) (1985) *In Defence of Welfare* (London: Tavistock)

Bebbington, A. and Davies, B. (1983) 'Equity and efficiency in the allocation of the personal social services', *Journal of Social Policy*, vol.12, no.3, pp.309–30

Beenstock, M. (1979) 'Taxation and incentives in the UK', *Lloyd's Bank Review*, no.134

Bell, D. (1976) *The Cultural Contradictions of Capitalism* (New York: Basic Books

Benn, T. (1980) 'The Inheritance' in Mullins, C. (ed.) *Arguments for Socialism* (Harmondsworth: Penguin)

Benton, S. (1988) 'Citizen Cain's silenced sisters', *New Statesman and Society*, 2 December

Beresford, P. and Croft, S. (1986) *Whose Welfare: Private care or public services?* (Brighton: Lewis Cohen Centre)

Boleat, M. (1985) *National Housing Finance Systems* (London: Croom Helm)

Borchorst, A. and Siim, B. (1987) 'Women and the advanced welfare state – a new kind of patriarchal power?' in Sassoon, A. Showstack (ed.), *Women and the State* (London: Hutchinson)

Bourdieu, P. (1984) *Distinction: a Social Critique of the Judgement of Taste* (London: Routledge and Kegan Paul)

Bradshaw, J. (1972) 'A taxonomy of social need' in *New Society* no.496, 30 March, pp.640–3

Bradshaw, J. (1985) 'Social security policy and assumptions about patterns of work' in Klein, R. and O'Higgins, M. (eds.), *The Future of Welfare* (Oxford: Basil Blackwell)

Bradshaw, J. and Deacon, A. (1984) *Reserved for the Poor* (Oxford: Martin Robertson)

Bradshaw, J. and Holmes, M. (1989) *Living on the Edge* (Newcastle: Tyneside Child Poverty Action Group)

Brook, L., Taylor, B. and Prior, G. (1990) *British Social Attitudes, 1989 Survey: Technical Report* (London: Social and Community Planning Research)

Brown, C. (1980) *Taxation and the Incentive to Work* (Oxford: Oxford University Press)

Brown, C. (1988) 'Will the 1988 tax cuts either increase incentives or raise more revenue?' *Fiscal Studies*, vol.9, no.4, pp.93–107

Brown, P. and Sparks, R. (eds.) (1989) *Beyond Thatcherism: Social policy, politics and society* (Milton Keynes: Open University)

Browning, E. (1975) 'Why the social insurance budget is too large in a democracy', *Economic Inquiry*, no.13, pp.373–87

Brownmiller, S. (1975) *Against Our Will* (London: Secker and Warburg)

Bryson, L. (1988) 'Women as welfare recipients: women, poverty and the state' in Baldock C. and Cass, B. (eds.), *Women, Social Welfare and the State* (Sydney: Allen and Unwin)

Buck, N. (1989) 'Polarization and inequality in Britain: a statistical analysis of the labour force survey' (mimeo: paper presented to the annual conference of the British Sociological Association, Exeter, July, 1989)

Bulmer, M., Lewis, J. and Piachaud, D. (eds.) (1989) *The Goals of Social Policy* (London: Unwin Hyman)

Burrows, R. and Butler, T. (1989) 'The middle mass and the pit: notes on the new sociology of consumption', *Sociological Review*, vol.37, no.1, pp.338–65

Bury, M. (1988) 'Arguments about ageing: long life and its consequences' in Wells and Freer (eds.), *The Ageing Population: Burden or Challenge?* (London: Macmillan)

Busfield, J. (1990) 'Sectoral divisions in consumption: the case of medical care', *Sociology*, vol.24, no.1, pp.77–98

Butler, D. and Stokes, D. (1969) *Political Change in Britain: Forces shaping electoral choice* (London: Macmillan)

Calnan, M. and Cant, S. (1990) *Principles and Practice: the case of private health insurance* (mimeo: paper delivered at the British Sociological Association Conference, University of Surrey, March, 1990)

Cameron, D. (1984) 'Social democracy, corporatism, labour quiescence and the representation of economic interest in advanced capitalist society', in Goldthorpe (ed.), *Order and Conflict in Contemporary Capitalism* (Oxford: Clarendon)

Cameron, D. (1985) 'Public expenditure and economic performance in international perspective' in Klein, R. and O'Higgins, M. (eds.), *The Future of Welfare* (Oxford: Basil Blackwell)

Canto, V., Jones, D. and Laffer, A. (1983) 'Tax rates, factor employment, market productivity and welfare' in Canto, V., Jones, D. and Laffer, A. (eds.), *Foundations of Supply-side Economics* (New York: Academic Books)

Carter, E. (1990) 'Material deprivation and its association with childhood hospital admission in the East End of London', *Community Medicine*, vol.15 no.6

Cartwright, A. (1967) *Patients and Doctors: A study of general practice* (London: Routledge and Kegan Paul)

Cass, B. (1990) 'Gender and social citizenship', paper presented at the 24th. annual Social Policy Association conference, University of Bath

Castles, F. (ed.) (1989) *The Comparative History of Public Policy* (Oxford: Polity Press)

Castles, F. (1990) 'The dynamics of policy change: what happened to the English-speaking nations in the 1980s', *European Journal of Political Research*, vol.18, no.5, pp.491–514

Castles, F. and McKinlay, R. (1979) 'Public welfare provision, in Scandinavia: the sheer futility of a sociological approach to politics', *British Journal of Political Science*, vol.9 no.2, pp.157–71

Castles, F., Widmaier, U. and Wildenmann R. (1989) 'The political economy of the peoples' welfare: an initial presentation', *European Journal of Political Research*, vol.17, no.4, pp.361–6

Central Statistical Office (CSO) 1974, 1989, 1990 and 1991 *Social Trends* (annual), (London: HMSO)

Central Statistical Office (CSO) 1985, 1989b, 1990b and 1991b *The Family Expenditure Survey* (annual: surveys up to 1989 issued by the Department of Employment) (London: HMSO)

Central Statistical Office (CSO) (1990c) *Economic Trends*, October (London: HMSO)

Chamberlayne, P. (1990) 'Alternative models of welfare – new directions in Europe?' paper presented at the 24th annual Social Policy Association Conference, University of Bath

Charlesworth, A., Wilkin, D. and Durie, A. (1984) 'Carers and services: a comparison of men and women caring for dependent elderly people', *Equal Opportunities Commission* (Manchester)

Chodorow, N. (1978) *The Reproduction of Mothering: Psychoanalysis and the sociology of gender* (Berkeley: University of California Press)

Coates, D. and Hillard, J. (1987) *The Economic Revival of Modern Britain: the debate between left and right* (Aldershot: Edward Elgar)

Coates, K. and Silburn, B. (1973) *Poverty: the forgotten Englishmen* (Harmondsworth: Penguin)

Cole, G.D.H. (1920) *Guild Socialism Restated* (London: Lawrence Parsons)

Collins, E. and Klein, R. (1980) 'Equity and the NHS: self-reported morbidity, access and primary care', *British Medical Journal*, no.281, pp.1111–15

Collins, E. and Klein, R. (1984) 'Self-reported morbidity, socio-economic factors and general practitioner consultations' (mimeo: *University of Bath*, Bath)

Connerton, P. (ed.) (1976) *Critical Sociology*, (Harmondsworth: Penguin)

Conservative Party (1987) *The Next Moves Forward: 1987 Election Manifesto* (London: Conservative Central Office)

Cooke, F.L. (1979) *Who Should be Helped?* (New York: Sage)

Cooke, K. (1987) 'The withdrawal from paid work of the wives of unemployed men: a review of research', *Journal of Social Policy*, vol.16, no.3, pp.371–82

Coote, A., Harman, H. and Hewitt, P. (1990) *The Family Way*, Social Policy Paper no.1 (London: Institute for Public Policy Research)

Coutts, K. and Godley, W. (1989) 'The British economy under Mrs Thatcher', *Political Quarterly*, vol.60, pp.137–51

Craig, G. and Glendinning, C. (1990) 'Parenting in poverty', *Community Care*, 15 March

Cranston, M. (1976) 'Human rights, real and supposed' in Timms, M. and Watson, D. (eds.), *Talking about Welfare*, (London: Routledge and Kegan Paul)

Crossland, R. (1964) *The Future of Socialism* (London: Jonathon Cape)

CSO *see* Central Statistical Office

Dahrendorf, R. (1987) 'The underclass and the future of Britain', Tenth Annual Lecture, *St George's House*, Windsor Castle

Dale, J. and Foster, P. (1986) *Feminists and State Welfare* (London: Routledge and Kegan Paul)

Davey-Smith, G., Bartley, M. and Blane, D. (1990) 'The Black report on socioeconomic inequalities in health 10 years on', *British Medical Journal* vol.301, 18–25 August

Davidoff, L., L'Esperance, J. and Newby, H. (1976) 'Landscape with figures: home and community in English society' in Mitchell, J. and Oakley, A. (eds.), *The Rights and Wrongs of Women* (Harmondsworth: Penguin)

Deacon, A. (1978) 'The scrounging controversy: public attitudes towards the unemployed in contemporary Britain', *Social and Economic Administration*, vol.12, no.2

Deacon, R. and Hyde, M. (1986) 'Working-class opinion and the welfare state: beyond the state and the market', *Critical Social Policy*, no.18, Winter, 1986–7, pp.15–31

Deakin, N. (1987) *The Politics of Welfare* (London: Methuen)

Dean, H. (1990) *Social Security and Social Control* (London: Routledge and Kegan Paul)

Delphy, C. (1984) *Close to Home* (London: Hutchinson)

Dennis, N. (1975) *Reading Rawls* (Oxford: Basil Blackwell)

Department of Employment (1989) *Employment Gazette*, April

Department of Employment (1990) *Employment Gazette*, April

Department of Health (1989) *Working for Patients* (London: HMSO)

Department of Health (1989b) *Caring for People: Community care in the next decade and beyond*, Cm.849 (London: HMSO)

Department of Health and Social Security (1983) *Social Security Statistics for 1981* (London: HMSO)

Department of Health and Social Security (1985) *The Future of Social Security*, vol.1, Cmnd 9517 (London: HMSO)

Department of Health and Social Security (1986) *Low-income Families: 1981–83* (London: HMSO)

Department of Health and Social Security (1988) *Households below Average Income 1981–1985* (London: HMSO)

Department of Social Security (1990) *Social Security Statistics for 1989*, (London: HMSO)

Department of Social Security (1990) *Households Below Average Incomes, 1981–87: A Statistical Analysis* (London: HMSO)

Dex, S. and Shaw, L. (1986) *British and American Women at Work: Do Equal Opportunity Policies Matter?* (London: Macmillan)

Dilnot, A. and Kell, M. (1988) 'Top rate tax cuts and income – some empirical evidence', *Fiscal Studies*, vol.9, no.4, pp.70–92

Donzelot, J. (1980) *The Policing of Families* (London: Hutchinson)

Douglas, J.D. (1989) *The Myth of the Welfare State* (Brunswick, NJ.: Transaction Books)

Doyal, L. and Gough, I. (1984) 'A theory of human needs', *Critical Social Policy*, no.10, Summer, pp.6–33

Duke, V. and Edgell, S. (1984) 'Public expenditure cuts in Britain and consumption sectoral cleavages', *International Journal of Urban and Regional Research* vol.8, no.2, pp.177–201

Dunleavy, P. (1979) 'The urban basis of political alignment: social class, domestic property ownership and state intervention in consumption processes', *British Journal of Political Science*, vol.9, no.4, pp.409–43

Dunleavy, P. (1980), 'The political implications of sectoral cleavages and the growth of state employment: Part 1, the analysis of production cleavages and Part 2, Cleavage structures and political alignment', *Political Studies*, vol.28, no.3, pp.364–83, and no.4, pp.527–49

Dunleavy, P. and Husbands, C. (1985) *British Democracy at the Crossroads* (London: George Allen and Unwin)

Dunleavy, P. and O'Leary, B. (1987) *Theories of the State* (London: Macmillan)

Economic and Social Research Council (1990) 'Report on the Social Change and Economic Life Initiative', *Newsletter*, no.6, July, pp.5–6

Economist (1988) 'The New Edwardians', Leading Article, 9 April, 1988

Edwards, M. (1981) *Financial Arrangements in Families* (Canberra, Australia: National Women's Advisory Council)

Eisenstadt, S. and Ahimer, O. (eds.) (1985) *The Welfare State and its Aftermath* (London: Croom Helm)

Epstein, T. (1986) *Women, Work and Family in Britain and Germany* (London: Croom Helm)

Ermisch, J (1990) *Fewer Babies, Longer Lives* (York: Joseph Rowntree Foundation)

Esping-Anderson, G. (1990) *The Three Worlds of Welfare Capitalism* (Oxford: Polity Press)

Esping-Anderson, G. and Korpi, W. (1984) 'Social policy as class politics in post-war capitalism: Scandinavia, Austria and West Germany', in Goldthorpe (ed.), *Order and Conflict in Contemporary Capitalism* (Oxford: Clarendon)

ESRC *see* Economic and Social Research Council

Evandrou, M. (1987) *The Use of Domiciliary Services by the Elderly: A survey*, Welfare State Programme Discussion Paper no.15, London School of Economics

Evandrou, M. (1990) *Challenging the Invisibility of Carers*, Welfare State Programme Discussion Paper no.49, London School of Economics

Evandrou, M., Falkingham, J. and Glennerster, H. (1990) 'The personal social services: "everybody's poor relation, but nobody's baby" ' in Hills, J. (ed.), *The State of Welfare* (London: London School of Economics)

Evandrou, M., Falkingham, J., Le Grand, J. and Winter, D. (1990) *Equity in Health and Social Care*, Social Policy Association annual conference, University of Bath

Evans, P., Rueschmeyer, D. and Skocpol, T. (eds.) (1985) *Bringing the State Back In* (Cambridge: Cambridge University Press)

Eversley, D. (1982) 'Some aspects of ageing in Britain' in Hereven, T. (ed.), *Ageing and the Life Cycle Course in a Cross-Cultural Interdisciplinary Perspective* (New York: Guildford Press)

Eysenck, K. (1954) *The Psychology of Politics* (London: Routledge and Kegan Paul)

Falkingham, J. (1987) 'Britain's ageing population' *Suntory Toyota International Centre for Economics and Related Disciplines*, Welfare state programme paper no.17, London School of Economics

Falkingham, J. (1989) 'Dependency and ageing in Britain: a re-examination of the evidence', *Journal of Social Policy*, vol.18, no.2, pp.211–34

Fieghan, S. and Reddaway, M. (1981) *Companies, Incentives and Senior Managers*, Oxford University Press for Institute for Fiscal Studies

Field, F. (1989) *Losing Out: the emerging British underclass* (Oxford: Basil Blackwell)

Finch, J. and Groves, D. (1980) 'Community care and the family: a case for equal opportunities?' *Journal of Social Policy*, vol.9, no.4, pp.487–513

Finch, J. and Groves, D. (1983) *A Labour of Love: Women, work and caring* (London: Routledge and Kegan Paul)

Finch, J. (1989) *Family Obligations and Social Change* (Cambridge: Polity)

Flora, P. (1985) 'On the history and current problems of the welfare state', in Eisenstadt and Ahimer *The Welfare State and its Aftermath* (London: Croom Helm)

Fox, J. and Goldblatt, P. (1982) *Longitudinal Study: Socio-demographic mortality differences* (London: OPCS)

Franklin, M. and Page, E. (1984) 'A critique of the consumption sector cleavage approach in British voting studies', *Political Studies*, vol.32, no.4, pp.521–36

Freer, C. (1988) 'Old Myths: frequent misconceptions about the elderly', in Wells and Freer (eds.), *The Ageing Population: Burden or Challenge?* (London: Macmillan)

Friedman, M. (1962) *Capitalism and Freedom* (Chicago: Chicago University Press)

Friedmann, R., Gilbert, N. and Sherer, M. (eds.) (1987) *Modern Welfare States* (Brighton: Wheatsheaf)

Fries, F. (1980) 'Ageing, natural death and the compression of morbidity', *New England Medical Journal*, vol.303, no.3, p.130

Furnham, A. and Lewis, A. (1986) *The Economic Mind* (Brighton: Wheatsheaf)

Furniss, N. and Tilton, T. (1979) *The Case for the Welfare State* (Bloomington: Indiana University Press)

Gallie, W. (1956) 'Essentially contested concepts' *Proceedings of the Aristotelian Society*, supp.vol.no.48

Galtung, J. (1980) 'The basic needs approach', in Lederer, K. (ed.) *Human Needs* (Cambridge Massachussetts: Harvard University Press)

Gamble, A. (1985) (second edition) *Britain in Decline* (London: Macmillan)

George, V. and Wilding, P. (1976; second edition 1986) *Ideology and Social Welfare* (London: Routledge)

George, V. and Wilding, P. (1984) *The Impact of Social Policy* (London: Routledge and Kegan Paul)

Gershuny, J. and Miles, I. (1983) *The New Service Economy* (London: Frances Pinter)

Gerth, H. and Mills, C. (eds.) (1948) *From Max Weber: Essays in Sociology, Wirtschaft und Gesellschaft* (London: Routledge and Kegan Paul)

Gewirth, H. (1987) 'Political philosophy and positive rights', in Frankel, E., Miller, F., Paul, J. and Ahrens, J. (eds.), *Beneficence, Philanthropy and the Public Good* (Oxford: Basil Blackwell)

Giddens, A. (1976) *New Rules of Sociological Method* (London: Hutchinson)

Gilder, G. (1981) *Wealth and Poverty* (New York: Basic Books)

Glazer, N. (1988) *The Limits of Social Policy* (Harvard, Mass.: Harvard University Press)

Glendinning, C. (1990) 'Dependency and interdependency; the incomes of informal carers and the impact of social security' *Journal of Social Policy*, vol.19, no.4, pp.469–98

Glendinning, C. and Millar, J. (1987) *Women and Poverty in Britain* (Brighton: Wheatsheaf)

Glennerster, H. (1989) 'Swimming against the tide: the prospects for social policy', in Bulmer, M., Lewis, J. and Piachaud, D. (eds.), *The Goals of Social Policy*

Glennerster, H. (1990) 'Social policy since the second world war', in Hills, J. (ed.), *The State of Welfare* (Oxford: Clarendon Press)

Glennerster, H., Falkingham, J. and Evandrou, M. (1990) *How Much Do We Care? A Comment on the Government's Community Care Proposals*, Welfare State Paper no.46, London School of Economics

Godfrey, L. (1975) *Theoretical and Empirical Aspects of the Effect of Taxation on the Supply of Labour* (Paris: OECD)

Golding, P. and Middleton, S. (1982) *Images of Welfare* (Oxford: Martin Robinson)

Goldthorpe, J. (ed.) (1984) *Order and Conflict in Contemporary Capitalism* (Oxford: Clarendon)

Goldthorpe, J., Lockwood, D., Bechhofer, F. and Platt, J. (1969) *The*

Affluent Worker in the Class Structure (Cambridge: Cambridge University Press)

Good, F. (1990) 'Estimates of the distribution of personal wealth', *Economic Trends*, no.444, pp.137–49

Goodin, R. (1985) *Protecting the Vulnerable* (Chicago: Chicago University Press)

Goodin, R. and Le Grand, J. (eds.) (1987) *Not Only the Poor* (London: Allen and Unwin)

Gordon, C. (1988) *The Myth of Family Care*, Welfare State Paper no.29, London School of Economics

Gough, I. (1979) *The Political Economy of the Welfare State* (London: Macmillan)

Gough, I. (1990) *International Competitiveness and the Welfare State: a case-study of the UK*, SPRC Report no.85, Social Policy Research Centre (Sydney: University of New South Wales)

Government Actuary (1984) *Population, Pension Costs and Pensioners' Incomes* (London: HMSO)

Graham, H. (1983) 'Caring: a labour of love' in Finch, J. and Groves, D. (eds.), *A Labour of Love: Women, work and caring* (London: Routledge and Kegan Paul)

Gray, J. (1989) *Limited Government: a Positive Agenda*, Hobart Paper 113 (London: Institute of Economic Affairs)

Green, D. (1990) 'Foreword' in Murray, C. (1990) *The Emerging British Underclass*, Choice in Welfare Series, no.2 (London: Institute of Economic Affairs)

Greve, J. with Currie, E. (1990) *Homelessness in Britain*, (York: Joseph Rowntree Memorial Trust)

Gribbin, J. (1988) *The Hole in the Sky: Man's threat to the ozone layer*, Friends of the Earth

Guillemard, A. (ed.) (1983) *Old Age and the Welfare State* (London: Sage)

Habermas, J. (1970) 'On systematically distorted communication', *Inquiry*, vol.13, pp.205–18

Habermas, J. (1973) *Knowledge and Human Interests* (London: Heinemann)

Habermas, J. (1976) *Legitimation Crisis* (London: Heinemann)

Hadley, R. and Hatch, S. (1981) *Social Welfare and the Failure of the State* (London: George, Allen and Unwin)

Hage, J., Hanneman, R. and Gargan, E. (1989) *State Responsiveness and State Activism* (London: Unwin Hyman)

Hakim, C. (1989) 'Workforce restructuring, social insurance coverage and the black economy', *Journal of Social Policy*, vol.18, no.4, pp.471–504

Hall, P., Land, H., Parker, R. and Webb, A. (1975) *Change, Choice and Conflict in Social Policy* (London: Heinemann)

Halsey, A. (ed.) (1988) *British Social Trends since 1900* (London: Macmillan)

Halsey, A., Heath, A. and Ridge, J. (1980) *Origins and Destinations* (Oxford: Clarendon Press)

Hansard (1981–) *Parliamentary Debates, Sixth Series*, vol. 1 (London: Hansard Society)

Harding, S. (1989) 'The changing family', in Jowell, R., Witherspoon, S. and Brook, L. (eds.), *International Social Attitudes* (Aldershot: Gower)

Harris, D. (1987) *Justifying State Welfare: the new right versus the old left* (Oxford: Basil Blackwell)

Harris, R. and Seldon, A. (1987) *Welfare Without the State*, Hobart Paperback, no.26, Institute of Economic Affairs

Hartmann, H. (1987) 'Changes in women's economic and family roles' in Beneria, L. and Stimpson, C. (eds.), *Women, Households and the Economy* (New Brunswick: Rutgers University Press)

Hattersley, R. (1987) *Choose Freedom: the Future for Democratic Socialism* (Harmondsworth: Penguin)

Haveman, R. (1987) 'US anti-poverty policy and the non-poor' in Goodin and Le Grand (eds.), *Not Only the Poor* (London: Allen and Unwin)

Hayek, F. (1944) *The Road to Serfdom* (London: G. Routledge and Sons Ltd)

Hayek, F. (1948) *Individualism and Economic Order* (London: Routledge and Kegan Paul)

Hayek, F. (1960) *The Constitution of Liberty* (London: Routledge and Kegan Paul)

Hayek, F. (1979) *Law, Legislation and Liberty: vol.3* (London: Routledge and Kegan Paul)

Heath, A., Jowell, R. and Curtice, J. (1985) *How Britain Votes* (Oxford: Pergamon Press)

Hegel, G. (1942) *The Philosophy of Right*, (translated by Knox, T.) (Oxford: Oxford University Press)

Hegel, G. (1976) 'The phenomenology of mind: excerpt on the master and slave', in Connerton, P. (ed.), *Critical Sociology* (Harmondsworth: Penguin) pp.41–50

Heidenheimer, A., Heclo, H. and Adams, C. (1990) *Comparative Public Policy: the politics of social choice in America, Europe and Japan* (New York: St Martins Press)

Hendricks, J. and Clalasanti, T. (1986) 'Social policy on ageing in the US', in Phillipson and Walker (eds.), *Ageing and Social Policy* (Aldershott: Gower)

Henwood, M. and Wicks, M. (1984) *The Forgotten Army: Family care and elderly people*, (London: Family Policy Studies Centre)

Henwood, M. and Wicks, M. (1985) 'Community care, family trends and social change' *The Quarterly Journal of Social Affairs*, vol.1, no.4, pp.357–71

Hicks, A. and Swank, D. (1984) 'On the political economy of welfare expansion: a comparative analysis of 18 advanced capitalist democracies', *Comparative Political Studies*, vol.17, no.1, pp.81–119

Hicks, A., Swank, D. and Ambuhl, M. (1989) 'Welfare expansion revisited: policy routines and their mediation by party, class and crisis', *European Journal of Political Research*, vol.17, no.4, pp.401–30

Hicks, C. (1988) *Who Cares? Looking After People at Home* (London: Virago)

Higgins, J. (1988) *The Business of Medicine* (London: Macmillan)

Hill, M. (1990) *Social Security Policy in Britain* (Aldershot: Edward Elgar)

Hills, J. (1990) *The State of Welfare: the welfare state in Britain since 1974* (Oxford: Clarendon Press)

Hindess, B. (1987) *Freedom, Equality and the Market* (London: Tavistock)

Hirsch, F. (1977) *Social Limits to Growth* (London: Routledge and Kegan Paul)

Hirschman, A. (1970) *Exit, Voice and Loyalty* (Cambridge, Mass.: Harvard University Press)

Holloway, J. and Picciotto, S. (1978) *State and Capital: a Marxist Debate* (London: Edward Arnold)

Hume, D. (1963) *An Enquiry Concerning Human Understanding* (Selby-Brigg, L.) (ed.) (Oxford: Oxford University Press)

Hunt, A. (1970) *The Home Help Service in England and Wales* (London: HMSO)

Ignatieff, M. (1989) 'Citizenship and moral narcissism', *Political Quarterly* vol.60, no.1, pp.63–74

Illsley, R. and Le Grand, J. (1987) *Measurement of Inequality in Health*, Welfare State Paper, no.12, London School of Economics

Jacobs, M. (1990) *Sustainable Development: Greening the economy*, Fabian Tract 538, (London: Fabian Society)

Jenkins, S. (1989) 'Some recent trends in UK income inequality', paper presented at the 1989 annual conference of the Social Policy Association, University of Bath

Johnson, N. (1987) *The Welfare State in Transition* (Brighton: Wheatsheaf)

Johnson, N. (1990) *Reconstructing the Welfare State: 1980–1990, a decade of change* (Brighton: Wheatsheaf)

Johnson, P. and Webb, S. (1990) *Poverty in Official Statistics: Two reports*, commentary no.24, Institute for Fiscal Studies

Jones, P. (1982) 'Freedom and the redistribution of resources', *Journal of Social Policy*, vol.11, no.2, pp.217–38

Joseph, K. and Sumption, J. (1979) *Equality* (London: John Murray)

Joshi, H. (1986) 'Participation in paid work – evidence from the women and employment survey' in Blundell, R. and Walker, I. (eds.), *Unemployment, Job Search and Labour supply* (Cambridge: Cambridge University Press)

Joshi, H. (1990) 'The cash opportunity costs of childbearing: an approach to estimation using British data', *Population Studies*, no.44, pp.52–3

Jowell, R., Witherspoon, S. and Brook, L. (1984–90; Annual) *British Social Attitudes* (Aldershot: Gower)

Judge, K. (1987) 'The British welfare state in transition', in Friedmann, R., Gilbert, N. and Sherer, M. (eds.), *Modern Welfare States*

Judge, K., Smith, G. and Taylor-Gooby, P. (1983) 'Public opinion and the privatisation of welfare', *Journal of Social Policy*, vol.12, no.4

Kant, I. (1959) *Foundations of the Metaphysics of Morals* (translated by L. Beck) (New York: Liberal Arts Press)

Keane, J. (1988) *Democracy and Civil Society* (London: Verso)

Kell, M. (1988) 'Top rate tax cuts, incentives and revenue', *Economic Review*, September, pp.30–2

Kemeny, J. (1981) *The Myth of Home Ownership* (London: Routledge and Kegan Paul)

Kiernan, K. and Wicks, M. (1990) *Family Change and Future Policy*, (London: Family Policy Studies Centre)

Klein, R. (1984) 'Privatisation and the welfare state', *Lloyd's Bank Review*, no.151

Klein, R. and O'Higgins, M. (1985) *The Future of Welfare* (Oxford: Blackwell)

Laing and Buisson (1987, 1990; annual) *Laing's Review of Private Health Care* (London: Laing and Buisson)

Land, H. (1989) 'The social construction of dependency' in Bulmer, M., Lewis, J. and Piachaud D. (eds.), *The Goals of Social Policy* (London: Unwin Hyman)

Land, H. and Rose, H. (1985) 'Compulsory altruism for some or an altruistic society for all?' in Bean, P., Ferris, J. and Whynes D. (eds.) *In Defence of Welfare* (London: Tavistock)

Langan, M. and Ostner, I. (1991) *Gender and Welfare*, (mimeo: Bremen University)

Lash, S. and Urry, J. (1987) *The End of Organized Capitalism* (Cambridge: Polity Press)

Layard, R. and Nickell, S. (1990) *The Thatcher Miracle?* (mimeo: paper presented at the Centre for Labour Economics, London School of Economics, 9 December)

Le Grand, J. (1982) *The Strategy of Equality* (London: Allen and Unwin)

Le Grand, J. (1990) 'Conclusion: the state of welfare', in Hills, J. (ed.) *The State of Welfare* (Oxford: Clarendon Press)

Le Grand, J. and Estrin, S. (1989) *Market Socialism* (Oxford: Oxford University Press)

Le Grand, J., Winter, D. and Woolley, F. (1990) 'The National Health Service: safe in whose hands?' in Hills, J. (ed.) *The State of Welfare* (Oxford: Clarendon Press)

Leibfried, S. (1990) 'The classification of welfare state regimes in Europe', Plenary Session Paper, Social Policy Association Annual Conference, University of Bath, July

Lewis, A. (1980) 'Attitudes to public expenditure', *Political Studies*, vol.29, no.2

Lewis, J. (1984) *Women in England, 1870–1950*, (Brighton: Wheatsheaf)

Lewis, J. (1989) 'Introduction: social policy and the family', in Bulmer, M., Lewis, J. and Piachaud D. (eds.) *The Goals of Social Policy* (London: Unwin Hyman)

Lewis, J. and Meredith, D. (1988) *Daughters Who Care: Daughters caring for mothers at home* (London: Routledge)

Lewis, J. and Piachaud, D. (1987) 'Women and poverty in the twentieth century', in Glendinning and Millar (eds.) *Women and Poverty* (Brighton: Wheatsheaf)

Lister, R. (1990) 'Women, economic dependency and citizenship', *Journal of Social Policy*, vol.19, part 4, pp.445–68

Lister, R. (1990b) *The Exclusive Society: Citizenship and the poor* (London: Child Poverty Action Group)

Local Government Information Unit (LGIU) (1990) *Poll Tax Focus Extra* (London: LGIU, no.11)

Lockwood, D. (1966) 'Sources of variation in working-class images of society', *Sociological Review*, vol.14, pp.249–67

Loney, M., Bocock, R., Clark, J., Cochrane, A., Graham, P. and Wilson, M. (eds.) (1987) *The State or the Market* (London: Sage)

Lynch, J. (1986) *Multicultural Education* (London: Routledge and Kegan Paul)

Mack, J. and Lansley, S. (1985) *Poor Britain* (London: Allen and Unwin)

Mack, J. and Lansley, S. (1991) *Breadline Britain* (London: Unwin Hyman)

McNicol, J. (1987) 'In pursuit of the underclass', *Journal of Social Policy*, vol.16, no.3, pp.293–318

Manning, N. (1989) 'Social Policy in the USA', paper presented at the annual conference of the Social Policy Association, University of Bath, June

Marmor, T., Mashaw, J. and Harvey, P. (1989) *America's Misunderstood Welfare State* (New York: Basic Books)

Marquand, D. (1988) *The Unprincipled Society* (London: Jonathon Cape)

Marsh, C. (1979) 'Opinion polls – social science or political manoeuvre?', pp.268–88 in Irvine, J., Miles, I. and Evans, J. (eds.), *Demystifying Social Statistics* (London: Pluto Press)

Marshall, G., Rose, D., Vogler, C. and Newby, H. (1985) 'Class, citizenship and distributional conflict in modern Britain', *The British Journal of Sociology*, vol.36, no.2 pp.259–84

Marshall, G., Newby, H., Rose, D. and Vogler, C. (1988) *Social Class in Modern Britain* (London: Hutchinson)

Marshall, T. (1950) *Sociology at the Cross-Roads and other Essays* (London: Heinemann)

Martin, J. and Roberts, C. (1984) *Women and Employment: a lifetime perspective*, Department of Employment/OPCS (London: HMSO)

Martin, J., White, A. and Melzer, H. (1989) *Disabled Adults: Services, transport and employment*, OPCS Survey Report no.4, OPCS (London: HMSO)

Marx, K. and Engels, F. (1976) *The German Ideology* (translated by Arthur, C.), (London: Lawrence and Wishart)

Maslow, A. (1943) 'A theory of human motivation', *Psychological review*, no.50, pp.370–96

Maynard, A. (1985) 'Welfare: who pays?' in Bean, P., Ferris, J. and Whynes, D. (eds.), *In Defence of Welfare* (London: Tavistock)

Mead, L. (1986) *Beyond Entitlement: the social obligations of citizenship* (New York: Free Press)

Metcalfe, D. (1982) 'Employment and Unemployment' in Prest, A. and Coppock, D. (eds.) *The British Economy: A Manual of Applied Economics* (London: Weidenfeld and Nicholson)

Michnik, A. (1985) *Letters from Prison and Other Essays* (Berkeley: University of California Press)

Miliband, R. (1971) *The State in Capitalist Society* (London: Quarto)

Millar, J. (1987) 'Lone mothers' in Glendinning, C. and Millar, J. (eds.) *Women and Poverty in Britain* (Brighton: Wheatsheaf)

Millar, J. and Glendinning, C. (1987) 'Invisible women, invisible poverty' in Glendinning, C. and Millar, J. (eds.), *Women and Poverty* (Brighton: Wheatsheaf)

Minford, P. (1987) 'The role of the social services: a view from the New Right', in Loney *et al.* (ed.), *The State or the Market* (London: Sage)

Minford, P. (1988) 'Outlook after the budget', *Fiscal Studies*, vol.9, no.2, pp.30–7

Mintel International (1990) *Inherited Wealth* (London: Mintel)

Mishra, R. (1977) *Society and Social Policy* (London: Macmillan)

Mishra, R. (1984) *The Welfare State in Crisis* (Brighton: Wheatsheaf)

Mishra, R. (1990) *The Welfare State in Capitalist Society* (Hemel Hempstead: Harvester Wheatsheaf)

Moore, J. (1988) 'Welfare Policy in an Opportunity State', Speech given on 8 June, Conservative Party Constituency Association's annual meeting, Conservative Central Office, London

Mouffe, C. (1988) 'The civics lesson', *New Statesman and Society*, 7 October

Mueller, D. (1979) *Public Choice* (Cambridge: Cambridge University Press)

Murray, C. (1984) *Losing Ground; American Social Policy, 1950–1980* (New York: Basic Books)

Murray, C. (1989) 'The Underclass', *The Sunday Times Magazine*, 26 November, 1989

Murray, C. (1990) *The Emerging British Underclass*, Choice in Welfare Series no.2 (London: Institute of Economic Affairs)

National Audit Office (1990) *The Elderly: Information Requirements for Supporting the Elderly and Implications of Personal Pensions for the National Insurance Fund*, Report by the Comptroller and Auditor General (London: HMSO)

National Federation of Housing Associations (1991) *Housing London: Issues of Finance and Supply*, London

National Institute for Economic and Social Research (1989) *National Institute Economic Review*, no.129, August

National Institute for Economic and Social Research (1991) *National Institute Economic Review*, no.135, February

Navarro, V. (1988) 'Welfare states and their redistributive effects' *Political Quarterly*, vol.59 no.2, pp.219–35

Nelson, B. (1984) 'Women's poverty and women's citizenship: some political consequences of economic marginality', *Signs: Journal of Women in Culture and Society*, vol.10, no.2 (Winter)

Newby, H., Marshall, G., Rose, D. and Vogler, C. (1986) 'From class structures to class action' in Roberts, R., Finnegan, R. and Gallie, D. *New Approaches to Economic Life* (Manchester: Manchester University Press)

Nicholl, J., Williams, B., Thomas K. and Knowelden, J. (1984) 'Contribution of the private sector to elective surgery in Britain', *The Lancet*, 14 July

Nissel, M. and Bonnerjea, L. (1982) *Family Care of the Handicapped Elderly: Who Pays?* (London: Policy Studies Institute)

Norman, R. (1976) *Hegel's Phenomenology: a Philosophical Introduction* (London: Chatto and Windus)

Norman, R. (1987) *Free and Equal* (Oxford: Oxford University Press)

Novak, T. (1988) *Poverty and the State* (Milton Keynes: Open University Press)

Nozick, R. (1974) *Anarchy, State and Utopia* (Oxford: Basil Blackwell)

O'Connor, J. (1973) *The Fiscal Crisis of the State* (New York: St Martin's Press)

O'Connor, J. (1988) 'Convergence or divergence: change in welfare effort in OECD countries, 1960–80', *European Journal of Political Research*, vol.16, no.2, pp.277–99

O'Connor, J. and Brym, R. (1988) 'Public welfare in OECD countries: towards a reconciliation of inconsistent findings', *British Journal of Sociology*, vol.39, no.1, pp.47–68

O'Donnell, O. and Propper, C. (1989) *Equity and the Distribution of National Health Service Resources*, Welfare State Paper no.45, London School of Economics

OECD (Organisation for Economic Cooperation and Development) (1981), *The Crisis of Welfare* (Paris: OECD)

OECD (1985), *Social Expenditure, 1960–90* (Paris: OECD)

OECD (1988) *The Future of Social Protection* (Paris: OECD)

OECD (1988b) *Economic Outlook* (Paris: OECD)

OECD (1988c) *OECD Observer*, no.43 (Paris: OECD)

OECD (1988d) *Ageing Populations* (Paris: OECD)

OECD (1990) *OECD Observer* no.48 (Paris: OECD)

Offe, C. (1984) in Keane, J. (ed.), *Contradictions of the Welfare State* (London: Hutchinson)

O'Higgins, M. (1985) 'Inequality, redistribution and the recession', *Journal of Social Policy*, vol.14 no.3, pp.279–307

O'Higgins, M. and Patterson, A. (1985) 'The prospects for public expenditure: a disaggregate analysis', in O'Higgins, M. and Klein, R. (eds.), *The Future of Welfare* (Oxford: Blackwell)

O'Higgins, M. and Jenkins, S. (1989) 'Poverty in Europe: estimates for 1975, 1980 and 1985' (mimeo: unpublished paper presented to the European Community summit, 9 December, 1989)

Okrasa, W. (1987) *Social Justice and the Redistributive Effect of Social Spending in Poland*, Welfare State paper, no.18, London School of Economics

Olson, M. (1982) *The Rise and Decline of Nations* (Yale: Yale University Press)

O'Mahony, B. (1988) *A Capital Offence: the plight of single young homeless people in London* (London: Routledge)

OPCS (1978) *The General Household Survey for 1976* (London: HMSO)

OPCS (1987) *The General Household Survey for 1985* (London: HMSO)

OPCS (1989) *The General Household Survey for 1987* (London: HMSO)

Oppenheim, C. (1990) *Poverty: the Facts* (London: Child Poverty Action Group)

Owen, S. and Joshi, H. (1987) 'Pensions and gender: the significance of lifetimes earnings differentials', (mimeo, paper presented at the Social Policy Association Conference, July, 1987, University of Edinburgh

Pahl, J. (1984) 'The allocation of money within the household' in

Freeman, M. (ed.), *The State, the Law and the Family* (London: Tavistock)

Pahl, J. (1988) 'Earning, sharing and spending: married couples and their money', in Walker, R. and Parker, G. (eds.), *Money Matters* (London: Sage)

Pahl, J. (1989) *Money and Marriage* (London: Macmillan)

Pahl, J. (1990) 'Household spending, personal spending and the control of money in marriage', *Sociology*, vol.24, no.1, pp.119–38

Pahl, R. (1984) *Divisions of Labour* (Oxford: Blackwell)

Pahl, R. (1990) 'The search for social cohesion: from Durkheim to the European Commission', (mimeo: paper presented at the ESRC/CNRS Conference on Citizenship, Social Order and Civilising Processes, Cumberland Lodge, Windsor Great Park, 3–5 September, 1990)

Pahl, R. and Wallace, C. (1986) 'Forms of work and privatisation on the Isle of Sheppey' in Roberts, B., Finnegan, R. and Gallie, D. (eds.), *New Approaches to Economic Life*, (Manchester: Manchester University Press)

Paloheimo, H. (1984) 'Distributive struggle and economic development in the 1970s in developed capitalist countries', *European Journal of Political Research*, vol.12, no.2, pp.171–90

Papadakis, E. (1990) *Attitudes to State and Private Welfare*, Report no.18, Social Policy Research Centre, (Sydney: University of New South Wales)

Papadakis, E. and Taylor-Gooby, P. (1987) *The Private Provision of Public Welfare* (Brighton: Wheatsheaf)

Parker, G. (1985) *With Due Care and Attention: a review of research in informal care* (London: Family Policy Studies Centre)

Parker, S. (1980) *Older Workers and Retirement* (London: HMSO)

Parry, R. (1985) 'Britain: stable aggregates, changing composition', in Rose, R. (ed.) *Public Employment in Western Nations* (Cambridge: Cambridge University Press)

Pascall, G. (1986) *Social Policy: a feminist analysis* (London: Tavistock)

Pateman, C. (1989) 'The patriarchal welfare state', in *The Disorder of Women* (Chicago: Polity Press)

Patten, J. (1988) 'Active Citizenship', *Sunday Times*, 11 December, 1989

Payne, S. (1951) *The Art of Asking Questions?* (Princeton, N.J.: Studies in Public Opinion, no.3)

Pearce, D. (1989) *Blueprint for a Green Economy* (London: Earthscan)

Pemberton, A. (1990) 'Rescuing the good Samaritan: an exposition and a defence of the samaritan principle in welfare', *Journal of Social Policy*, vol.19 part 2, pp.221–34

Phillipson, C. (1978) *The Emergence of Retirement* (Durham: University of Durham)

Phillipson, C. and Walker, A. (eds.) (1986) *Ageing and Social Policy* (Aldershot: Gower)

Piachaud, D. (1981) 'Peter Townsend and the Holy Grail', *New Society*, no.57, pp.419–22

Piachaud, D. (1990) 'Poverty and social security' (mimeo, paper presented to Suntory-Toyota Seminar of Issues in Social Policy, London School of Economics)

Plant, R. (1985) 'The very idea of a welfare state', in Bean, P., Ferris, J. and Whynes D. (eds.), *In Defence of Welfare* (London: Tavistock) pp.3–30

Plant, R., Lesser H. and Taylor-Gooby, P. (1980), *Political Philosophy and Social Welfare* (London: Routledge and Kegan Paul)

Popper, K. (1962) *The Open Society and its Enemies*, (2 vols.) (London: Routledge and Kegan Paul)

Poulantzas, N. (1978) *Classes in Capitalist Society* (London: Verso)

Procter, I. (1990) 'The privatisation of the working class: a dissenting view', *British Journal of Sociology*, vol.41, no.2, pp.137–80

Randall, G. (1989) *Homeless and Hungry; a sign of the times* (London: Centrepoint)

Rawls, J. (1973) *A Theory of Justice* (Oxford: Oxford University Press)

Rentoul, J. (1989) *Me and Mine: the triumph of the new individualism?* (London: Unwin Hyman)

Rentoul, J. (1990) 'Individualism' in Jowell, R., Witherspoon, S. and Brook, L. (eds.), *British Social Attitudes, the 1990 Report* (Aldershot: Gower)

Ringen, S. (1987) *The Possibility of Politics* (Oxford: Clarendon Press)

Roberts, B., Finnegan, R. and Gallie, D. (eds.) (1986) *New Approaches to Economic Life* (Manchester: Manchester University Press)

Room, G. (1979) *The Sociology of Welfare* (Oxford: Blackwell)

Room, G., Lawson, R. and Laczko, F. (1989) 'New poverty in the European Community', *Policy and Politics*, vol.17, no.2, pp.165–76

Rousseau, J. (1973) *The Social Contract and Discourses* (London: Dent)

Rowbotham, S., Segal, L. and Wainwright, H. (1979) *Beyond the Fragments* (London: Merlin)

Sabel, C. (1982) *Work and Politics* (Cambridge: Cambridge University Press)

Saltman, R. and von Otter, C. (1991, forthcoming) *Planned Markets and Public Competition: Strategic reforms in Northern European health systems* (Milton Keynes: Open University Press)

Salvation Army (1989) *Sleeping Rough in London: Press release*, July, 1989

Sarlvik, B. and Crewe, I. (1983) *Decade of Dealignment* (Cambridge: Cambridge University Press)

Saunders, P. (1984) 'Beyond housing classes: the sociological significance of private property rights in means of consumption', *International Journal of Urban and Regional Research*, vol.8, no.2, pp.202–27

Saunders, P. (1986) *The Urban Question*, Second edition (London: Hutchinson)

Saunders, P. (1990) *A Nation of Home-owners* (London: Unwin Hyman)

Saunders, P. and Harris, C. (1989) *Popular Attitudes to State Services: a growing demand for alternatives?* Research Report 11, Social Affairs Unit

Sawyer, M. (1976) 'Income distribution in OECD countries' *OECD Economic Outlook: Occasional Studies*, July

Sayers, J. (1982) *Biological Politics* (London: Tavistock)

Scott, A. (1991) 'And never the twain shall meet? Life-time segregation of men and women' (mimeo, to be published in A. Scott (ed.) (1991) *Gender Segregation in British Labour Markets* (Cambridge: Cambridge University Press))

Scott, H. (1975) *Does Socialism Liberate Women: Experiences from Eastern Europe* (London: Beacon Press)

Seabrook, J. (1984) *The Idea of Neighbourhood* (London: Pluto Press)

The Sheffield Group: Alcock, P., Gamble, A., Gough, I., Lee, P. and Walker, A. (eds.) (1989) *The Social Economy and the Democratic State* (London: Lawrence and Wishart)

Skocpol, T. (1985) 'Bringing the state back in: strategies of analysis in current research', in Evans, P., Rueschemeyer, D. and Skocpol, T. (eds.), *Bringing the State Back In* (Cambridge: Cambridge University Press)

Skocpol, T. (1989) *Targeting within Universalism*, Occasional Paper no.89/2, Centre for American Political Studies, Harvard University, Cambridge, Massachussetts.

Skocpol, T. and Amenta, E. (1986) 'States and social policies', *Annual Review of Sociology*, vol.12

Smart, C. (1987) 'Securing the family?' in Loney, M., Bocock, R., Clark, J., Cochrane, A., Graham, P. and Wilson, M. (eds.) *The State or the Market* (London: Sage)

Smeeding, T., O'Higgins, M. and Rainwater, L. (eds.) (1990) *Poverty, Inequality and Income Distribution in Comparative Perspective* (Hemel Hempstead: Harvester Wheatsheaf)

Smith, D. (1989) *North and South: Britain's Growing Divide* (Harmondsworth: Penguin)

Smith, G. (1988) *Social Needs: Policy practice and research* (London: Routledge)

Smith, T. (1989) 'Inequality and welfare', in Jowell, R., Witherspoon, S. and Brook, L. (eds.), *International Social Attitudes* (Aldershot: Gower)

Social Services Select Committee (1989) *Report on the Social Security Changes Implemented in April, 1989*, House of Commons Paper no.437–i, 1988–9 session (London: HMSO)

Social Services Select Committee (1990) *Community Care: Carers*, House of Commons Paper no.410, 1989–90 session (London: HMSO)

Soper, K. (1981) *On Human Needs* (Brighton: Harvester Press)

Speaker's Commission on Citizenship (1990) *Encouraging Citizenship* (London: HMSO)

Stedman-Jones, G. (1971) *Outcast London* (Oxford: Clarendon Press)

Stephens, J. (1979) *The Transition from Capitalism to Socialism* (London: Macmillan)

Sullivan, M. (1987) *Sociology and Social Welfare* (London: Allen and Unwin)

Sullivan, O. (1989) 'Housing tenure as a consumption-sector divide: a critical perspective', *International Journal of Urban and Regional Studies*, vol.13, no.2, pp.183–200

Svenson, M. and MacPherson, S. (1988) 'Real losses and unreal figures: the impact of the 1986 Social Security Act' in Becker, S. and MacPherson, S. (eds.), *Public Issues, Private Pain: Poverty, Social Work and Social Policy* (London: Social Services Insight books) pp.41–53

Tawney, R. (1935) *Equality* (London: Allen and Unwin)

Taylor, C. (1971) 'Interpretation and the science of man', *Review of Metaphysics*, vol.25, no.3, pp.1–45

Taylor, C. (1979) *Hegel and Modern Society* (Cambridge: Cambridge University Press)

Taylor, M. and Ward, H. (1982) 'Chickens, whales and lumpy public goods: alternative models of public goods provision', *Political Studies*, vol.30 no.3, pp.350–70

Taylor-Gooby, P. (1985) *Public Opinion, Ideology and State Welfare* (London: Routledge and Kegan Paul)

Taylor-Gooby, P. (1987) 'Citizenship and welfare' in Jowell, R., Witherspoon, S. and Brook, L. (eds.), *British Social Attitudes: the 1987 Report* (Aldershot: Gower)

Taylor-Gooby, P. (1989) 'The role of the state', in Jowell, R., Witherspoon, S. and Brook, L. (eds.), *International Social Attitudes* (Aldershot: Gower)

Taylor-Gooby, P. (1989b) 'Disquiet and state welfare: clinging to nanny', *International Journal of Urban and Regional Research*, vol.13, no.2, pp.201–16

Taylor-Gooby, P. (1990) 'The unkindest cuts', in Jowell, R., Witherspoon, S. and Brook, L. (eds.), *British Social Attitudes: the Seventh Report* (Aldershot: Gower)

Taylor-Gooby, P. (1991) 'Poverty and inequality' in Fainstein, S.,

Gordon, I. and Harloe, M. (eds.), *A Tale of Dual Cities: London and New York* (London: Blackwell)

Taylor-Gooby, P. (1991b) 'Polarisation and citizenship' in Townsend, P. (ed.), *Poverty in London*, vol.2 (London: Low Pay Unit)

Taylor-Gooby, P. and Dale, J. (1981) *Social Theory and Social Welfare* (London: Edward Arnold)

Thane, P. (1982) *The Foundations of the Welfare State* (London: Longman)

Thatcher, M. (1978) *TV Interview*, reported in the *Guardian*, 31 January

Thatcher, M. (1981), *Welfare and the Family*, speech to Womens' Royal Voluntary Service, 19 January

Therborn, G. (1986) *Why Some People are more Unemployed than Others* (London: Verso)

Timmins, N. (1988) *Cash, Crisis and Cure* (London: Newspaper Publishing)

Titmuss, R. (1955) 'The social division of welfare', in *Essays on the Welfare State* (London: Allen and Unwin)

Titmuss, R. (1970) *Social Policy* (London: Allen and Unwin)

Townsend, P. (1973), *The Social Minority* (London: Allen Lane)

Townsend, P. (1979), *Poverty* (Harmondsworth: Penguin)

Townsend, P. (1981) 'The structured dependency of the elderly: a creation of social policy in the twentieth century', *Ageing and Society*, vol.1 no.1 pp.5–28

Townsend, P. (1986) 'Ageism and social policy', in Phillipson, C. and Walker, A. (eds.), *Ageing and Social Policy* (Aldershot: Gower)

Townsend, P., Corrigan, P. and Kowarzik, U. (1987) *Poverty and Labour in London* (London: Low Pay Unit)

Townsend, P., Davidson, N. and Whitehead, M. (eds.) (1988) *Inequalities in Health: The Black report and the health divide* (Harmondsworth: Penguin)

Treasury (1979) *The Government's Expenditure Plans, 1980–81*, Cmnd., 7746 (London: HMSO)

Treasury (1989) *The Government's Expenditure Plans, 1989–90 – 91/2*, Cm., 288–1 (London: HMSO)

Treasury (1990) *The Government's Expenditure Plans, 1990/91 – 92/3*, Cm., 1021 (London: HMSO)

Treasury (1991) *Public Expenditure Analysis to 1993/4*, Cm., 1520 (London: HMSO)

Treasury and Civil Service Select Committee (1983) *The 1983 Budget*, House of Commons Paper 286, session, 1983–4

Turner, B. (1986) *Citizenship and Capitalism* (London: Allen and Unwin)

Turner, B. (1988) *Status* (Milton Keynes: Open University Press)

Turner, B. (1989) 'Ageing, status politics and social theory', *British Journal of Sociology*, vol.40 no.4, pp.588–606

Turner, B. (1990) 'Outline of a theory of citizenship', *Sociology*, vol.24, no.2, pp.189–217

Unemployment Unit (1991) *Working Brief*, April (London: Unemployment Unit and Youthaid)

Ungerson, C. (1987) *Policy is Personal* (London: Tavistock)

Uusitalo, H. (1984) 'Comparative research on the determinants of the welfare state', *European Journal of Political Research*, vol.12, no.4, pp.403–22

Wacquaint, L. and Wilson, W.J. (1989) 'The cost of racial and class exclusion in the inner city', in Wilson, W.J. (ed.), *Special Issue of the Annals of the American Academy of Social and Political Science on the Ghetto Underclass*, vol.501, January

Waerness, K. (1989) 'Dependency in the welfare state' in Bulmer, M., Lewis, J. and Piachaud, D. (eds.], *The Goals of Social Policy* (London: Unwin Hyman)

Walker, A. (1984) *Social Planning* (Oxford: Blackwell)

Walker, A. (1987) 'The social construction of dependency' in Loney, M., Bocock, R., Clark, J., Cochrane, A., Graham, P. and Wilson, M. *The State or the Market* (London: Sage)

Walker, A. (1990) 'Blaming the victims', in Murray, C. *The Emerging British Underclass*, Choice in Welfare Series no.2 (London: Institute of Economic Affairs)

Walker, A. and C. (1987) *A Divided Nation?* (London: Child Poverty Action Group)

Walker, R. and Parker, G. (eds.) (1988) *Money Matters: Income, wealth and financial welfare* (London: Sage)

Ward, H. with Samways, D. and Benton, T. (1990) 'Environmental politics and policy' in Dunleavy, P., Gamble, A. and Peele, G. (eds.), *Developments in British Politics 3* (London: Macmillan)

Watson, S. (1987) 'Ideas of the family in the development of housing forms' in Loney, M., Bocock, R., Clark, J., Cochrane, A., Graham, P. and Wilson, M. (eds.), *The State or the Market* (London: Sage)

Weale, A. (1983) *Political Theory and Social Welfare* (London: Macmillan)

Weir, M., Orloff, A.S. and Skocpol, T. (1988) 'Introduction' in Weir, M., Orloff, A.S. and Skocpol, T. (eds.), *The Politics of Social Policy in the United States* (Princeton: Princeton University Press)

Wells, N. and Freer, C. (eds.) (1988) *The Ageing Population: Burden or challenge?* (London: Macmillan)

Wenger, C. (1985) 'Care in the community: changes in dependency and use of domiciliary services: a longitudinal perspective', *Ageing and Society*, vol.5, pp.143–59

Wicks, M. (1987) *A Future for All: Do we need a welfare state?* (Harmondsworth: Penguin)

Wilensky, H. (1975) *The Welfare State and Equality* (Berkeley: California University Press)

Wilkinson, M. (1986) 'Tax expenditure and public expenditure in the UK', *Journal of Social Policy*, vol.15, no.1, pp.23–50

Wilkinson, R. (1989) 'Class mortality differentials, income distribution and trends in poverty, 1921–81', *Journal of Social Policy*, vol.18, no.3, pp.307–36

Williams, F. (1989) *Social Policy* (Oxford: Polity Press)

Wilson, W. Julius (1987) *The Truly Disadvantaged* (Chicago: University of Chicago Press)

Witherspoon, S. (1988) 'A woman's work' in Jowell, R., Witherspoon, S. and Brook, L. (eds.), *British Social Attitudes: the 5th Report* (Aldershot: Gower)

Wittgenstein, L. (1958) *Philosophical Investigations* (Oxford: Basil Blackwell)

Wolfe, A. (1989) *Whose Keeper? Social Science and Moral Obligation* (Berkeley: University of California Press)

Wollstonecraft, M. (1970) *A Vindication of the Rights of Women* (first pub. 1792) (London: Dent)

World Commission on Environment and Development (1987) *Our Common Future* (The Brundtland Report) (Oxford: Oxford University Press)

NAME INDEX

SUBJECT INDEX